Mood

Mood is a phenomenon whose study is inherently interdisciplinary. While it has remained resistant to theorisation, it nonetheless has a substantial influence on art, politics, and society. Since its practical omnipresence in everyday life renders it one of the most significant aspects of affect studies, it has garnered an increasing amount of critical attention in a number of disciplines across the humanities, sciences, and social sciences in the past two decades. *Mood: Interdisciplinary Perspectives, New Theories* provides a comprehensive theoretical and empirical exploration of the phenomenon of mood from an interdisciplinary angle. Building on cutting-edge research in this emerging field and bringing together established and new voices, it bridges the existing disciplinary gap in the study of mood and further consolidates this phenomenon as a crucial concept in disciplinary and interdisciplinary study. By combining perspectives and concepts from the literary studies, philosophy, musicology, the social sciences, artistic practice, and psychology, the volume does the complexity and richness of mood-related phenomena justice and benefits from the latent connections and synergies in different disciplinary approaches to the study of mood.

Birgit Breidenbach is currently a Lecturer in Literature and Philosophy at the University of East Anglia. After earning a B.A. at the University of Giessen and an M.A. at the University of Warwick, she completed a Ph.D. in English and Comparative Literary Studies at Warwick in 2017 with a thesis on the role of mood in the literature of European modernity. Her published and presented work focuses on literary and aesthetic theory, affect, and the interplay between philosophy and literature.

Thomas Docherty is a Professor of English and of Comparative Literature at the University of Warwick. He is the author of many books, including, most recently, *Literature and Capital* (Bloomsbury, 2018), *The New Treason of the Intellectuals* (Manchester University Press, 2018), *Complicity* (Rowman & Littlefield, 2016), *Universities at War* (Sage, 2015), and *Confessions* (Bloomsbury, 2012). *Political English* will appear from Bloomsbury in 2019. He is currently completing a study of *Censorship*, and a novel, provisionally titled *Of Silence and Slow Time*. In 2016, he was awarded an honorary degree, Doctor of Letters, from the University of Kent.

Warwick Series in the Humanities
Series Editor: Christina Lupton

Titles in this Series

For more information about this series, please visit: https://www.routledge.com/Warwick-Series-in-the-Humanities/book-series/WSH

Mood
Interdisciplinary Perspectives, New Theories

Edited by Birgit Breidenbach
and Thomas Docherty

 Routledge
Taylor & Francis Group

NEW YORK AND LONDON

First published 2019
by Routledge
605 Third Avenue, New York, NY 10017

and by Routledge
2 Park Square, Milton Park, Abingdon, Oxon, OX14 4RN

First issued in paperback 2021

Routledge is an imprint of the Taylor & Francis Group, an informa business

Library of Congress Cataloging-in-Publication Data
Names: Breidenbach, Birgit, editor.
Title: Mood : interdisciplinary perspectives, new theories / edited by Birgit Breidenbach and Thomas Docherty.
Description: New York : Taylor and Francis, 2019. | Series: Warwick series in the humanities | Includes bibliographical references and index. |
Identifiers: LCCN 2019005917 (print) | LCCN 2019011282 (ebook) | ISBN 9780429259432 (Ebook) | ISBN 9780429535116 (epub) | ISBN 9780429521645 (pdf) | ISBN 9780429549816 (Mobi) | ISBN 9780367200664 (hardback : alk. paper)
Subjects: LCSH: Mood (Psychology) | Emotions.
Classification: LCC BF521 (ebook) | LCC BF521 .M66 2019 (print) | DDC 155.5/124—dc23
LC record available at https://lccn.loc.gov/2019005917

ISBN 13: 978-1-03-209310-9 (pbk)
ISBN 13: 978-0-367-20066-4 (hbk)

Typeset in Sabon
by codeMantra

Contents

List of Figures

List of Contributors

Jon Arcaraz Puntonet is an architect and earned a Ph.D. in architecture from the Department of Design, Urbanism, Theory and History in the School of Architecture of the University of Navarra (2015) with a thesis titled *Fernando Higueras: a Syncretic Architecture.*

Birgit Breidenbach is currently a Lecturer in Literature and Philosophy at the University of East Anglia. After earning a B.A. at the University of Giessen and an M.A. at the University of Warwick, she completed a Ph.D. in English and Comparative Literary Studies at Warwick in 2017 with a thesis on the role of mood in the literature of European modernity. Her published and presented work focuses on literary and aesthetic theory, affect, and the interplay between philosophy and literature.

Joshua Burraway is a post-doctoral Research Associate in Anthropology at the University of Virginia. His work focuses on medical anthropology, anthropology of the body, homelessness and mental health.

Mary Cappello is the author of six books of literary nonfiction, including *Awkward* (a Los Angeles Times bestseller); *Swallow*, based on the Chevalier Jackson Foreign Body Collection in Philadelphia's Mütter Museum; and, *Life Breaks In: A Mood Almanack* (University of Chicago Press, 2016). A recipient of a Guggenheim Fellowship, a Berlin Prize, the Bechtel Prize for Educating the Imagination, and the Dorothea Lange-Paul Taylor Prize, she is Professor of English and Creative Writing at the University of Rhode Island.

Thomas Docherty is a Professor of English and of Comparative Literature at the University of Warwick. He is the author of many books, including, most recently, *Literature and Capital* (Bloomsbury, 2018), *The New Treason of the Intellectuals* (Manchester University Press, 2018), *Complicity* (Rowman & Littlefield, 2016), *Universities at War* (Sage, 2015), and *Confessions* (Bloomsbury, 2012). *Political English* will appear from Bloomsbury in 2019. He is currently completing a study of *Censorship*, and a novel, provisionally titled *Of Silence and Slow Time*. In 2016, he was awarded an honorary degree, Doctor of Letters, from the University of Kent.

Rex Ferguson, Ph.D., is a Senior Lecturer in English Literature at the University of Birmingham. His first monograph, *Criminal Law and the Modernist Novel*, was published by CUP in 2013. His work has often utilised phenomenological thinking in order to advance its discussion of modernist writing and he has published in journals such as *New Formations, Philosophy and Literature, Critical Quarterly*, and *Textual Practice*.

Edward M. Hill is a postdoctoral researcher in the Mathematics Institute and the Zeeman Institute for Systems Biology and Infectious Disease Epidemiology Research (SBIDER) at the University of Warwick. His work focuses on the application of mathematical and computational methods in epidemiology and he has published in journals such as *PLOS Computational Biology, Proceedings of the Royal Society B: Biological Sciences*, and *Epidemics*.

Thomas House is a Reader in the School of Mathematics at the University of Manchester. He is a Fellow of the Alan Turing Institute and holds a Royal Society Industry Fellowship with IBM Research. His work focuses on mathematical epidemiology, with a particularly interest in efficient statistical inference for these problems. He has published in journals such as *Journal of Mathematical Biology, Journal of the Royal Society Interface*, and *PNAS*.

Hagi Kenaan is a Professor of Philosophy at Tel Aviv University, specialising in phenomenology, aesthetics and the philosophy of art. He is the author of *The Present Personal: Philosophy and the Hidden Face of Language* (Columbia University Press, 2005); *The Ethics of Visuality: Levinas and the Contemporary Gaze* (I.B. Tauris, 2013), and *Photography and Its Shadow* (Stanford University Press, forthcoming 2020). His previous work on the place of moods in philosophy is the co-edited collection *Philosophy's Moods: The Affective Grounds of Thinking* (Springer, 2011).

Mikko Ketovuori is a Lecturer of Music Education in the teacher education department at the University of Turku, Finland. His earlier research dealt broadly with the arts, music and their role in education and in society. Ketovuori has given international keynotes and lectures in such places as India, Singapore, the U.S., Spain, Austria, Czech Republic and Romania. Currently, he is working on the issue of pain with a multidisciplinary team of anesthesiologists, computer scientists, and pharmacologists. The hypothesis of the project is that individual pain can be assessed and predicted in an analogous way that mood can be measured from society.

Matt Lampert is the director of research at the Socionomics Institute, a centre dedicated to understanding social mood's influence on social behaviour. A graduate of the University of Cambridge, Matt has spoken about social mood theory throughout the U.S. and Europe. He is a board member of the Socionomics Foundation and edits the monthly research magazine, *The Socionomist*. Matt's research has been supported by the National Academy of Sciences with funds from the National Science Foundation. He contributed to the recent books *The Socionomic Theory of Finance* and *Socionomic Causality in Politics*, and he served as a contributing editor for the volume *Socionomic Studies of Society and Culture*.

Jonathan Mitchell is a British Academy Post-Doctoral Research Fellow at the University of Manchester (Department of Philosophy). His research focuses on the intersection between philosophy of mind, emotion and value, and he is currently developing a new theory of emotions. He has published widely on these topics and others, specifically on the philosophy of Nietzsche and the nature of pain experiences.

Yasmine Richardson studied at Merton College, University of Oxford, where she wrote her doctoral thesis on the theme of awkwardness in Marcel Proust's *A la recherche du temps perdu*. She has taught literature and film both at Oxford and the American University of Paris, and now lives in Paris where she is training to be a portrait painter in the realist tradition.

Madeleine Scherer is an Early Career Fellow at the Institute of Advanced Studies and the Department of English and Comparative Literature of the University of Warwick, specialising in the reception of Graeco-Roman mythology in twentieth century postcolonial literature. Her dissertation focuses on the reception of the classical underworld in Irish and Caribbean literature, comparing how the ancient trope of Hades is used by postcolonial writers as a way to interrogate mnemonic reconstructions of the past. Throughout her work, she attempts to show the overlapping concerns of classical reception, memory studies and postcolonial literature.

Erik Wallrup is an Associate Professor in Musicology at Stockholm University. He also works as an editor for the Royal Swedish Academy of Music in the project 'Swedish Musical Heritage.' Wallrup has written *Being Musically Attuned: The Act of Listening to Music* (Ashgate/Routledge 2015), a book on the concept of *Stimmung*/mood/attunement in music. Among his earlier publications are a book-length essay on Nietzsche's philosophy of listening ('Nietzsches tredje öra' [Nietzsche's Third Ear]) and articles within the fields of musical aesthetics and artistic research. His current research project is entitled 'The Affective Shift of Music in the Gustavian Era.'

Acknowledgements

We would like to thank the Humanities Research Centre—in particular Tim Lockley and Sue Rae—as well as the Department of English and Comparative Literary Studies and the Centre for Research in Philosophy, Literature and the Arts at the University of Warwick for their generous financial support of the 2016 *Mood* conference, which enabled us to collaboratively produce this work. In addition to this, we extend our gratitude to all speakers and attendees of the conference for having provided intellectual impulses and diverse perspectives which have shaped the contributions in this volume in many ways.

Introduction

Birgit Breidenbach and Thomas Docherty

Teresa Brennan's influential book *The Transmission of Affect* (2004) opens with a scenario all too familiar to any reader: one enters a room and instantly 'feels' a certain atmosphere, be it tension, anxiety, or exhilaration.[1] Brennan argues that this atmosphere immediately changes one's body; something that was not present before is added, and it actively envelops and alters one's affective state:

> [i]f I walk back into the atmospheric room in which I started [...] and it is rank with the smell of anxiety, I breathe this in. Something is taken in that was not present, at the very least not consciously present, before. But no matter how thoroughly my system responds to the presence of this new affect, it is the case that something is added. Whether this in itself makes me afraid, or whether I respond to fear by producing it within myself after I have smelt it around me (and probably both things occur) the phenomenon cannot be explained by the simple postulate that I am acting out something I already felt or was driven toward feeling by my 'individual drives'.[2]

The atmosphere situates the person who entered the room in the midst of what is, by definition, a social phenomenon, which then goes on to affect that person's possibilities for action. Imagine that you arrive at your workplace in the morning, running a little late after struggling to find a parking space for an extended period of time. You may feel annoyed, mildly embarrassed, and keen to share the reason for your lateness to point out that you are not responsible for it. As you enter the shared office space, you instantly register that your work colleagues seem unusually quiet and uncomfortable. They are quietly looking at one of your co-workers, whose body language suggests that they are deeply upset and struggling to speak. Would you continue to greet your colleagues as you would usually do and explain your lateness? Would you express your annoyance at the inadequate parking provision at your workplace? You will, more likely, attune your actions to this new and unexpected atmosphere—you may greet your colleagues quietly and wait to see how the situation unfolds, or you may inquire whether everything is in order.

You will probably feel different now; your annoyance and embarrassment may have made way to a new sense of concern or discomfort, and your actions will change to adjust to the new mood in the room. If you were to proceed with your earlier intention to address the parking provision, your lack of affective attunement to this social situation may result in you being perceived as 'tone-deaf' or inconsiderate.[3]

Brennan concludes her example by stating that '[t]he affect *in the room* is a profoundly social thing. How exactly does it get there?'[4] This final question, which addresses the origin of the modes and *moods* of our daily encounters with one another, is the key consideration for this book, as it aims to interrogate the formation—as well as the social, aesthetic, and political dimensions—of the affective states and relationships that we describe as 'moods.' Alongside this pivotal problem, a number of other questions that we can derive from Brennan's example and our own will be central to our inquiry: the atmosphere, or mood, in the room seems to be more than merely the sum of the different states of feeling that the individuals present bring into the room, although their behaviour, disposition, and attitudes would, naturally, impact on the 'profoundly social' presence felt in the room—what is, then, the relationship that exists between the mood of an individual and that of a group? As the one entering the tense atmosphere in your office space, your mood is altered by this atmosphere, but you simultaneously add a new presence to the affective fabric of the group. This aspect reveals another pivotal dimension of mood: its temporal structure and changeability.

Further, perhaps the nature of the room, too, plays into the formation of this mood: would the atmosphere not differ if the room is not an office space but a chapel in a medieval Gothic cathedral or a kindergarten playroom? If the lighting is bright and cheerful or dark and gloomy? Physical and geographical spaces appear to have an intimate, yet elusive, connection to our affective states, which goes beyond mere pathetic fallacy. We commonly speak about moods as if they are containers that 'envelop' us spatially, as we think of a person being 'in a mood,' or not being 'in the mood.' These conceptual metaphors are indicative of the close relationship between space and affect, which Brennan stresses by evoking a room 'rank with the smell of anxiety.' The mood in it is thus experienced as a *physical* presence that is specific to the 'atmospheric room.' How do spaces thus impact or determine the formation and experience of moods?

Finally, what impact does the mood in the room have on those who experience it? What are its effects on an individual as well as a social—and by extension, political—level? If mood is of a profoundly social nature, it transcends the individual, going beyond the notion of the self-contained subject and revealing its fluid boundaries with physical spaces and other subjects. Due to this, moods can be, and often are, contagious and collective. If the impact of the atmosphere in the room changes the individual's behaviour and their possibilities for action or the actions that seem appropriate within a given context, how does it, on a larger scale, affect the opinions, attitudes, and actions of a group? And how does the mood 'spread' and unfold within the collective?

Before we entered that room, something had already been happening within it. A mood had already been established, without our presence. Yet, given the simple fact that there is a temporal dimension to mood, my arrival makes me aware of the immediate past, occurrences within the room giving it its complete dynamic and form, when I was absent from this mood. Although my physical presence was not necessary for the prevailing mood in the room, my entrance now—necessarily—provokes a sense that mood, as such, is dialectically set. There is an interplay between my own mood and that of the previously existing collective, and both interfere with each other. Of necessity, my entrance is a moment of dissonance, and my decision to attune my mood to that in the room is an attempt to discover what has been going on prior to my arrival. It stimulates a curiosity, and a decision to listen. To give this a special edge, imagine the scenario in which the conversation that is taking place in the room is actually about you, and you enter just before the others are able to complete what they were saying, behind your back, in your supposed absence.

The dialectic that informs any specific mood is always political, in that it is concerned with the establishment of a new collective. T.S. Eliot famously argued that, when a new poet or 'individual talent' arrives, she or he rearranges the entire history of poetry: the individual talent, as it enters the space of poetry, affects and reshapes the tradition; just as the tradition had helped to inform and shape the predilections and preferences of the poet.[5] At issue in this is mood in the very precise sense of 'attunement', or Martin Heidegger's concept of *Stimmung*. To become a poet, for the modern and modernist Eliot, one had to have acquired already the tradition, and this involves great labour, as it cannot simply be inherited in some neutral fashion. The individual talent—the person entering the room—makes a determined effort at a form of attunement, simply in order to make herself heard and to make what she has to say 'available' to the existing language or lexicon of moods. The effort and transformative labour is one of listening, of trying to hear and understand what the prevailing language says or means.

We might say, then, that mood is fundamental to each and every single act of human interaction and communication, and that it is determining of the condition of any and all human community. Mood thus speaks to the Being-with others, in Heideggerian terms—or, as Maurice Merleau-Ponty describes it, our shared 'basis of co-existence'[6]—which Jean-Luc Nancy has given centre stage in his concept of 'plural singularity': by definition, we always exist 'with' others and '[t]here is no meaning if meaning is not shared.'[7] When Nancy further states that '[e]verything, then, passes *between us*,'[8] it is that very *between* which mood indicates on an existential, affective, and social level. Mood, we might say, is literally and intrinsically 'interesting' (*inter-esse*): it stands as the ground of our being together in the world. Mood quite specifically 'interests' us, calling us into a social being, but a being that is necessarily conditioned by the changing of moods that is established as the dialectical play between 'the room' (or Eliot's tradition) as it stands and we who enter, at the moment of entry (identified by that entry as a new and specific subject). To learn a language, as an infant, is to attune oneself to the prevailing language in the room, as it were; yet, as soon as one has gained some competence in that listening, one is in a position to re-tune, to change one's tune, to become thereby fully individual. And this is a process without end, and even—technically—without beginning.

Attunement is never stable, but is always intrinsically linked to change: it is dynamic, kinetic, as well as potential. Consider the tuning of a musical instrument (a process signified by the German word *Stimmung* alongside the word's primary meaning of affective 'mood'). There is a specific vibration of strings, say, that one needs if one is to play and hear a middle C. It is physical; as a vibration, it involves movement in space and across time; it contains within itself the very wave-motion—change *as motion or movement*—that makes the sound as it reaches our ear. The frequency of the vibration is what makes the sound, but the sound itself is formed by internal and intrinsic motion and movement. How awkward it becomes, then, to get two instruments to attune with each other. Attunement is hard work. My piano is joined by your guitar, and all is well. But then a voice enters. It is out of tune with us, but the singer is in tune with herself. Dissonance results. The singer sings of her difficulty in parking, and we realise that she is not part of this tune, not attuned to this community. She is, as it were, speaking a foreign tongue in the very midst of our attempts to attune with each other, and we name her as a foreigner, 'barbarian,' a maker of sounds that disturb our conventions and norms.

Alternatively, however, 'a voice comes to one in the dark.'[9] Alone in the dark. It breaks the silence. Silence also was conditioned by a mood. In Beckett, it might be a mood of failure. The response, however, can never be another silence. Mood is and was always there, and all we can do is to engage productively or otherwise with it.

*

We live a distinctly 'moody' age: one that is not only acutely perceptive towards individual, social, political, and psychiatric forms of mood, but one that actively seeks to interrogate the nature of these moods and the questions and concerns in relation to it that have been formulated above. Collectively, we seem to be growing increasingly aware of the impact that moods have on our daily lives, be it through the widespread psychiatric 'mood disorders' of the twenty-first century or through cultural moods whose dissemination has ostensibly been facilitated by the speed and ease of digital means of communication. At the same time, attempts to influence, intensify, and regulate mood are becoming ever more common, such as pharmaceutical 'mood stabilisers,' 'mood playlists' on popular music streaming services like Spotify, and the use of 'mood lighting' in public and private spaces.[10] Likewise, political and social processes are progressively considered through their relation to communal attitudes and modes of feeling: the so-called 'Mood of the Nation' poll at Pennsylvania State University attempted to trace the development of political attitudes and perceptions in the run up to the 2016 US presidential election.[11] Likewise, a *New York Times* article titled 'An American Mood' sought to grasp the nation's mood through artistic representations of different individuals' feelings and opinions on and after the 2016 Election Day.[12] Similarly, in her official birthday message on 17 June 2017, Queen Elizabeth II suggested that in the wake of the terror attacks in Manchester and London as well as of the Grenfell Tower Disaster, it was 'difficult to escape a very sombre national mood.'[13] The discipline of economics, as it notices the importance of these and similar phenomena, attends increasingly to issues of 'wellbeing' or the 'economics of happiness,' attempting to measure what it had previously seen as metaphysical values instead of the simple materiality of financial wealth.[14]

There can be a clear political dimension to mood, then, as these examples suggest. As we now know—or at least suspect—mood has interfered fundamentally with the principles of democratic politics. The recent scandals concerning the harvesting of personal and private data, via Facebook and Cambridge Analytica, for example, have led to a suggestion that the covert manipulation of mood is possible, that its consequences can be massive, and in ways that might be detrimental to democratic politics. Yet, at the same time, we have always known that political rhetoric depends upon shifting and swaying the moods of the citizen. That is what political persuasion is about, and, at least since Aristotle, we have known that logos or reason works alongside pathos or feeling. Both of these work alongside ethos, our sense of belonging to a shared community of interests, a common identity. The difference with contemporary technology is that both ethos and pathos have effectively reduced the standing of logos itself, to the point where our reason is shaped by our emotion and by our preferred social and political identity. Identity politics—where I am fully attuned, as it were, to a particular mood or model of how to live—leads to a condition in which reason is subsumed under identity. Tribalism is the result, and we sometimes call this either tunnel vision or 'confirmation bias' or 'silo thinking' in the echo-chamber of social media.

Confirmation bias leads to political conformity, and it is this—and the consequent opportunity for political control by those armed with the necessary algorithms and in control of the technology—that provides the new concern about the nature of politics. If we can decide to change the constitutional status of 65 million people, say, through an emotional response to the EU as in Brexit, without recourse to reason, then we have to ask who is calling the tune, who is playing the pipe? Likewise, if 310 million people can be led into a war, say, thanks to Donald Trump waking up one morning and feeling that his masculinist identity is threatened by the 'Rocket Man' Kim Jong-un, then we are entering a new phase of politics. In her 2014 essay 'Not in the Mood,' Sara Ahmed comments on the circulation of mood through political discourses, arguing that political actors do not merely attribute forms of feeling to political collectives, but give form to existing feelings and thereby make them imperatives for the formation of a national identity. Using the example of a speech delivered in 2011 by the then Prime Minister of the UK, David Cameron, Ahmed observes:

> At the time of the speech the security minister Baroness Neville-Jones said to the *Today* radio programme on BBC 1: 'There's a widespread feeling in the country that we're less united behind values than we need to be'. Speeches like Cameron's are affective because they pick up on feelings, and give them form. In giving them form, they direct those feelings in specific ways. Feelings of nervousness or anxiety might be prevalent, they might even be widespread (we are living in times which make such feelings *make sense*). Political discourse transforms feeling by giving that feeling an object or target. We could call this projection: negative feelings are projected onto outsiders, who then appear to threaten from without, what is felt as precariously within. But projection is not the right word insofar as it implies an inside going out. I think these feelings are in some way *out and about*. They circulate at least in part through being understood as in circulation (the speech act which says the nation feels this or that way does something, it becomes an injunction to feel that way in order to participate in the thing being named, such that to participate in feeling or with feeling becomes a confirmation of feeling).[15]

If mood is thus instrumental to political change and collective identity—be it through the attribution, evocation, or manipulation of collective attitudes and forms of feeling—we need to be wary of it, but first of all, we need to become more aware of it.

The present volume is indicative of a recent shift in our perception of mood and its pivotal role in our personal and political lives. Increasingly, there is a widespread sense both in the media and in academic inquiries that cultural moods are not simply reactive towards particular events or descriptive of certain ways in which people feel at a specific moment in time; rather, these moods actively shape not only forms of individual and collective feeling but also political, social, and economic actualities. Simultaneously, the study of mood has been growing into a new field of inquiry in its own right within a number of academic disciplines, including psychology, cognitive science, philosophy, political science, and aesthetics. This volume places itself within the growing body of a literature that aims to investigate the nature of mood: its psychological and philosophical stature, its aesthetic forms and functions as well as its political, social, and ethical dimensions. Furthermore, it considers mood as a phenomenon whose study is, by definition, of an interdisciplinary nature.

To some extent, the recent surge in academic attention that has been dedicated to mood across the humanities and social sciences could be seen as a result of the so-called 'affective turn,' a term that has been used to describe the proliferation of work focusing on feeling, the body, and emotions as a source for producing knowledge and insight into aesthetic, social, and political phenomena since the 1990s. The works of leading figures in the field of affect studies, such as Brian Massumi, Eve Kosofsky Sedgwick, Patricia Clough, and Teresa Brennan, are oftentimes indebted to and inspired by Gilles Deleuze and Félix Guattari's postmodern philosophy of the body[16] as they consider the feeling body and its modes of affectedness alongside technoscientific and biopolitical concerns. Affect studies' ethos of elevating feeling to the status of an epistemological tool that can account for complex sociopolitical and cultural systems has enabled and encouraged a similar reconsideration of mood as a related field of enquiry.

Over the course of the past ten years, mood has become a topic in various disciplines that has sparked sustained academic interest, proving that—as Matthew Ratcliffe has phrased it—mood 'matters'[17] and, at the same time, makes things matter to us. Much of the work that has been produced in a number of disciplines over the recent period emphasises the potential for subverting established forms of understanding and knowing that a mood-based perspective can offer. The *New Literary History*'s 2012 special edition *In the Mood*, edited by Rita Felski and Susan Fraiman, is a crucial contribution to mood's raising stature in intellectual discourses. In their introduction to this special issue, Felski and Fraiman emphasise the extent to which mood allows us to reconsider phenomena whose study seems to have exhausted traditional, binary, and dialectical means of categorising experience and feeling:

> The concept of mood [...] circumvents the clunky categories often imposed on experience: subjective versus objective, feeling versus thinking, latent versus manifest. The field of affect studies is

sometimes taken to task for reinforcing such dichotomies, creating a picture of affect as a zone of ineffable and primordial experience that is subsequently squeezed into the rationalist straitjacket of language. The concept of mood, for the most part, avoids such difficulties. Definitions of mood often emphasize its role in modulating thought, acknowledging a dynamic and interactive relationship between reason and emotion. Mood is tied up with self-understanding and shapes thinking rather than being stifled by thinking. It makes intellectual work possible and inflects it in subtle and less subtle ways, informing the questions we ask, the puzzles that intrigue us, the styles and genres of argument we are drawn to. Mood impinges on method.[18]

Adopting a mood-based lens, then, means that not only the objects of our enquiry but also the methods and assumptions underlying that enquiry must change. If its vague, elusive nature challenges academic strategies for studying it, mood's very vagueness and intangibility can be a catalyst for forging new ways of understanding our fundamental modes of coexisting alongside each other in the world.

The prolific work on mood in contemporary philosophy often takes its inspiration from Martin Heidegger's influential theory of mood, or *Stimmung*, as developed in his *Being and Time* (1927). Mood, Heidegger proposes, is more than a subjective feeling or state-of-mind; it is the fundamental condition for our encounter with the world, and we need to recognise it as such. Heidegger thus proposes that 'it is necessary to see this phenomenon as a fundamental *existentiale*,'[19] i.e., a constitutive aspect of our existence. We are never not in a mood, and this mood—or 'attunement'—determines the way in which we will encounter, understand, and interact with the world. Writers such as Lars Svendsen,[20] Hagi Kenaan and Ilit Ferber,[21] Matthew Ratcliffe,[22] and Angelika Krebs and Aaron Ben-Ze'ev[23] have taken up Heidegger's philosophy of mood, oftentimes productively critiquing and refining it. Recent publications on mood in the field of philosophy have also taken Heidegger's proposition a step further in beginning to question the very moods underlying philosophical work itself. In their volume *Philosophy's Moods: The Affective Grounds of Thinking* (2011), Kenaan and Ferber raise the pivotal questions of 'how philosophical thought operates within and through mood' and what 'different roles moods play in the history of philosophy.'[24] The volume presents an important move towards the type of academic self-reflection that mood encourages, and the way in which—as Felski and Fraiman suggest—it impinges on the very methods that we use to study it.

Hans Ulrich Gumbrecht proposes that this, too, applies to our encounters with art. In his study *Atmosphere, Stimmung, Mood: On a Hidden Potential of Literature* (2011), a text that has influenced much contemporary work on mood in literary studies, Gumbrecht proposes a mode of reading that concentrates on reading for mood or *Stimmung*.[25] Gumbrecht considers this approach as a 'third position'[26] between the currently stagnating, opposed schools of deconstruction and cultural studies in literary theory. However, he suggests that a mood-based approach to literature and other art forms is in itself no novelty—instead, Gumbrecht argues, we are always already reading with mood in mind. Indeed, we might see some preliminary suggestions regarding the importance of mood, or *Stimmung*, in a text as early as Longinus's *On the Sublime*, written sometime in the first century CE, in which the stimulation of specific sublime moods is seen as instrumental in acts of persuasion, acts that make listeners or readers change their minds on some particular issue. Gumbrecht's aim, then, becomes to make readers and critics more perceptive towards these moods, to encourage them to register them and engage with them, thereby rediscovering a fundamental aspect of aesthetic experience: 'the objective is to follow configurations of atmosphere and mood in order to encounter otherness in intense and intimate ways.'[27] The question of mood's aesthetic dimension also lies at the heart of a growing body of work which considers it in relation to literature,[28] film,[29] music,[30] and other art forms, as well as in the formation of culture in general, as seen, for instance, in Ben Highmore's recent publication *Cultural Feelings: Mood, Mediation and Cultural Politics* (2017).[31]

Psychology and psychiatry, the disciplines that are probably the most closely associated with mood, have been instrumental in developing central contributions to our understanding of mood and how its relationship to other affective phenomena can be conceptualised.[32] In recent years, psychiatric studies of various mood disorders have increased considerably,[33] making them a key topic in contemporary psychiatric research. In addition to this, cognitive psychology and philosophy of mind have found a common ground in considering the affective structures of human existence. Neuroscientists such as Antonio Damasio and philosophers such as Giovanna Colombetti have been considering the architecture of the human mind and the role of mood and related forms of affect in cognitive processes.[34] At the same time, recent developments in neurobiological research include the application of computational models to the study of mood.[35]

In other areas of the social sciences, mood's role in sociopolitical processes has become subject to extensive study. The 'socionomic hypothesis'—developed by Robert Prechter[36]—considers social mood to be a key factor in financial and political developments, and this has inspired a steadily growing body of work dedicated to the impact of social mood on different areas of culture and politics.[37] A number of recent publications have also considered the relationship between mood and the internet,[38] in particular in relation to social media: for instance, Richard Coyne's

Mood and Mobility: Navigating the Emotional Spaces of Digital Social Networks (2016) proposes that digital social networks not only disseminate but also forge collective moods.[39] Work of this nature follows the idea that 'mood is a social phenomenon before it is individual'[40] and emphasises its pivotal role in collective and communal relationships.

Much of the work that has been described above is already, by virtue of its central theme, of an interdisciplinary nature. Indeed, it seems hardly possible to *not* study mood in an interdisciplinary way, considering its locatedness at the intersection of a number of disciplines, each of which attends to different aspects of mood: philosophy to its experiential and existential meaning; psychology to its cognitive and affective dimension; aesthetics to its undeniable impact on our experience and appreciation of art; and sociology, politics, and 'Socionomics' to its crucial role in the formation of social and political actualities. While each of these disciplines has produced its own understanding of mood, a concerted effort to bridge the gap between their approaches to mood and to create a dialogue between them needs to be made. As Felski and Fraiman suggest, mood has the potential to bridge existing distinctions: 'if moods seem to be everywhere and nowhere, their value may lie precisely in bridging distinctions and lubricating relations between ostensibly separate entities: self and other, films and viewers, thought and feeling, scholarship and daily life.'[41] The same can be said for disciplinary boundaries.

*

As scholars of literature, we encountered limitations within our own field when trying to attend to the phenomenon of mood: when attempting to 'read mood,' we soon felt that our disciplinary tools for doing so may at times hold back a deeper understanding of the processes at work when we speak about the 'mood of a text.' Reading Eliot's *The Waste Land,* for example, made us melancholic, nostalgic, but also somewhat amused, exalted, and delighted—but answering the questions of *why, how,* and *with what effect* it did so took us into a realm of inquiry that involves a plethora of phenomenological, psychological, ethical, historical, and political problems: how can we describe and account for these moods? How is language capable of evoking them? What actually happens in our bodies as we experience them? How do I know that not only myself but others also experience the same moods when reading this poem? Is there a way of going beyond a subjective experience of these moods and making sense of them through more objective and measurable means? Is it merely the poem that draws us into these moods or are there other factors at work? Historically, where do these moods come from? When and by whom were they invented, and have they to some extent contributed to the 'invention' of modernism?[42] What gives Eliot's poem the right to make us feel that way, and why would we let it? And, finally, what are the political implications of entering these moods? Do we experience them because they are collectively accepted, even encouraged, within Western culture, because they are what we are supposed to feel? If so, do they keep us from feeling other, more uncomfortable, or uglier moods?[43] Clearly, reading Celan, for example, gave us an entirely different mode—mood—of experience from the kind of moods that we made in the encounter with Eliot. We came to see that a philosophical reflection on the nature of mood and psychological and cognitive considerations of its workings would be crucial to conceptualising it aesthetically; at the same time, we realised that the kinds of relationships that literary mood forges—between reader and author, between reader and text, and between readers—were not only of an aesthetic, but of a social, ethical, even a political, nature.

The chapters included in this volume seek firstly, to provide an overview of the current developments and recent advancements in the study of mood in a number of fields, including philosophy, architecture, musicology, mathematical epidemiology, medicine, classics, translation studies, and literary studies. Furthermore, they recognise the interdisciplinary challenge that mood poses, and engage with this phenomenon in new and innovative ways. The majority of the chapters in the present collection were inspired by papers delivered at the conference *Mood: Aesthetic, Psychological and Philosophical Perspectives*, which was held at Warwick in 2016. Through this conference, we aimed to explore the interdisciplinary potential that we had found in mood and to create synergy between the insights that developments in different disciplines could offer. As a result of this, the contributions included in this volume make a conscious effort to bridge disciplinary gaps in approaching mood. Broadly speaking, the volume can be divided into two sections, the first of which is mainly concerned with the theory of mood while the other is dedicated to a more 'applied' study of specific moods; however, the boundaries between these two are fluid: each analysis of specific moods is inextricably tied to implicit or explicit theoretical reflections on how they can be conceptualised and understood and, at the same time, any theoretical reflection on the nature of mood draws on specific historical, experienced, and observed moods.

Hagi Kenaan's chapter 'Changing Moods' opens these reflections as it, first, revisits and explicates Heidegger's ontological concept of *Stimmung* and then goes beyond Heidegger's considerations in examining mood's temporality and inherent plurality: Kenaan provocatively suggests that 'there is no such thing as *a* mood' as moods are defined by their inherent processual nature and by the dynamic changes from one mood to another. To understand mood, we need to consider its instability and changeability, as well as the relationships between moods and the dynamic changes between them. Kenaan's essay is an impactful reminder that it is impossible to consider mood in an entirely abstract, isolated, and theoretical fashion[44]: only through observing the temporal unfolding from one mood to the next can we fully realise their experiential and existential significance.

Chapter 2, by Jon Arcaraz Puntonet, considers the very intersection of the two dimensions through which mood unfolds: temporality and spatiality. By analysing the relationship between Fernando Higueras's architectural project *10 Residencies for Artists on El Pardo Hill in Madrid* and Manuel de Falla's ballet *El Amor Brujo*, Arcaraz uncovers the intimate connection between rhythm, tempo, and space in provoking and eliciting a mood in the observer. Arcaraz thus traces the musical dimension of *Stimmung* back to the Pythagorean understanding of rhythm and shows how Higueras's project transposes musical rhythm into the experience of spatial objects. The essay's trajectory is both intensely specific to de Falla's and Higueras's pieces and makes an important contribution to an understanding of mood's spatio-temporal experientiality and actuality.

Jonathan Mitchell's essay 'The Varieties of Mood Intentionality' addresses a long-standing problem in the conceptualisation of mood. In attempting to distinguish between mood and other affective phenomena, scholars have often cited the idea that feelings and emotions are intentional, that they are always in some way directed toward something, whereas mood is a fundamentally non-intentional state, which encompasses one's total perspective without having intentional objects.[45] Conversely, by distinguishing between first-order and second-order levels of experience, Mitchell presents an understanding of personal-level intentionality that enables him to identify varying degrees of mood intentionality: mood's intentional objects, Mitchell argues, can be 'the self,' 'the body,' and 'the world.' Ultimately, Mitchell thus sheds light on the ways in which we can psychologically and philosophically make sense of moods as complex states emerging through our experiences of our own bodies, our sense of self and our directedness towards the world.

The fourth chapter, by Erik Wallrup, again revisits Heidegger's concept of *Stimmung*, which it considers from a musicological and historical point of view. Understanding *Stimmung* as attunement, Wallrup traces the conceptual history of attunement in Heidegger's works alongside Heidegger's paradoxical rejection of music as an art form. He thereby uncovers two dialectically opposed ways of thinking about music in relation to mood: traditionally, music has either been seen as pure mathematics (entirely 'rational') or pure feeling (entirely 'irrational'). By considering our affectedness by music as motion and emotion, Wallrup presents the act of listening as an act of fundamental attunement. As we have outlined above, our daily engagement with mood is negotiated through the act of listening, one that—Wallrup argues—attunes us to the world and others in a musical fashion.

Chapter 5, by Edward M. Hill and Thomas House, considers this attunement through a completely different, and yet related, lens: based on mathematical modelling, Hill and House present an analysis of how mood spreads in social networks and can thus be considered as being 'contagious.' The essay details the methodology and results of a number of innovative studies conducted by the authors and their collaborators, in which they set out to investigate the contagiousness of positive and negative moods in adolescent friendship networks. The studies and data collected shed light on the complex relationship between individual and social mood and enable a better understanding of mood from an epidemiological perspective with possible applications within the health-care sector. The chapter presents us with a nexus of ethical and cultural problems: if we can indeed say that mood spreads in a contagious way, the ethical, medical, and societal significance of mood is vast.

The social dimension of mood also lies at the heart of Chapter 6, by Mikko Ketovuori and Matt Lampert. Considering the relationship between politics, stock market developments, and cultural production, Ketovuori and Lampert analyse the moods reflected in Finnish popular music in the years 2006 and 2009, respectively. Following Prechter's socionomic hypothesis, they suggest a causal relationship between high and low aggregate moods found in Finnish pop songs with peaks and lows in stock market indexes, national economic performance, and consumer confidence as well as specific political developments in the respective years. Their analysis showcases the complex relationship between politics, economics, and aesthetic production, and, based on the example of Finland, it critically investigates the dynamics behind the notion of 'national moods,' carrying important implications for political, economic, and cultural inquiries into mood.

Madeleine Scherer's essay on mood in the *Odyssey* opens up another crucial dimension of moods: their historicity, and the historical dimension of the concept of 'mood' itself. When considering a text that was composed over two millennia ago, the historically and culturally conditioned nature of our understanding of mood comes into focus. By closely looking at the moods of the *Odyssey*, particularly that of *nostos*, Scherer not only considers the ways in which we as contemporary readers can make sense of the affective composition of Homer's epic, but also rigorously demonstrates how antiquity's understanding of the human being on the one hand and the social collective on the other hand feed into the ways in which mood is conceptualised. This transhistorical perspective gives us a better sense of the origins of specific moods, such as nostalgia, and their affective histories, thus offering important impulses for both the study of classical texts and for the study of mood's conceptual history.

Chapter 8, too, questions whether moods are universal and historically stable, but shifts the focus from a transhistorical to a transcultural point of view. By considering how the awkwardness of Marcel Proust's *In Search of Lost Time* has been rendered into English, Yasmine Richardson addresses the cultural specificity of moods and asks if it is possible to 'translate' them. Richardson provides a lucid analysis of the features that make Proust's *magnum opus* 'awkward,' examines the translational strategies that have been used to translate this awkwardness from its original French into English, and thus demonstrates the ways in which each language and culture creates its own affective vocabulary. Like the preceding chapter by Scherer, Richardson's essay thereby sensitises us to mood's contingency, and it opens up pressing questions for the study of mood, most importantly whether our different affective vocabularies indicate that different cultures experience different moods.

Joshua Burraway's 'Altering the Mood: Boredom and Anaesthesia in Itchy Park' continues the consideration of culturally, historically, and, in this instance, socially specific moods. The essay combines empirical work on the experience of boredom in the homeless community of London's 'Itchy Park' with an analysis of the relationship between intoxication, boredom, and existence through an anthropological lens. Burraway's interviews with homeless participants, whose boredom has oftentimes driven them into addiction, showcase the temporal and existential dimension of the 'deep' boredom they feel—a boredom that is indicative of late capitalism's complicity in forging specific affective modes of being. And yet, this intoxicated boredom is a mood that is radically rejected by the ethos of our society. It is not even dysphoric in the sense of our socially accepted 'ugly feelings,'[46] but fundamentally 'a-phoric' in its detached unbearableness.

Chapter 10, by Rex Ferguson, returns to the question of aesthetic mood and investigates its very nature. Ferguson therein revisits affect studies' and philosophy's attempts to conceptualise mood and considers how we can approach the project of 'mood-reading.' By analysing the atmospheric spatiality and intensely multisensory narrative of Lawrence Durrell's *The Alexandria Quartet*, Ferguson demonstrates how the quartet's plot becomes constitutive for the formation of a mood that makes itself 'felt' in the text. The text's immersive quality allows for a contagiousness which unfolds in the aesthetic process; the text's aura, its physical presence, envelops the reader and creates an atmosphere that they 'breathe' in. The material presence of aesthetic mood, its encodedness in textual form, thus become the powerful medium of yet another form of contagion—one that enters our bodies through the act of reading.

The final chapter presents an adapted excerpt from Mary Cappello's book *Life Breaks In: A Mood Almanack* (2016), a collection of lyric essays that, through its associative, affectively perceptive, and experimental modes of writing, both investigates and epitomises mood's essence. Cappello introduces us to her reasoning and intentions behind 'essaying' mood: the essay genre, Cappello explains, enables her to notice and

acknowledge mood 'without killing it in the process.' Her sonic repertoire of moods guides us through autobiographically inspired moods of
experience and reflection: from a dime hitting the floor unheard in a
restaurant via being submerged in a 'gong bath' as if in a liquid mood
to the mood-inducing quality of the word 'riffraff,' the text takes its
readers through the minute temporal changes, plurality, and flexibility
of our daily moods. Treading carefully so as not to break the moods it
evokes, Cappello's text provides the most organic reflection on mood
that this volume offers.

The chapters in the present volume thus present a comprehensive, although not exhaustive, selection of current developments and contributions to the study of mood. Other disciplines, such as linguistics (which
considers grammatical moods as well as the different affective vocabularies to which Richardson's chapter calls attention), human geography
(which looks at our affective relationship to space), religious studies (in
which religious congregations form affective communities that are constitutive for collective moods), and the life sciences (whose empirical work
on the physical basis of mood is crucial to understanding the notion of
contagious moods), to name but a few—and the dialogue between the disciplines that are represented in this volume and those beyond its scope—
can, and hopefully will, through future work, offer further insights into
the phenomenon at hand. While this introduction has attempted to set
the scene for the volume as a whole, by outlining the individual chapters'
shared concerns in relation to the spatial, temporal, social, political, and
aesthetic dimensions of mood, it has deliberately refused to provide a
single definition of mood, its nature, and meaning. Some of the essays in
this book demonstrate different ways of reconsidering mood that produce
tension, or are even mutually exclusive—which is perhaps a necessary
accompaniment of our interdisciplinary project. We believe that it is this
latent tension, a being 'out-of-tune' with one another, that will perhaps
allow the most productive modes of thinking about mood.

Notes

1 Teresa Brennan, *The Transmission of Affect* (Ithaca, NY and London: Cornell University Press, 2004), p. 1.
2 Ibid., p. 68.
3 As the person entering, your task is to '*read* the room'. Its atmosphere is
  legible, and one might say that this depends on a certain sense of affective
  literacy. Hence it is possible to speak of such as thing as 'mood-reading', as
  Rex Ferguson does in Chapter 10 of this volume.
4 Ibid.
5 T[homas] S[tearns] Eliot, 'Tradition and the Individual Talent' [1919], in
  The Waste Land and Other Writings (New York: The Modern Library,
  2002), pp. 99–108.
6 Maurice Merleau-Ponty, *Phenomenology of Perception*, trans. Colin Smith
  (London and New York: Routledge, 2002), p. 518.

7 Jean-Luc Nancy, *Being Singular Plural* [1996], trans. by Robert D. Richardson and Anne E. O'Byrne (Stanford, CA: Stanford University Press, 2000), p. 2.

8 Ibid., p. 5.

9 Samuel Beckett, *Company* (London: John Calder, 1980), p. 7.

10 Cf. Birgit Breidenbach, 'Grasping the Ineffable: Interdisciplinary Perspectives on Mood', *Exchanges: The Warwick Research Journal*, 4(2), 2017, pp. 309–15 (pp. 309f.). http://exchanges.warwick.ac.uk/index.php/exchanges/article/view/147 (accessed 31 March 2018).

11 *Mood of the Nation Poll*, Pennsylvania State University. http://election2016.psu.edu/tag/mood-of-the-nation-poll/ (accessed 31 March 2018).

12 Cari Vander Yacht, 'An American Mood', *New York Times*, 12 November 2016, www.nytimes.com/interactive/2016/11/12/us/racerelated-election-art.html (accessed 31 March 2018).

13 *BBC News* website, 'London Fire: Queen Reflects on "Sombre National Mood"', 17 June 2017. www.bbc.co.uk/news/uk-40310959 (accessed 31 March 2018).

14 Indeed, some recent accounts, even of Marxism, indicate that economic questions and issues of happiness are intertwined at the fundamental level of how bodies live and relate with each other and with nature. Terry Eagleton put this succinctly in his *The Ideology of the Aesthetic* (Oxford: Blackwell, 1990, p. 201): 'If communism is necessary, it is because we are unable to feel, taste, smell and touch as fully as we might.' The non-Marxist account of this can be found in Keynesian economic thinking, as in Edward Skidelsky and Robert Skidelsky, *How Much Is Enough?* (London: Penguin, 2013).

15 Sara Ahmed, 'Not in the Mood', *New Formations*, 82 (Summer 2014), *Mood Work*, 13–28 (p. 25).

16 Patricia Ticineto Clough, 'Introduction', in *The Affective Turn: Theorizing the Social*, ed. by Patricia Ticineto Clough and Jean Halley (Durham, NC and London: Duke University Press, 2007), pp. 1–33 (p. 1).

17 Matthew Ratcliffe, 'Why Mood Matters', in *The Cambridge Companion to Heidegger's "Being and Time"*, ed. by Mark A. Wrathall (Cambridge and New York: Cambridge University Press, 2013), pp. 157–76.

18 Rita Felski and Susan Fraiman, 'Introduction', *New Literary History*, 43(3), Summer 2012, *In the Mood*, pp. v–xii (p. vi). A similar position is held by Michel Haar as he suggests that '[t]o "listen to" *Stimmung*, it is necessary not only to eschew the definitions given by the rational faculty of understanding but to take one's distance from the egocentric *interiority* of feeling and its *intentionality*' in his *The Song of the Earth: Heidegger and the Grounds of the History of Being*, trans. by Reginald Lilly (Bloomington and Indianapolis: Indiana University Press, 1993), p. 41.

19 Martin Heidegger, *Being and Time*, trans. by John Macquarrie and Edward Robinson (New York et al.: Harper Collins, 1962), p. 173. See also Bruce W. Ballard, *The Role of Mood in Heidegger's Ontology* (London and Lanham, New York: University of America Press, 1991).

20 Cf. Lars Svendsen, *A Philosophy of Boredom*, trans. by John Irons (London: Reaction Books, 2005); see also Lars Svendsen, 'Moods and the Meaning of Philosophy', *New Literary History*, 43(3), Summer 2012, pp. 419–31.

21 Hagi Kenaan, and Ilit Ferber (eds.), *Philosophy's Moods: The Affective Grounds of Thinking* (Dordrecht et al.: Springer, 2011).

22 Matthew Ratcliffe, *Feelings of Being* (Oxford: Oxford University Press, 2008); Matthew Ratcliffe, 'Heidegger's Attunement and the Neuropsychology of Emotion', *Phenomenology and Cognitive Emotion*, 1, 2002, pp. 287–312; Matthew Ratcliffe, 'The Phenomenology of Mood and the Meaning of Life', in *The Oxford Handbook of Philosophy of Emotion*, ed.

by Peter Goldie (Oxford: Oxford University Press, 2010), pp. 349–71; and Ratcliffe, 'Why Mood Matters'.

23 Angelika Krebs, and Aaron Ben-Ze'ev (eds.), *The Meaning of Moods*, *Philosophia*, 45(4), December 2017, pp. 1395–708.

24 Hagi Kenaan, and Ilit Ferber, 'Moods and Philosophy', in *Philosophy's Moods: The Affective Grounds of Thinking*, ed. by Hagi Kenaan and Ilit Ferber (Dordrecht et al.: Springer, 2011), pp. 3–10 (p. 6).

25 Hans Ulrich Gumbrecht, *Atmosphere, Stimmung, Mood: On a Hidden Potential of Literature* [2011], trans. by Erik Butler (Stanford, CA: Stanford University Press, 2012).

26 Ibid., p. 3.

27 Ibid., pp. 12f.

28 Cf. Thomas Pfau, *Romantic Moods: Paranoia, Trauma, and Melancholy, 1790–1840* (Baltimore, MD: The Johns Hopkins University Press, 2005); Owen Earnshaw, 'Mood, Delusions and Poetry: Emotional 'Wording of the World' in Psychosis, Philosophy and the Everyday', *Philosophia*, 45(4), December 2017, *The Meaning of Moods*, pp. 1697–708.

29 Cf. Robert Sinnerbrink, 'Stimmung: Exploring the Aesthetics of Mood', *Screen*, 53(2), 1 June 2012, pp. 148–63; Carl Platinga, 'Art Moods and Human Moods in Narrative Cinema', *New Literary History*, 43(3), Summer 2012, *In the Mood*, pp. 455–75; John Rhym, 'Towards a Phenomenology of Cinematic Mood: Boredom and the Affect of Time in Antonioni's L'eclisse, *New Literary History*, 43(3), Summer 2012, *In the Mood*, pp. 477–501; Susanne Schmetkamp, 'Gaining Perspectives on Our Lives: Moods and Aesthetic Experience', *Philosophia*, 45(4), December 2017, *The Meaning of Moods*, pp. 1681–95.

30 Cf. Erik Wallrup, *Being Musically Attuned: The Act of Listening to Music* (Farnham and Burlington, VT: Ashgate, 2015).

31 Ben Highmore, *Cultural Feelings: Mood, Mediation and Cultural Politics* (New York and Abingdon: Routledge, 2017).

32 See, for instance, Richard J. Davidson, 'On Emotion, Mood, and Related Affective Constructs', in *The Nature of Emotion: Fundamental Questions*, ed. by Paul Ekman and Richard J. Davidson (Oxford: Oxford University Press, 1994), pp. 51–5, and Christopher Beedie, Peter Terry, and Andrew Lane, 'Distinctions between Emotion and Mood', *Cognition and Emotion*, 19, 2005, pp. 847–78.

33 On the psychiatric notion of mood disorders, see Robert J. DeRubeis and Daniel R. Strunk, eds. *The Oxford Handbook of Mood Disorders* (Oxford: Oxford University Press, 2017) and Leslie Matsukawa, 'Mood Disorders', in *Culture and Psychopathology: A Guide to Clinical Assessment*, ed. by Jon Streltzer, 2nd ed. (New York and Abingdon: Routledge, 2017), pp. 21–35.

34 See Antonio R. Damasio, *The Feeling of What Happens: Body, Emotion, and the Making of Consciousness* (London: Vintage, 1999) and Antonio R. Damasio, *Self Comes to Mind: Constructing the Conscious Brain* (London: Heinemann, 2010), as well as Giovanna Colombetti, 'The Embodied and Situated Nature of Moods', *Philosophia*, 45(4), December 2017, *The Meaning of Moods*, pp. 1437–51, and Giovanna Colombetti, *The Feeling Body: Affective Science Meets the Enactive Mind* (London and Cambridge, MA: The MIT Press, 2014).

35 James E. Clark, Stuart Watson, and Karl J. Friston, 'What is Mood? A Computational Perspective', *Psychological Medicine*, (2018), pp. 1–8. DOI:10.1017/S0033291718000430 (accessed 20 April 2018).

36 Robert R. Prechter, *The Wave Principle of Human Social Behavior and the New Science of Socionomics* (Gainesville, GA: New Classics Library, 1999). See also the contribution by Ketovuori and Lampert in this volume.

37 See, for instance, John L. Casti, *Mood Matters: From Rising Skirt Lengths to the Collapse of World Powers* (New York: Copernicus Books, 2010). Another important contribution to understanding the political dynamics of mood can be found in *Mood Work*, an issue of *New Formations* which considers mood's significance in economic developments and forms of labour. In this issue, see in particular Ben Highmore and Jenny Bourne Taylor, 'Introducing Mood Work', *New Formations*, 82 (Summer 2014), *Mood Work*, 5–12.

38 Cf. Jaap van Ginneken, *Mood Contagion: Mass Psychology and Collective Behaviour Sociology in the Internet Age* (The Hague: Eleven International Publishing, 2013).

39 Richard Coyne, *Mood and Mobility: Navigating the Emotional Spaces of Digital Social Networks* (London and Cambridge, MA: The MIT Press, 2016).

40 Ibid., p. 13.

41 Felski and Fraiman, 'Introduction', xii.

42 Studies of the moods of modernism—such as nostalgia, melancholia, and anxiety—can, for instance, be found in Tammy Clewell, ed., *Modernism and Nostalgia: Bodies, Locations, Aesthetics* (Basingstoke and New York: Palgrave Macmillan, 2013); Sara Crangle, 'Phenomenology and Affect: Modernist Sulking', in *A Handbook of Modernism Studies*, ed. by Jean-Michel Rabaté (Chichester: John Wiley & Sons, 2013), pp. 327–45; Sanja Bahun, *Modernism and Melancholia: Writing as Countermourning* (Oxford: Oxford University Press, 2014); and Rebecca Saunders's *Lamentation and Modernity in Literature, Philosophy, and Culture*. Clewell, for instance, argues that nostalgia is 'constitutive of the aesthetic practices and political aspirations of modernist literature,' thus suggesting that moods are a foundational element of modernism. See Tammy Clewell, 'Introduction: Past "Perfect" and Present "Tense": The Abuses and Uses of Modernist Nostalgia', in *Modernism and Nostalgia: Bodies, Locations, Aesthetics*, ed. by Tammy Clewell (Basingstoke and New York: Palgrave Macmillan, 2013), pp. 1–22 (p. 20). A similar argument is made by Saunders as she proposes that modernity has created and disseminated specific moods, cf. *Lamentation and Modernity in Literature, Philosophy, and Culture* (Houndsmills, Basingstoke, and New York: Palgrave Macmillan, 2007), p. 10.

43 In her book *Ugly Feelings*, Sianne Ngai argues that a number of 'ugly' or unpleasant feelings, such as anxiety, paranoia, and irritation, to some extent present 'the psychic fuel on which capitalist society runs,' meaning that dysphoric feelings have become integrated, even constitutive, for late capitalist economy. Cf. Sianne Ngai, *Ugly Feelings* (London and Cambridge, MA: Harvard University Press, 2007), pp. 3f.

44 Kenaan shares this sentiment with Gumbrecht, who argues that theoretical approaches to mood are problematic because 'every *Stimmung* is historically and culturally unique' (*Atmosphere, Mood, Stimmung*, pp. 16f.).

45 See William Fish, 'Emotions, Moods, and Intentionality', in *Intentionality Past and Future*, ed. by Gábor Forrai and George Kampis (New York: Rodopi Press, 2005), pp. 25–35 (p. 25).

46 See endnote 43.

Works Cited

Ahmed, Sara, '*Not in the Mood*', *New Formations*, 82 (Summer 2014), *Mood Work*, 13–28.

Bahun, Sanja, *Modernism and Melancholia: Writing as Countermourning* (Oxford: Oxford University Press, 2014).

Ballard, Bruce W., *The Role of Mood in Heidegger's Ontology* (London, Lanham, MD and New York: University of America Press, 1991).

BBC News website, 'London Fire: Queen Reflects on "Sombre National Mood"', 17 June 2017. www.bbc.co.uk/news/uk-40310959 [accessed 31 March 2018].

Beckett, Samuel, *Company* (London: John Calder, 1980).

Beedie, Christopher, Peter Terry, and Andrew Lane, 'Distinctions between Emotion and Mood', *Cognition and Emotion*, 19 (2005), 847–78.

Breidenbach, Birgit, 'Grasping the Ineffable: Interdisciplinary Perspectives on Mood', *Exchanges: The Warwick Research Journal*, 4, 2 (2017), 309–15. http://exchanges.warwick.ac.uk/index.php/exchanges/article/view/147 [accessed 31 March 2018].

Brennan, Teresa, *The Transmission of Affect* (Ithaca, NY and London: Cornell University Press, 2004).

Casti, John L., *Mood Matters: From Rising Skirt Lengths to the Collapse of World Powers* (New York: Copernicus Books, 2010).

Clark, James E., Stuart Watson, and Karl J. Friston, 'What is Mood? A Computational Perspective', *Psychological Medicine*, (2018), 1–8. DOI:10.1017/S0033291718000430 [accessed 20 April 2018].

Clewell, Tammy, ed., *Modernism and Nostalgia: Bodies, Locations, Aesthetics* (Basingstoke and New York: Palgrave Macmillan, 2013).

——, 'Introduction: Past "Perfect" and Present "Tense": The Abuses and Uses of Modernist Nostalgia', in *Modernism and Nostalgia: Bodies, Locations, Aesthetics*, ed. by Tammy Clewell (Basingstoke and New York: Palgrave Macmillan, 2013), pp. 1–22.

Colombetti, Giovanna, 'The Embodied and Situated Nature of Moods', *Philosophia*, 45, 4 (December 2017), *The Meaning of Moods*, 1437–51.

——, *The Feeling Body: Affective Science Meets the Enactive Mind* (London and Cambridge, MA: The MIT Press, 2014).

Coyne, Richard, *Mood and Mobility: Navigating the Emotional Spaces of Digital Social Networks* (London and Cambridge, MA: The MIT Press, 2016).

Crangle, Sara, 'Phenomenology and Affect: Modernist Sulking', in *A Handbook of Modernism Studies*, ed. by Jean-Michel Rabaté (Chichester: John Wiley & Sons, 2013), pp. 327–45.

Damasio, Antonio R., *Self Comes to Mind: Constructing the Conscious Brain* (London: Heinemann, 2010).

——, *The Feeling of What Happens: Body, Emotion, and the Making of Consciousness* (London: Vintage, 1999).

Davidson, Richard J., 'On Emotion, Mood, and Related Affective Constructs', in *The Nature of Emotion: Fundamental Questions*, ed. by Paul Ekman and Richard J. Davidson (Oxford: Oxford University Press, 1994), pp. 51–5.

DeRubeis, Robert J., and Daniel R. Strunk, eds., *The Oxford Handbook of Mood Disorders* (Oxford: Oxford University Press, 2017).

Eagleton, Terry, *The Ideology of the Aesthetic* (Oxford: Blackwell, 1990).

Earnshaw, Owen, 'Mood, Delusions and Poetry: Emotional 'Wording of the World' in Psychosis, Philosophy and the Everyday', *Philosophia*, 45, 4 (December 2017), *The Meaning of Moods*, 1697–708.

Eliot, T[homas] S[tearns], 'Tradition and the Individual Talent' [1919], in *The Waste Land and Other Writings* (New York: The Modern Library, 2002), pp. 99–108.

Felski, Rita, and Susan Fraiman, 'Introduction', *New Literary History*, 43, 3 (Summer 2012), *In the Mood*, v–xii.

Fish, William, 'Emotions, Moods, and Intentionality', in *Intentionality Past and Future*, ed. by Gábor Forrai and George Kampis (New York: Rodopi Press, 2005), pp. 25–35.

Gumbrecht, Hans Ulrich, *Atmosphere, Stimmung, Mood: On a Hidden Potential of Literature* [2011], trans. by Erik Butler (Stanford, CA: Stanford University Press, 2012).

Haar, Michel, *The Song of the Earth: Heidegger and the Grounds of the History of Being*, trans. by Reginald Lilly (Bloomington and Indianapolis: Indiana University Press, 1993).

Heidegger, Martin, *Being and Time*, trans. by J. Macquarrie and E. Robinson (New York et al.: Harper Collins, 1962).

Highmore, Ben and Jenny Bourne Taylor, 'Introducing Mood Work', *New Formations*, 82 (Summer 2014), *Mood Work*, ed. Jeremy Gilbert, 5–12.

Highmore, Ben, *Cultural Feelings: Mood, Mediation and Cultural Politics* (New York and Abingdon: Routledge, 2017).

Kenaan, Hagi, and Ilit Ferber, eds., *Philosophy's Moods: The Affective Grounds of Thinking* (Dordrecht et al.: Springer, 2011).

——, 'Moods and Philosophy', in *Philosophy's Moods: The Affective Grounds of Thinking*, ed. by Hagi Kenaan and Ilit Ferber (Dordrecht et al.: Springer, 2011), pp. 3–10.

Krebs, Angelika, and Aaron Ben-Ze'ev, eds., *Philosophia*, 45, 4 (December 2017), *The Meaning of Moods*, 1395–708.

Matsukawa, Leslie, 'Mood Disorders', in *Culture and Psychopathology: A Guide to Clinical Assessment*, ed. by Jon Streltzer, 2nd ed. (New York and Abingdon: Routledge, 2017), pp. 21–35.

Merleau-Ponty, Maurice, *Phenomenology of Perception*, trans. Colin Smith (London and New York: Routledge, 2002).

Mood of the Nation Poll, Pennsylvania State University. http://election2016.psu.edu/tag/mood-of-the-nation-poll/ [accessed 31 March 2018].

Nancy, Jean-Luc, *Being Singular Plural* [1996], trans. by Robert D. Richardson and Anne E. O'Byrne (Stanford, CA: Stanford University Press, 2000).

Ngai, Sianne, *Ugly Feelings* (London and Cambridge, MA: Harvard University Press, 2007).

Pfau, Thomas, *Romantic Moods: Paranoia, Trauma, and Melancholy, 1790–1840* (Baltimore, MD: The Johns Hopkins University Press, 2005).

Platinga, Carl, 'Art Moods and Human Moods in Narrative Cinema', *New Literary History*, 43, 3 (Summer 2012), *In the Mood*, 455–75.

Prechter, Robert R., *The Wave Principle of Human Social Behavior and the New Science of Socionomics* (Gainesville, GA: New Classics Library, 1999).

Ratcliffe, Matthew, 'Why Mood Matters', in *The Cambridge Companion to Heidegger's "Being and Time"*, ed. by Mark A. Wrathall (Cambridge and New York: Cambridge University Press, 2013), pp. 157–76.

——, 'The Phenomenology of Mood and the Meaning of Life', in *The Oxford Handbook of Philosophy of Emotion*, ed. by Peter Goldie (Oxford: Oxford University Press, 2010), pp. 349–71.

——, *Feelings of Being* (Oxford: Oxford University Press, 2008).

——, 'Heidegger's Attunement and the Neuropsychology of Emotion', *Phenomenology and Cognitive Emotion*, 1 (2002), 287–312.

Rhym, John, 'Towards a Phenomenology of Cinematic Mood: Boredom and the Affect of Time in Antonioni's L'eclisse', *New Literary History*, 43, 3 (Summer 2012), *In the Mood*, 477–501.

Saunders, Rebecca, *Lamentation and Modernity in Literature, Philosophy, and Culture* (Houndsmills, Basingstoke, and New York: Palgrave Macmillan, 2007).

Schmetkamp, Susanne, 'Gaining Perspectives on Our Lives: Moods and Aesthetic Experience', *Philosophia*, 45, 4 (December 2017), *The Meaning of Moods*, 1681–95.

Sinnerbrink, Robert, 'Stimmung: Exploring the Aesthetics of Mood', *Screen*, 53, 2 (Summer 2012), 148–63.

Skidelsky, Edward, and Robert Skidelsky, *How Much is Enough? The Love of Money, and the Case for the Good Life* (London: Penguin, 2013).

Svendsen, Lars, 'Moods and the Meaning of Philosophy', *New Literary History*, 43, 3 (Summer 2012), *In the Mood*, 419–31.

——, *A Philosophy of Boredom*, trans. by John Irons (London: Reaction Books, 2005).

Ticineto Clough, Patricia, 'Introduction', in *The Affective Turn: Theorizing the Social*, ed. by Patricia Ticineto Clough and Jean Halley (Durham, NC and London: Duke University Press, 2007), pp. 1–33.

Vander Yacht, Cari, 'An American Mood', *New York Times*, 12 November 2016. www.nytimes.com/interactive/2016/11/12/us/racerelated-election-art.html [accessed 31 March 2018].

van Ginneken, Jaap, *Mood Contagion: Mass Psychology and Collective Behaviour Sociology in the Internet Age* (The Hague: Eleven International Publishing, 2013).

Wallrup, Erik, *Being Musically Attuned: The Act of Listening to Music* (Farnham and Burlington, VT: Ashgate, 2015).

1 Changing Moods

Hagi Kenaan

Introduction

We are all familiar with the fact that moods change. But what is the significance of this familiar fact? Is change merely a factual characteristic of moods, or can it also offer us a lens for gaining a deeper understanding of mood's essence? The central point of this chapter is that the changing of moods is a key for the understanding of moods' inner structure and consequently of what it means to be *in* a mood.

The changing of moods is clearly not a new topic for philosophy, whose interest in this subject goes back to antiquity and is, in this sense, as old as its interest in moods themselves. For Seneca and Plutarch, for example, moods and their proneness to change are thematised in the context of a discussion of questions about how to regulate and adequately negotiate the effects that moods have on the human soul, a discussion that is ultimately inseparable from a horizon of questions about the living of the good life. In both Seneca and Plutarch, the quest for a tranquillity of mind grows out of a sensitive understanding of the intrinsic volatility of moods. But since both thinkers frame the unpredictability of moods and their proneness to change as a problem that needs to be overcome, the changing of moods never receives specific attention as a positive phenomenon and only appears in the negative form of that which philosophy aims at doing away with (Plutarch 1962; Seneca 2004).

Philosophers have not always been as pronounced regarding their partiality for certain kinds of mood. But even when the question of moods' value remains unspoken, philosophy typically operates with the assumption that certain moods are more evocative of philosophical reflection or more conducive to doing philosophy than others. Philosophy's manner of grounding itself in a mood is at times accompanied by an explicit privileging of a specific mood *as* philosophical (e.g., wonder in Plato and Aristotle or anxiety in Kierkegaard and Heidegger). However, also in those many other cases when the question of mood does not at all surface, the underlying presence of a regulating mood can often be traced out. When Descartes, for example, experiments with doubt in the *Meditations* (Descartes 1999), his renowned suspension of the immediacy and efficacy of the surrounding world would not have been possible without an enabling condition of detachment. It is, in other words, a mood of radical disengagement that enables the thinker to distance himself from the ordinary and radically challenge the rootedness of his thinking in the habits of the everyday. I have dealt elsewhere with the question of how philosophy relates to its moods apropos certain mood paradigms that, in my view, have been essential to the philosophical tradition (Kenaan and Ferber 2011). What I did not pay attention to in that discussion and wish to underscore here, however, is that the very possibility of a 'philosophical mood' (whether implicit or explicit) is itself dependent on a shift in moods. That is, when embracing a specific mood as conducive to doing philosophy, the new orientation created by this mood—the opening of new reflective possibilities—first of all means that a change has occurred in one's standing vis-à-vis the ordinary. In this respect, it is also, but not only, in addressing the question of philosophy's moods that we first need to come to terms with the structure that allows moods to change and to do so while considering the implications that this grounding structure carries for our understanding of moods.

Before I begin to discuss the question of change, however, let me say something more general about how I understand moods, apropos the renewed philosophical interest in them in recent years. The immediate backdrop for the contemporary discussion of moods is the significant wave of philosophical literature on the emotions in the past few decades. One of the central focal points of that philosophical preoccupation with the emotions was their cognitive dimension. This implied not only an integration of emotions into our intricate space of reason but also, more generally, an understanding of emotions as unique forms of knowing the world,[1] which, in a corollary manner, underscored the need to problematise and offer alternatives to an age-old paradigmatic distinction between the conceptual and the affective. Being one of the upshots of that discussion, the current philosophical turn to moods is typically construed in terms of moods' affinity to, and their ways of differing from, the emotions. While moods are typically framed as emotional phenomena—'to understand the nature of moods one has to first understand the nature of emotions' (Solomon 1993: 71)—they are concomitantly marked as distinct from full-fledged emotions. Moods are taken to 'share many properties with other emotions, especially in their physiological and motivational aspects,' but they are ultimately taken to form a class apart. The main reason for thinking of them in contradistinction to emotions is that, unlike emotions, moods seem to lack a clear structure of directedness towards an object. They are not intentional states. As De Sousa put it, a mood is what affects 'how you feel about everything, [but] isn't about anything specific' (De Sousa 2015). Underlining the non-intentional structure of moods, the 'grammar of moods' is thus typically severed (or at least, distanced) from the logic of objects, its commitment to objectivity and dependency on thought.[2]

The divide between intentional and non-intentional mental states is motivated indeed by a discerning intuition, but it all too easily covers up two important dimensions of moods that I wish to underline in making a beginning.[3] First, it blurs the presence of the dynamic relationship that exists between emotions and moods and that, as such, complicates any clear-cut distinction between the two: with a certain degree of intensity, emotions and moods not only tend to influence each other, but, under certain conditions, emotions may develop into moods just as moods may take on the distinctiveness of an emotion. Furthermore, what the common aforementioned distinction all too often obfuscates is the difference between the experiential orders in which moods and emotions operate. This means that while a clear-cut distinction between the two is lacking, emotions cannot serve as the benchmark for understanding moods. Unlike a distinction that can be made, for example, between different kinds of geometrical shapes on a plain, emotions and moods are not two kinds of phenomena that are jointly and uniformly positioned in the same field of experience: whereas emotions occupy a (more or less) determined place *in* experience, moods manifest themselves as experiential frameworks, as embodied schemas that pervade, anchor, and, in a certain sense, hold together the multifaceted aspects of our field of experience. In other words, moods are not episodes in our field of experience but basic modes of that field. Furthermore, by framing moods as non-intentional, we need to overcome the temptation to identify the non-intentional with the merely affective. Moods are modes of experience that typically bear an affective dimension, but they are not simply modes of affect. What kind of modes are they? They are modes—and here I bring Heidegger into the picture—of our being-in-the-world.

Moods as Modes of Attunement

To make the point briefly through Heidegger, let us recall his basic motivations in turning to moods. Heidegger's famous treatment of moods appears in *Being and Time* in a chapter titled 'Being-in as Such' (Chapter V, Part I, Division I) which is the last in a sequence of chapters analysing the existential structure termed 'being-in-the-world' (Heidegger 1996). In this context, the novelty of Heidegger's analysis of 'being-in' stems from his ability to reinterpret the term 'in' in a manner that is no longer founded on the common model of physical containment. For him, our human situatedness *in* a world cannot be understood in terms that are typically used for describing a relation that exists between an object and the factual confines of the given space in which it is located (as, for example, a chair's being in a room or a key in a drawer). These terms would be inadequate for capturing the intrinsically human essence of our embeddedness in the meaningfulness of our surrounding. And, this is primarily because human existence is not a closed, self-identical, and self-sufficient entity, but rather a process of self-determination, one that depends on a ceaseless interaction with its surroundings. Being-in a world is thus a condition of immersion and involvement through which the human being can fulfil itself and become what it is. Or, in other words, 'being-in' signifies the essentially entangled character of human existence that is always already caught in a web of relations whose on-going determination is the condition for its meaningfulness and whose originality is ineluctably lost when the idea of being human is conceptualised as independent and prior to that relationality.

In Division 1 of *Being and Time*, Heidegger gradually unpacks the structure of being-in-the-world by posing and answering three consecutive questions: What? Who? And how? What is world or what is worldliness? Who is that being which finds itself in the world, i.e., who is Dasein? And finally, in Chapter V, how—in what manner—is Dasein *in* the world? What are the basic parameters of our human situatedness? How does our entanglement *in* a world manifest itself? The 'how?' is the question of mood, a question that allows Heidegger to focus on the phenomenal dimension of our human entanglement which he terms *Befindlichkeit* (translated by J. Stambaugh as 'attunement'). Attunement is a fundamental existential structure that manifests itself in the fact that our existence is always already affected by—always finding itself in—some mood.

> What we indicate ontologically with the term attunement (*befindlichkeit*) is ontically what is most familiar and an everyday kind of thing: mood, being in a mood. Prior to all psychology of moods ... we must see this phenomenon as a fundamental existential and outline its structure.
>
> (Heidegger 1996: 126)

For Heidegger, moods are concrete manifestation of the existential structure of attunement that 'discloses Dasein in its thrownness.' Moods are not a consequence of, or a sign derivative from, that structure but rather the very actuality, the burden, of being unavoidably entangled in a surrounding that always already touches us, matters to us, and is meaningful to us in ways we can never fully contain. In moods, human existence 'is always already brought before itself' (p. 128), but this does not mean that moods enable us to understand ourselves or the structure of our entanglement which 'has become manifest as a burden' (p. 127).

> One does not know why. And Dasein cannot know why because the possibilities of disclosure belonging to cognition fall far short of the primordial disclosure of moods.
>
> (p. 127)

In their own unique, non-cognitive, way, moods have a disclosing capacity. They not only exhibit the psychological/anthropological 'how' of our being-in the world, but they primarily have an ontological lesson to teach us. What they disclose on the ontological level is that attunement lies at the heart of our ability to be touched by the world and, as such, grounds the possibility of having and encountering a world that matters to us. 'In attunement lies existentially a disclosive submission to the world out of which things that matter to us can be encountered' (p. 129).

The fact that things matter to us is not a given. It is, rather, made possible by the structure of our relatedness to them, one that draws us in. We are never neutral spectators, because our being-in the world is always already involved, implicated, affected in one way or another.

> Being affected ... by the character of things at hand is ontologically possible only because being-in as such is existentially determined beforehand in such a way that what it encounters in the world can matter to it in this way. This mattering to it is grounded in attunement, and as attunement it has disclosed the world, for example, as something by which it can be threatened.
>
> (p. 129)

For Heidegger, 'the moodedness of attunement constitutes existentially Dasein's openness to world' (p. 129). That is, we can experience the world in ways that matter to us only because we are always attuned to the world. In other words, the world appears to us in ways that touch us and that are meaningful to us only because of the attuned form of our being-in the world. Moods, in this sense, constitute the openness of the world to Dasein. But where or when can we most clearly recognise the actuality of attunement? The locus of such recognition is the changing of moods.

> The way we slide over from one to another or slip into bad moods, are by no means nothing ontologically although these phenomena remain unnoticed as what is supposedly the most indifferent and fleeting in Dasein. The fact that moods can be spoiled and change only means that Dasein is always already in a mood.
>
> (p. 126)

As we undergo a mood change, it becomes clear that we are always attuned in one way or another, 'always already in a mood' and, in this sense, the allegedly trivial fact that moods change is an indication of attunement's underlying structure. Heidegger is thus fully aware of the changing of moods to which he even attaches a philosophical significance. And yet, this change does not interest him in and of itself, but becomes relevant to his project only in being indicative of the permanent underlying structure that ultimately concerns him. In other words, when Heidegger argues that 'the fact that moods can ... change, only means that Dasein is always already in a mood,' he frames our ordinary shifts in mood as indicators of a fundamental existential structure that underlies the specificity of any particular mood. For him, a proper understanding of moods can be gained only once we recognise the basic human condition of always already being-in some mood, always bearing the touch of affect. Yet, is the changing of moods only a means to reveal the inherent depth of our permanent givenness to some mood, or is it a dimension significant onto itself? Putting the question in this way is already suggestive of the direction I wish to take here. Indeed, this is precisely where I wish to part ways from Heidegger who ultimately ends up privileging the changeless core (rather than the changeability) of our experience with moods. The fact that Heidegger has no further regard for the changing of moods is not coincidental, but reflects his wider concerns in *Being and Time* which include a notion of authenticity that is based on Dasein's being-a-whole and, in a corollary manner, on the privileging of only one kind of mood as ontologically fundamental.

Moving beyond Heidegger, I wish to make a case for the need to understand change as the grounding condition of our being-in-a-mood, and consequently, to draw out some of the implications of what it means to philosophically embrace this condition of change. But let's take things one step at a time.

When Moods Change

In growing up, we typically develop some understanding of our shifting moods. We usually become acquainted with the general fact that our moods change and we develop a certain level of understanding of how change is essential to our emotional life.[4] This kind of understanding often comes in handy when trying to get through a bad mood or when comforting others: 'Things will look brighter in the morning,' 'Tomorrow is another day,' etc. But the volatility of moods may also be experienced as threatening and unsettling—'Please don't sink into that despair again'—especially, for people who have a history of dramatic mood changes. Our moods are commonly experienced within a horizon of a future change and against the background of the mood changes we have already undergone. As such, the experience of moods typically involves in-built dimensions of plurality and relationality. The mood we're in is always one option among others, always related to other moods (our own moods but also, of course, the moods of others). And, thus, even in times in which we feel captivated by a mood and find it difficult to envision the possibility of a mood change, the option of change is nevertheless structurally part of the horizons of our being in any given mood.

As already suggested, moods are not mere affects or subjective states and their changing too is hardly ever experienced as pertaining only to our inner life. Changes in mood may often not register in us as such and appear rather as a change occurring in our surrounding. When we fall in love, a city that usually seems boring and gloomy suddenly appears joyful and full of potential. When we are very stressed, a person with whom we usually feel comfortable may suddenly appear to be annoying. It is only upon reflection that we recognise that it is not our friend who has changed but that his turning into a nuisance had to do with the kind of mood we are in. With the change of mood, the world around us seems to change.[5] Yet, the correlation between mood and world is not always apparent at first sight. And, even when it does become apparent, the character of this intertwining still poses a question for the understanding. An understanding of this kind is what Antoine Roquentin, the protagonist of Sartre's *Nausea*, searches for, for example, once he recognises that an unexplained change has pervaded his world. Roquentin's need to examine this disturbing sense of change is the explicit reason why he begins writing the journal of which *Nausea* is comprised:

> The best thing would be to write events from day to day. Keep a diary to see clearly – let none of the nuances or small happenings escape... I must tell how I see this table, this street, the people, my packet of tobacco, since *those* are the things which have changed. I must determine the exact extent and nature of this change.
>
> (Sartre 2007)

Roquentin searches for an understanding by attending to how specific manifestations of his everyday have changed. Yet, detailing these specific changes leaves him unsatisfied, since they cannot explain the fact that his whole modality of being-in-the-world has changed. As he turns to look for a psychological explication of his condition, however, he is again puzzled by the fact that he cannot pinpoint the change to any specific aspect of his inner, subjective, world. Roquentin thus wavers between two unsatisfying options:

> So a change has taken place during these few weeks. But where? It is an abstract change without object. Am I the one who has changed? If not, then, it is this room, this city and this nature: I must choose.
>
> (p. 4)

Roquentin is ultimately unable to choose, however, between an 'internal' and 'external' explanation since the very opposition between the two realms cannot do justice to his experience. His world has changed but this change lends itself to a conceptualisation neither in terms of a mere subjective occurrence nor in terms of the objectivity of things.

Roquentin's difficulty in finding proper terms for describing the mood he is in is revealing. And, as Sartre's novel makes clear, Roquentin will not be able to come close to answering the question that baffles him as long as he continues to think of the structure of being in a mood in binary terms. In other words, there's a philosophical lesson to be gleaned from Roquentin's struggle to understand. And, the lesson is that mood is the form of our intertwining with the world, an intertwining that precedes the subjective/objective dichotomy.

Modes of Intertwining: Two Analogies

Yet, going beyond Sartre, in what terms should we think of this intertwining? And, specifically, how should we understand the manner in which the changing of moods opens for us different dimensions of the world? A relatively common way for articulating this correlation and its changing possibilities is to think of moods as experiential filters working in ways that are analogical to what technological filters do for us. Take, for example, the standard filtering apps that are built into our most common cellphone cameras and are typically used to modify photographed images before uploading them to social networks.[6] These modular filters do not typically affect the picture's visual contents but apply rather to their spectrum of colours and lighting conditions. As such, the photo of the young boy holding his dog can be made to appear 'nostalgic' or with a 'retro' feel to it, but it can also appear as a translucent, even bland representation of an ordinary situation. In either case, the objects seen (the boy, the dog, etc.) are typically taken to be invariant, while their manner of appearance changes in correlation to the different filtering options. In this context, the efficacy of visual filters of this kind invites an understanding in terms of the distinction between what is seen in the picture and the manner of appearance of what is seen (between the 'what' and the 'how').

The analogy to moods is clear. Filters like moods are modalities of seeing-through. Their intrinsic features determine our viewing conditions and thus also certain aspects of the world's appearance. The visual grammar of colour and changing light gradations is pertinent to the way we commonly speak of moods. 'I'm blue.' 'These are dark times.' 'Today, after a long period, the world suddenly seems brighter,' etc. But the analogy continues further: while certain aspects of the world's appearance change with the changing of moods, the world's factual structure seems to remain invariant under these transformations. (In traditional philosophical parlance, one may want to use here the distinction between primary and secondary properties of objects: primary properties belong to the objects themselves, and secondary properties are dependent on the conditions of encountering these objects.)

The filter analogy is intuitive and gives a concrete sense of the correlation between the changing plurality of moods and the correlative ways through which the world shows itself to us. At the same time, however, there is something in the filter analogy that I ultimately find to be unsatisfying: what seems to suggest itself in the idea of a filter is that there is a primary structure to our encounter with the world that is prior to its filtering, i.e., independent of a mood. When the analogy to filters is taken literally, it may all too easily tempt us to think of moods as a supplement to a more basic structure of openness to the world that can supposedly be conceptualised without mood and that involves the changing of moods only incidentally. Hence, in looking for an alternative image that could make better sense of the intrinsic belongingness of mood to the heart of the world's unfolding, I arrived at an alternative, one that comes from music and that, as such, may also serve as a reminder of the initial musical connotations of the term *Stimmung* (or for our purpose *Stimmungen*). What I have in mind is the analogy between moods and musical keys.

A musical key anchors the musical composition in a system of relations between pitches that functions as a schema for the melody's embodiment in its concrete musical surrounding. Clearly, a key determines which specific notes/pitches are available for a given melody, but the significance of a change of key cannot be reduced to the positivity of the pitches that it renders available. The key grounds the melody in its tonic chord which is, in itself, already part of a more elaborate harmonic system with its hierarchies, inner and outer relations as well as its correlations with other—e.g., parallels, relative—keys.[7] Consequently, with a change of key, the tune's concrete sphere of attunement changes. In this sense, the relation between keys is never only formal. A move to a new key is an opening of a new mode of being for the tune, a mode through which a tune unfolds in its movement from relief to tension and from tension to relief. This mode is interesting for our purposes since it exemplifies the intrinsic relationality by which a tune's being—its unfolding—is connected to its musical surround which, like the world in the case of moods, is never just a given. Indeed, a tune's concrete environment includes certain positive/objective elements such as the series of pitches available for a tune, but this positivity is only part of a complex matrix of relationships between presences and absences, audible and inaudible dimensions, always already appearing within horizons of meaning that are open and never fully determinate. Moods, like musical keys, are, in this respect, relational modes of being anchored in the world— an anchoring whose determinate structural features function both in closing off ranges of possibilities and, at the same time, in shaping an environment, an intricate web of possibilities that can be articulated and realised in infinite ways. Think, in this context, of how Mozart's famous variations 'Ah, vous dirai-je Maman,'[8] unfold in correlation with their different keys, each variation unfolding within the potentialities embedded in the topography of its own space. In a mood as in a musical key, things and events can become meaningful only within the relational bounds of a mode of attunement that is always already part of a larger plurality and thus embodies the intrinsic possibility of change.

"There Is No Such Thing as a Mood"

Moods, as suggested, are modalities of a primary intertwining between subjectivity and world. They function as concrete schemas that delimit the world's spectrum of appearance while allowing the world to appear (as if) boundless in the richness of its possibilities. Certain moods allow us to see the tenderness of a gesture or the beauty of a place. Other moods may desensitise us to these aspects of the world, while concomitantly opening for us other perspectives that have previously remained unnoticed, thus revealing, for example, the practical confines or economical implications of a given situation. In their ways of enfolding or holding together the aforementioned intertwinings, moods are never given as simple self-identical states, but appear as constellations of a dynamism, an ongoing process of interaction, that makes them intrinsically volatile. When philosophy reflects on moods, however, it typically does not recognise that their proneness to change belongs to their inner structure and thus often overlooks the role played by change in determining the ways in which they become meaningful *as* moods.

As exemplified by the above analogies, an understanding of mood's dynamics of change requires a re-articulation of the common space in which the question of mood is posed. In particular, it requires a bracketing of the common 'what is x?' question (what is a mood? What is being in a mood? Or, what is this or that specific mood?) in order to allow us to come to terms with two constitutive dimensions of our experience with moods: plurality and relationality. To put this in another, more direct way, we may say that the first methodological step to be taken here is to realise that in a fundamental sense 'there is no such thing as *a* mood.'[9] Moods never come alone, and the question about them is, to begin with, a question about the workings of a relational plurality.

Indeed, the starting point for describing this relational matrix was the idea that moods never appear solely on their own, but always as part of more complicated mood trajectories in which the relationship of preceding and superseding another mood is already part of any elementary mood unit.

To put this schematically, in any sequence of moods

$$\cdots \rightarrow \text{Mood (E)} \rightarrow \text{Mood (F)} \rightarrow \text{Mood (G)} \rightarrow \text{Mood (H)} \rightarrow \cdots$$
the basic mood unit is: $[\rightarrow \text{Mood (X)} \rightarrow]$

Yet, if we follow this idea to its full consequences, we will see that it hides an even more radical core, one that no longer allows us to conceptualise the trajectory of our moods as a given sequence of static self-sufficient and self-enclosed consecutive states. The changing of moods is not a move in between given emotional or affective posts. When our moods change, we do not exit one given mood frame and enter another given frame that is waiting there, in stock, for us. What mood changes consist in, rather, is a transformation that a mood undergoes in becoming, from within itself, another mood. And, in a corollary manner, a change in mood means an active alteration of our being, a transmutation of the way in which we are in the world, of the 'how' of that in-world being.

Once we address the actuality of change in this way, however, moods' constitution no longer appear to be self-contained. This is because change requires an underlying structure: in order to change into another mood, the changing mood must be disposed towards such a change and, in this sense, carry within itself the possibility of becoming that other mood. As such, moods are never fully determined, closed, emotional frameworks, but always have transcendence—the possibility of infringing on and reaching beyond their own bounds—as part of their essence. Moods are not only structurally flexible, but they are open-ended and intrinsically interconnected to those mood possibilities that may ultimately supersede them and that in the meantime belong to their in-built potential.[10]

Considering moods in light of the structure that makes their changeability possible opens for us a range of new and interesting questions that invite further explorations. These questions address the ethical, pedagogical, and therapeutic implications carried by the understanding that the changing of moods is an infrastructure for us. What would it mean to embrace a subjectivity of changing moods? Or, to live in a meaningful way the non-reducible plurality, the constant alterations, intrinsic to our emotional make up? Would coming to terms with our intrinsic plurality affect our understanding of the moods we privilege? Can we embrace our changing moods and, at the same time, privilege specific moods? What kind of sense would the changing of mood allow us to make of situations in which we find ourselves captivated by one unchanging mood? How does a structural understanding of changing moods illuminate questions about the freedom and responsibility we have in and over our moods? How does it illuminate the possibilities we have in helping others who are unable to escape, to change, their confinement to a mood? I shall not attempt to answer these questions here, but only suggest that the promise of responding to these questions carries the potential of changing moods conceptually.

Notes

1 Consider, in this context, Martha Nussbaum's *Love's Knowledge* (Oxford: Oxford University Press, 1990).
2 Today, there are more and more voices that see this as a gradual rather than a categorical distinction. In the context, Peter Goldie holds the interesting position. For his argument, see *The Emotions: A Philosophical Exploration*

(Oxford: Oxford University Press, 2002), p. 17. In this context, see also Martha Nussbaum, *Upheavals of Thought: The Intelligence of Emotions* (Cambridge: Cambridge University Press, 2001), pp. 1–19, 129–37.

3 On the conditions of the blending of emotions into moods, see Hanna Pickard, 'Emotions and the Problem of Other Minds', in *Philosophy and the Emotions*, ed. by Anthony Hatzymoisis (Cambridge: Cambridge University Press, 2003), pp. 87–104 (p. 96).

4 On the temporality, duration, and change in emotions and, more generally, in affective attitudes, see Aaron Ben-Ze'ev's 'Does Loving Longer Mean Loving More? On the Nature of Enduring Affective Attitudes', *Philosophia*, 45, 4, December 2017, pp. 1541–62.

5 The idea that the world opens up to us in ways that are dependent on our moods is a commonplace that is often articulated also in popular culture. Think, for example, of the way this idea is expressed in the beautiful song from the depression era, 'When You're Smiling' (written by L. Shay, M. Fisher, and J. Goodwin and popularised in Louis Armstrong's recording at the end of the 1920s): 'When you're smiling, when you're smiling/The whole world smiles with you/When you're laughing, when you're laughing/The sun comes shining through/But when you're crying, you bring on the rain/So stop that sighing, be happy again.'

6 The popularity of these filters is underscored by those few images that are explicitly tagged 'unfiltered.'

7 In traditional classical music, the prototypical difference between keys is manifest in the difference between a major and a minor structure. Indeed, for an untrained ear, the difference between a C major and a C minor key, for example, would typically seem to be much more evident and pronounced than the difference between a C major and another major key that, by definition, retains the intrinsic (major) relationship between pitches. And yet, while the difference between major and minor keys is often clear and distinct—think of the Beatles' 'Hey Jude' played in a minor key—the transposition of a tune from one major key (or from one minor key) to another is not less significant and also brings about, even if in more subtle ways, a significant transformation in a tune's 'being-in-the-world.'

8 I thank Shira Yasur for discussing with me different aspects of musical keys and for suggesting the Mozart example.

9 I have borrowed here a rhetorical gesture famously used by psychoanalyst D.W. Winnicott who declares that 'there is no such thing as a baby.' What Winnicott's snappy statement conveys is that for the psychologist, the relevant contours of a baby's existence cannot be limited to the baby itself but must include a more complex structure: as a psychological entity the baby is what it is only in relation to—as part of—the mother-child dyad. See Donald W. Winnicott, *The Child, The Family and the Outside World* (London: Perseus Books, 1984), p. 17.

10 An alternative way of unpacking this structure would be in temporal terms. The present of being in a mood is never a narrow one but a present that is on its way to giving way to another mood. The future, in other words, is part of the present of the mood in a very distinct way.

References

Ben-Ze'ev, Aaron, 'Does Loving Longer Mean Loving More? On the Nature of Enduring Affective Attitudes', *Philosophia*, 45, 4 (December 2017), 1541–62.

De Sousa, Ronald, *Love: A Very Short Introduction* (Oxford: Oxford University Press, 2015).

Descartes, René, *Meditations of First Philosophy, the Philosophical Writings of Descartes*, Vol. 2, trans. by John Cottingham, Robert Stoothoff, and Dugald Murdoch (Cambridge: Cambridge University Press, 1999), pp. 12–16.

Goldie, Peter, *The Emotions: A Philosophical Exploration* (Oxford: Oxford University Press, 2002).

Heidegger, Martin, *Being and Time*, trans. by J. Stambaugh (New York: SUNY Press, 1996).

Kenaan, Hagi, and Ilit Ferber, 'Moods and Philosophy', in *Philosophy's Moods: The Affective Grounds of Thinking*, ed. by Hagi Kenaan and Ilit Ferber (New York: Springer, 2011), pp. 3–11.

Nussbaum, Martha, *Love's Knowledge* (Oxford: Oxford University Press, 1990).

——, *Upheavals of Thought: The Intelligence of Emotions* (Cambridge: Cambridge University Press, 2001).

Pickard, Hanna, 'Emotions and the Problem of Other Minds', in *Philosophy and the Emotions*, ed. by Anthony Hatzymoisis (Cambridge: Cambridge University Press, 2003), pp. 87–104.

Plutarch, Phillip De Lacy, *On Tranquillity of Mind, Moralia VI*, trans. by William C. Helmbold (Cambridge, MA: Harvard University Press, 1962).

Sartre, Jean-Paul, *Nausea*, trans. by Richard Howard (New York: New Directions, 2007).

Seneca, Lucius Annaeus, *On Tranquillity of Mind*. in *Dialogues and Letters*, trans. by Charles Desmond Nuttall Costa (London: Penguin Classics, 2004).

Solomon, Robert, *Not Passions' Slave* (Oxford: Oxford University Press, 1993).

Winnicott, W. Donald, *The Child, the Family and the Outside World* (London: Perseus Books, 1984).

This chapter was originally published in *Philosophia*, December 2017, Volume 45, Issue 4, pp. 1469–79. Reproduced with permission.

2 The Composition of a Mood

Jon Arcaraz Puntonet

This chapter explores the *idea of* rhythm as a quality that induces in the observer a mood and a behaviour that reveal the emotion and meaning of a work. It compares Fernando Higueras's project of *10 Residences for Artists on El Pardo Hill in Madrid* (1960) (Figure 2.1) with Manuel de Falla's ballet *El Amor Brujo* (1915).

Figure 2.1 Model of Fernando Higueras's project of *10 Residences for Artists on El Pardo Hill in Madrid*, 1960. © Archivo Fundación Fernando Higueras.

The point of departure is the Greek concept of rhythm, which involves an approach to form from its spatio-temporal condition. To do so, it uses music as its discipline of study. Music is composed using basic elements that follow on from each other in time, and which use groupings to structure the piece. Hence the work can be broken down into its component parts. Yet to fully understand it, to feel it, requires perceiving it as a whole, with this totality triggering the emotion that is inherent to a musical piece. In other words, the piece consists of a formal structure that gives shape to the various parts, but it cannot be understood without its complete and significant form, as a totality of relationships that operationalises the excess of expression that emotion arouses.

Greek culture reached the outcome of this duality between form and structure following a protracted evolution that began with the Pythagorean School. Pythagoras based himself on the formal principles of reality.

> Pythagoras [...] was the first to maintain that the origin of all things lay in number. The Pythagoreans had a sort of holy dread of the infinite and of that which cannot be reduced to a limit, and so they looked to numbers for the rule capable of limiting reality, of giving it order and comprehensibility. [...] all things exist because they are ordered and they are ordered because they are the realisation of mathematical laws....[1]

The notion of proportionality implicit in mathematics referred to the structure-form duality. In search of this order through which to structure reality, Pythagoras studied the mathematical relationships that governed musical intervals. Based on this study, as a direct transposition of musical principles, he arrived at his dimensional and spatial understanding:

> [...] the idea of passing from the arithmetical concept of number to the spatio-geometrical concept between the ratios of a variety of points is a Pythagorean concept.[2]

Based on these spatio-temporal precepts, the Greeks established their harmonious definition of reality. The Pythagoreans initially understood harmony to be the absence of contrasts. Yet once Heraclitus had understood harmony as equilibrium, the concept of symmetry changed. As opposed to a rigid principle based on the equilibrium of two equal elements, Polykleitos introduced the criterion of symmetry as *conmodulatio*. Rather than the concept of equilibrium as *equal weight*, Greek symmetry understood it as *the relationship between the parts and the whole*.

Following this organic criterion that related the parts to each other and to the whole, Vitruvius went one step further by linking symmetry to the perceived effect, bringing subjectivity into the equation.

The principle of symmetry, from *eurhythmy*, is the adaptation of proportions to the requirements of sight.[3] The Greeks thus completed their idea of form.

Many centuries later, German modernity recovered Greek thinking as one of the pillars of its culture. This influence led to the emergence of Gestalt psychology. In 1890, its precursor, Christian von Ehrenfels described the notion of Gestalt as the relationship between structure, understood as order in the arrangement of the parts, and form, understood as the whole constructed by the receiving subject. A few years later, other artistic expressions appeared that were similar to this approach, such as primitivism in the early twentieth century and the Neo-Platonism or Neo-Pythagoreanism of the 1920s, with a major referent being the studies by Matila C. Ghyka, which had such an influence on the Le Corbusier's *Modulor*.

Pythagorean Rhythms in the Study by Matila C. Ghyka

In his book *Le nombre d'or: Rites et rythmes pythagoriciens dans le développement de la civilisation occidentale*,[4] the neo-Pythagorean Matila C. Ghyka studied the notion of rhythm. This referred, theoretically, to the periodicity of events in time: a perceived periodicity, involving the recurrence of elements. Nevertheless, the rhythm could also be assimilated as the transposition of the Greek concept of symmetry or *conmodulatio*. This concept, theoretically referring to the mutual relationships of the elements and of the whole in a spatial succession, was defined as the concatenation of the commensurabilities between the different parts and between these parts and the whole. As the Greeks established, the nexus between the notions of rhythm (time) and symmetry (space) was rooted in the idea of proportion.

In his book, Ghyka broke rhythm down into different factors for analysing the project's structure: background rhythm, tonic rhythm, dynamic rhythm, and timbre rhythm. This classification is explained by the difference between the attributes of the perception of form and formal attributes.

The purpose of the attributes of the perception of form, namely, rhythm, harmony, and equilibrium, was their reference to the whole of the piece. It was no coincidence that they referred to the senses: sense of rhythm, sense of harmony, sense of equilibrium, etc. They achieved this by resorting to formal attributes: durations, accents, and intensities or timbre. These were the basic qualities used to compose the various parts of the piece.

Form was composed according to the unitary elements grouped into larger series. This composition involved the aforementioned attributes. The project was based on the smallest unit of expression, the motif, built up using a certain number of measures, which were developed in phrases that finally composed a period, the basic building block of a musical piece.

> The smallest unit of expression and meaning, the motif, is made up of a certain number of measures; the period contains several motifs in a unity of higher meaning. The regrouping of sounds into measures, into motifs, (we also add phrases) and into periods equals a semantic analysis of music, and cannot be determined by the simple act of counting the notes or times.[5]

This breakdown of rhythms into formal attributes may be studied in the architectural example chosen for this essay: *10 Residences for Artists on El Pardo Hill in Madrid*. Its analysis first involves identifying the unitary components grouped into a series. In this example, the measures are the unitary constructive elements, such as the tetrahedrons and the curved walls that support them; the motifs are formed from the helical geometry that underlies the composition of each dwelling; several grouped dwellings are ordered according to a range of sentences whose trajectory and punctuation define them as a curve, line, and dot; and all those sentences constitute the complete project as a period (Figure 2.2).

Once the sundry components have been identified, a study of their composition in larger groups will help us to understand, first, the work's syntax and then, second, its semantics. This renders it expedient to begin by analysing the formal attributes of the form mentioned earlier: background rhythm, tonic rhythm, dynamic rhythms, and rhythm of the timbre.

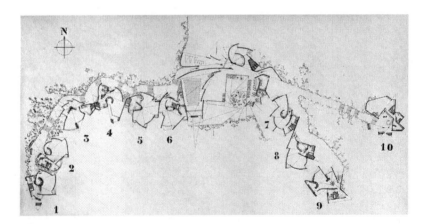

Figure 2.2 Plan of Fernando Higueras's project of *10 Residences for Artists on El Pardo Hill in Madrid*, 1960. © Archivo Fundación Fernando Higueras.

Background and Tonic Rhythm: The Periodicity of the Motif in the Series

The composition of the architectural example is characterised by a double periodicity: a linear recurrence and a rotating recurrence inherent in the motif's configuration and concatenation. That is to say, it looks towards both the motif and the totality, or to put it another way, towards the motif to compose the totality.

First there is a background rhythm with a clear intent. The ten residences were meant to constitute a community of artists on El Pardo hill. Each resident artist would have a private dwelling-workshop space in which to live and work. Each residence comprised two distinct zones: on the one side a bedroom, bathroom, and kitchen, and on the other, a workshop and a living room with a fireplace. Moreover, the artists would all share a communal area where they could discuss ideas with their neighbours. The gathering of ten creative minds in a community would favour team learning. Conversely, the decision to isolate each studio in an independent geometry was made because of the conviction that *artists were persons of enormous individuality.*[6] This individualisation of the studios compromises the design in the form of a series (Figures 2.1 and 2.2).

The series, composed by the succession of residences, is deployed in space and in time alluding to a discontinuous linear movement. Like the sequential photographs of Eadweard Muybridge, the residences have slight differences between them as if they form a sequence.

With these photographs, taken in the 1880s and published under the title *The Human Figure in Motion*, the photographer set out to record all the stages of the movement of a body in motion.

> [...] attached one after the other, and observed through a strobe cylinder, the photographs resembled for the first time animated images. Muybridge himself projected his images on a canvas with a device of this kind. This is the reason why he is considered one of the precursors of cinematography.[7]

Like Muybridge's experiments, the project *Ten Residences for Artists on El Pardo Hill* plays with a single piece, different variations of which animated it like a movement. It is an event understood as the activity of a thing.[8]

However, this event, understood as the activity of a thing, can only be explained from a specific idea of a series. The series needs to contain the characteristic of periodicity to be understood as an event. Periodicity means the *reproduction and return of form and similar images (repeated, not identical) in cadences of time and in an alternating resource of movements, achieving an integration of all the elements.*

The prior linear movement does not consist of a sequence of distinct pieces or of a monotonous repetition of an identical one, but rather of a recurrence of similar ones: a tonic rhythm. To obtain this similarity, the different elements of the series follow the same pattern: a helical geometry on top of which the elements are composed with different variations.

This dynamic geometry enables the recurrence of similar elements thanks to two intrinsic qualities: on the one hand, the geometry's continuous periodicity, whereby each unit in the series can be developed in a similar way to all the others, and on the other hand, the openness characterised by this geometry, thanks to which the units may be concatenated.

This generative geometry of Euclidean origin reflects the way the natural world is created. Its form is developed on the basis of a homothetic, open geometry, in a rotation that increasingly spreads out, while maintaining the same curvature. The helicoidal geometry that provides the units in the series therefore has an internal periodicity in its growth. This geometry's rhythm is not a discontinuous one as the sum of fragments, but instead the very proportion of this curve's development generates its own recurrent rhythm: a continuous periodicity.

In addition to the periodicity of the Euclidean form, there is the sum of the succession that the series establishes. This means that the helicoid's condition of openness allows the different units to become concatenated. Through this geometry, each dwelling is positioned on the hillside, individualised, while its curved arrangement around a vertical centre in movement and its openness as a dynamic form allow concatenation. This is structured thanks to the return to the helicoidal shape.

As the 'vitalist' philosopher Ludwig Klages explained in his theory on rhythm:

> Just as (in the binary measurement) the accentuated element follows the non-accentuated one, the valley follows the peak; both correspond to the bodies that served as the boundaries to an interval of time, without considering, in the present case, the beats that are not marked. Passing through an infinite number of stages, the ascent is followed immediately by a fall and the other way around, whereby neither the level of the higher point of inflection nor the level of the lower point of reflection form a crest. Instead of this, we see a curve, which clearly represents the unbounded continuity of an unquestionably structured movement, caused by the interrupted oscillation on both sides of the axis of departure.[9]

With a view to explaining this continuous quality of rhythm as concatenation, Ludwig Klages juxtaposes rhythm with metre. Etymologically speaking, metre comes from the Latin *tangere* which means to touch, while rhythm comes from the Greek *rheein* meaning to flow.

This definition of rhythm is related to a phenomenon that is fluid, continuous, uninterrupted, while at the same time, structured. The motif involves a rotation around a vertical axis that is turning. The recurrent rotary and repetitive movement marks the tonic rhythm.

By working with a series of autonomous but concatenated elements, superimposing the linear and helical recurrence, the design deals with both the subordination to the series and the autonomy or emancipation of the helical unit. The result is a deliberate ambiguity: the coexistence of agreement (unity) and difference (diversity). This differentiation between the whole and the part enables the project to play with similarities and differences in a freer, more open way.

Dynamic Rhythms: Variation and Variety of the Motif

Once the union/separation between the motif and the totality is achieved, some Gestalt principles are needed to enable us to understand the notions of variation and variety, which are inherent to the dynamic rhythms of the sequence. The principle of similarity enables each dwelling to be understood as a variation on the previous one. The prior strategy of periodicity is fundamental to the achievement of this temporal effect of variation:

> Similarity only acts as a structural principle if it is in conjunction with separation, namely, as a force of attraction between segregated things.[10]

Variation refers to each of the melodic imitations of a theme. A motif is *the theme or the subject of a composition that moves and has the efficacy and virtue to move.*[11] However, this idea of movement is left for later on in order to focus on syntactic order. In any case, at this stage of the explanation it is important to underline the importance of the motif in the overall composition.

As mentioned above, the motif is made up of the pieces located around each helical shape. The plan of each studio is divided into eight sectors through seven radii that organise the development of the helix. Both the tetrahedron of the roof and the bearing walls suit this partition. The tetrahedrons are arranged face to face, each fragment with its inherent peculiarities, to use that juxtaposition to deploy in space according to the helical geometry. The walls are either curved to contain the centre of the shape (to protect it, acting on the perimeter) or arranged in a radial formation, coinciding with the organising radii (Figure 2.4).

The harmony of the discourses of the different families of construction elements is superimposed over the melody. Thanks to the non-deformable nature of the tetrahedrons and the curved walls, three independent but harmonised layers (basement, ground floor, and roof) come together. The melody takes place horizontally, and the harmony vertically.

The non-deformable nature of the tetrahedrons and the stability of the curved walls lead to an articulated stacking, liberated of the restrictions of an identical structural continuity.

> If you take a sheet of cardboard and stand it up, it falls over. But if you bend it, giving it a curved shape, it becomes more stable and does not tip over. In addition, if you make the walls curved and it is a painter's studio, the incoming light does not shine on the painting in a distracting way.[12]

This articulated stacking leads to an agreement, or accord, among the different basic vertical elements. This articulation informs three discourses based on three different core elements that nonetheless form accords among different ones, both constructive, on a smaller scale, and formal ones governed by the constriction of helicoidal geometries, on a larger scale. Although there are three different planes, the vertical harmony remains intact thanks to the periodicity's underlying order. Periodicity and harmony mutually support each other to maintain the form. In both cases, the structure the helicoidal geometry gives to the motif is essential.

Compared to the compositions by Iannis Xenakis or John Cage, who removed the periodicity of musical serialism to concentrate on the study of the changes, fluctuations, and compositions of masses and other amorphous elements, Fernando Higueras would maintain such periodicity as a structuring principle. These musicians used probability or indeterminacy to achieve a full opening. With periodicity broken, differences and dissonances floated in space-time, and harmony was intermittently lost and recovered. This arrangement went over the limit and was then recovered. In this sense, they differed from the work by Fernando Higueras. In his work, form maintained its equilibrium thanks to periodicity. Thus, the observer's perception was capable of imbuing the whole with the necessary intelligibility.

However, this equilibrium is also carried beyond its limits. The striving to preserve the dynamic form, ruled by the principle of similarity, is countered by the opposing force that defends the variety of the design. Variation renders the ten dwellings similar, but there is also the opposite strategy: the differentiation of some elements with respect to others.

'Similarity is a pre-requisite to notice the differences,' argued Rudolf Arnheim.[13] The Gestalt principle of difference is defined as *difference within unity, (as a) set of diverse things, and not as the inconstancy, instability or mutability of things or as the removal or alteration in the substance of things.*[14]

The same opening that permits the concatenation of the discontinuous also facilitates the appearance of differences. By contrast with classical Pythagorean thinking that seeks to limit the project, this other Baroque side seeks to deploy the infinite possibilities of this order. It is not reductionist but expansionist. Rhythm enables it to bend the rules.

Differences are worked out through the resource of syncopation or the resource of the different tempos given to each sentence. These dynamic rhythms, as their name suggests, enliven the work. Matila C. Ghyka refers to syncopation as follows:

> In music, the deliberate displacement of the regular beat enables an effect of rupture, strangulation or extension of the expected rhythm to be obtained that is named syncopation. The corresponding effect in prosody is likewise obtained by rejecting, jumping, displacing and sliding regular tonic accents.[15]

The rhythmic effect of syncopation as an offbeat may be assimilated into the poetic effect of enjambment. This feature seeks to break up identical metrics and thus favour difference. Etymologically the term comes from the French *enjambement*, at the root of which is *jambe*, which means 'leg.' It alludes to the action of striding over something.

The poetic effect occurs when the pause at the end of a verse does not coincide with a morphosyntactic pause, that is, with one produced by punctuation. The incomplete phrase therefore straddles two verses. The metric licence that enjambment provides:

> involves linking the end of one verse to the beginning of another [...] This gap needs to be sufficiently abrupt so that the reader, when perceiving it, does not introduce any expiratory time between the two verses[...] In rhyming verses, the sense of measurement—forgotten by the enjambment—is recovered when another rhyme rekindles the memory of the previous one.[16]

The following example by Federico García Lorca, between the second and third verses, is clear:

> Llena, pues, de palabras mi locura
> o déjame vivir en mi serena
> noche del alma para siempre oscura.[17]

> [So now fill with words my madness
> or let me live in the tranquil
> night of my soul, forever in darkness.][18]

In the case of the architectural example, the tetrahedrons are arranged according to the order of the helix, but at the same time, in some specific cases they break it down, and thus sit astride two elements of the series. As can be seen in an overhead view of a model of the project, there are elements at both roof level and on the ground floor that ride up over the following ones, producing an ambiguous effect that contradicts the prevailing order. In the case of the roof, dwelling 7 overlaps the next one, giving greater importance to the linear movement of the displacement than to the concatenation of the helicoidal movement. Regarding the layer of freestanding walls, some of them are raised in continuity with others, linking two different helicoidal arrangements (Figures 2.1 and 2.2).

As can be seen, phrasing is also influenced by enjambment: they work on the tempo or speed of the action. The project takes advantage of the distinctness of each sentence to accelerate, slow, or stop the pace. Thus, the units located lower down the hillside are concatenated in a rotating movement as far as the communal building, where a pause is introduced. That pause acts as a node from which another rhythm connects three elements in a linear shape. And to end the movement, one last unit is configured on top as a full stop.

These superimposed, combined dynamic rhythms produce frequencies that can be delimited via punctuation criteria. The handling of spaces, pauses, and suspensions defines each group. Dwelling number 10 is isolated at the top of the hill, where it opens onto a courtyard, standing as a dot in the landscape. From the communal building, which also opens up to signify its importance, the other series are developed. On the one hand, the linear series, formed by dwellings 7, 8, and 9, is completed when the last dwelling is separated from all the others. On the other hand, another series, formed by dwellings 1 to 6, accentuates its rotational feature to mark out a longer route and adapt to the topography. The units go down the hillside in a sentence that repeatedly insists upon the rotation of each motif, terminating in the form of a pairing that like the previous sentence also distances itself from all the other dwellings. This pairing forms a set, and does not constitute two separate units: the sheltered porch on dwelling 2 harbours a door, an entrance archway, which presents itself to dwelling 1 (Figures 2.1 and 2.2).

Each sentence then expresses a tempo beyond metre. That tempo is concerned with the speed, with the energy with which the performance takes place. The rotating rhythm of the dwellings that descend along the slope contrasts with the linear rhythm, as a give and take, of the three dwellings on the same level. The tonic rhythm accelerates: it becomes an *allegro*. Thus, the nuances of the tempo qualify the sentences that the punctuation of the dynamic quantitative rhythms has established, introducing a criterion of intensity or expression.

The Rhythm of the Timbre and Resolving the Contradiction

Following this syntactic reading of the work, characterised by the motif's periodic movement in the series, the analysis now focuses on the choice of this motif for revealing the work's true meaning. The formal rhythmical attributes studied thus far affect the form or the change in form of a unit or motif: an action that may be understood as an event. Yet the observer's perception of this event depends on the movement it provokes in them.

It is the moment of love, as Matila C. Ghyka describes that

> transposition of the state of ecstasy of the person subject to the action of the spell, who becomes receptive and is overcome by the rhythm of passion, of bliss, or of simple euphoria that had thrilled the composer upon creating the work.[19]

Matila C. Ghyka summarises this final leap as the passage from enchantment to love, that is, from the automatism of the compositional value to the inspiration that the expressive imagination triggers or, to put it another way, to the mood that the work evokes. The author's aim was to make the observer experience similar feelings to his own. It is a lyrical work in that the author's feelings and emotions remain veiled within it.

To achieve this mood, the project alludes to different images. The specialised critics of the time interpreted the project as a flock of birds ready to take wing.[20] Nevertheless, our aim here is to interpret the project in a different way. The synthetic image it refers to involves a dance, a ritual. In this case, the motif alludes to the image of a flamenco dancer expressing her art. Considered in this way, with the stress on mood as such, it becomes reminiscent of the ballet *El Amor Brujo* by Manuel de Falla. The composition of the tetrahedrons, some of which are raised upon the others, reflects the movement of the dancer's arms, the expressive movement of her arms in the air, her hands and fingers accompanying the swirling movement, which contrasts with the uprightness of the body, maintaining the axis the dancer needs to perform on the stage. A whirling movement that is mirrored by the train on the dancer's dress and her petticoat, which ultimately portray the same idea, flying around the same structural axis (Figure 2.3–2.5).

In this sense, it may also bring to mind the arm movements of the dancer, Isadora Duncan. Her Dionysiac dance shared a lyricism with the flamenco of *El Amor Brujo* that Fernando Higueras sought to use to compose the ritual.

Irrespective of the final image conjured up, the common ground between the interpretation the critics made at the time and the new

Figure 2.3 Nathalie Gontcharova's cover of the first edited score of Manuel de Falla's ballet *El Amor Brujo*. Libretto by Maria Lejarraga. London. Chester Ltd. 1921. © Nathalie Gontcharova, VEGAP, Bilbao, 2017.

Figure 2.4 View of Fernando Higueras's model of *10 Residences for Artists on El Pardo Hill in Madrid,* 1960. © Archivo Fundación Fernando Higueras.

appreciation provided here is the work's materiality. The airiness of the dance's movement, or the weightlessness of taking flight, impacts upon the act's lightness. By contrast, the material used to build the project testifies to its weight. Set against the form or change in form is the material. It is this other rhythm: the rhythm of the timbre.

Weight is expressed through the raw material of the large volumes of roofing, of the walls built using what is referred as to *universal lightweight formwork*:

> I went to a place where they sold roller blinds made of old wood, I bought them all, placed them upright, and this made the ground plan, and I used some wires, chicken-wire, poured the concrete, in a curved shape, then removed it, and because it was a stiff curve shape it doesn't fall over. Then you add the pane of glass, you make another one, you add another pane, you make another one [...][21]

As this description shows, the finish is defined by the grain of the shuttering. The burring and other features produced by the rendering of the material remain visible. What matters is not a perfectly smooth finish, but the material itself.

As expressed in the pictorial discipline, contrasting with the structuring of the boundary geometries is the limited material content. This struggle between line and mass was brilliantly depicted by Pablo Picasso in *Les Demoiselles d'Avignon*. As Santiago Amón clearly explains:

> synthetic cubism lays the arrangement of the colours on the floating fraction of black [...], the waxing and waning of the line, interwove like a fabric, and the expressionist impetus is boosted, turning its back on geometric dogma, and invigorating the return of the *Les Demoiselles d'Avignon*, a crucial point in the simplification, disassociation and rupture, its passion will be heightened through the loss of the black, and its disappearance will become increasingly more obvious.[22]

This disappearance, specific to the crudeness of the mass, is set against the clarity of the pure geometries making up the work. Following on from the previous lightness, there now appears the slow transformation of the material, its erosion and decomposition: the gravity of death. There is therefore a juxtaposition of lightness and weight, duration and durability.

In turn, the architect Luis Moya described the project in the following terms:

> [...] in its violent embracing of the earth and its struggle to free itself from this embrace.[23]

There is a further appearance of the struggle referred to in the interpretations made so far. Nevertheless, this last explanation more clearly
reveals the notion of crystallographied nature that resolves the previous
contradictions. As material crystallises, becomes embodied, life is born.
It appears as a material that seeks to crystallise in the sense of *clearly
and precisely giving shape, forgoing any indeterminacy, to the ideas,
feelings or desires of a person or collective.*[24] From this perspective, the
contradiction between the two opposites is resolved through a productive potentiality.

Along these lines, the opposition used by both Manuel de Falla and
Federico García Lorca of the devices of the small and the pretty, which
address the concept of lightness, and therefore of the gravity of a fate
that runs contrary to the individual's will, leads to an act in the making
with an unresolved tension informing a mood. The latter reveals the
tragedy of the human condition, the unbearable lightness of being when
love is impossible or unrequited, bewitched, or dark.

When composing this work, Falla is dealing with a universal emotional conflict: love hurts.

> Lo mismo que el fuego fatuo,
> Lo mismito es el querer,
> Le huyes y te persigue,
> Le sigues y echa a correr.[25]

> [The same as the will-o'-the-wisp,
> Love is really the same!
> You flee from it and it chases you
> You call it and it runs away.]

This conflict consists of a triple rhythm of flamenco *bulerías*, or to put it
another way, an overlay of rhythms with a background rhythm, one of
flames, a yearning and melodic motif that represents the obsession the
work seeks to convey, which is repeated at regular intervals, obsessively,
and then repeated, like a ritual set against the one created by the old
gypsy women's spells.

In the case of the ten dwellings for artists on the hill in El Pardo, the obsessive motif deals with the start of movement, which contrasts the gravity of the inert with the lightness of the nascent. This movement towards
life is based on the act's potentiality, on the life force for achieving it.

> What was life, really? [...] Out of overcompensation for its own in-
> stability, yet governed by its own inherent laws of formation [...]
> what we call flesh ran riot, unfolded, and took shape, achieving
> form [...] substances awakened to lust via means unknown, by de-
> composing and composing organic matter itself, by reeking flesh.[26]

Figure 2.5 View of Fernando Higueras's project of *10 Residences for Artists on El Pardo Hill in Madrid*, 1960. © Archivo Fundación Fernando Higueras.

At that moment, life makes its presence felt. Impression and expression, the work itself on the one hand and the observer on the other, become harmonious.

This relationship can only be understood through the notion of primitivism. If we look back, all the elements that rhythm uses to compose the project's syntax—that is, the open arrangement that the helicoids' continuous proportion creates, the basic shapes of the tetrahedrons, or crude materiality as an unfinished form—all refer to the idea of primitivism.

Primitivism is understood to be that which lies in the origin, structured but as yet not fully formed. In turn, it is understood as the possibility of releasing what humans carry inside. Humans feel an impression, and they release it, they convey it to the outside as an expression. The possibility of expression is one of the principles of primitivism. And it is directly related to the original rhythm that each person harbours inside. Each individual's true self is reflected in their temperament, that inner rhythm that sets each one apart from all the others. According to this premise, impression and expression are part of the same process, which develops according to the receiver's own rhythm. As Hermann Bahr explains in his book *Expressionismus*, impressionism and expressionism are integrated. They are the two sides of the same reality.

> He understood how [...] the artist and the scientist were closely linked, how both created from the same expressive imagination, which acts according to the well-known idea of living transformation.[27]

In conclusion, primitivism is fundamental to our understanding of rhythm as a factor that underlies a mood that stirs emotion. This difficult agreement between impression and expression, between the Dionysian and the Apollonian, between classical thought and scholastic thought, between number and nature, between the measurable and the measureless is ultimately resolved by means of the plasticity of the work. That plasticity, which is built up by the imagination from the perception of (spatial) temporality, triggers a catharsis in the observer, understood as movement, which becomes a lyrical experience.

Notes

1 Umberto Eco, *Historia de la belleza a cargo de Umberto Eco* (Barcelona: Editorial Lumen S.A., 2004), p. 61. This quotation and all subsequent quotations have been translated by the author (unless otherwise indicated).

2 Ibid., p. 64.

3 Ibid., p. 75.

4 Matila C. Ghyka, *El número de oro: los ritmos. Ritos y ritmos pitagóricos en el desarrollo de la civilización occidental* (Buenos Aires: Editorial Poseidon, 1968).

5 Olivier Hanse, *Rythme et civilisation dans la pensée allemande autour de 1900*, PhD dissertation in the field of Germanic studies at the University of Rennes 2, Haute Bretagne, 2007, p. 88.

   Translated from the French: 'La plus petite unité d'expression et de sens, le motif, est constitué d'un certain nombre de mesures; la période réunit plusieurs motifs dans une unité de sens supérieure. Le regroupement des sons en mesures, en motifs et en périodes équivaut à une analyse sémantique de la musique, et ne peut être établi par le simple fait de compter les notes ou les temps.'

6 Fernando Higueras, *Hogar y arquitectura no. 42* (September–October 1962), p. 23.

7 V.V.A.A., *La fotografía del siglo XX* (Museum Ludwig Colonia, Colonia: Taschen, 2002), p. 456.

8 Rudolf Arnheim, *Arte y percepción visual* (Madrid: Alianza Editorial, 1979), p. 409.

9 Hanse, *Rythme*, p. 308.

   Translation from the French: 'De même que (dans la mesure binaire) l'élément accentué fait suite à l'élément non accentué, le creux fait suite au sommet; tous deux correspondent aux corps qui servaient de frontières à un laps de temps, mis à part que, dans le cas présent, les coups ne sont pas marqués. En passant par un nombre infini d'étapes, l'ascension est suivie sans transition par une chute puis inversement, de telle façon que, ni au niveau du point d'inflexion supérieur, ni au niveau du point d'inflexion inférieur, une arête ne se forme. Au lieu de cela, nous observons une courbe, qui représente de façon évidente la continuité sans limite d'un mouvement incontestablement structuré, causée par une oscillation ininterrompue de part et d'autre d'un axe de départ.'

10 Rudolf Arnheim, *Arte y percepción visual* (Madrid: Alianza Editorial, 1979), p. 96.

11 *Diccionario de la lengua española*. Real Academia Española (21st ed. 1992).

12 Ibid.

13 Arnheim, *Arte*, p. 97.

14 *Diccionario de la lengua española*, 1992.

15 Ghyka, *El número de oro*, p. 163.
16 *Larousse Enciclopedia* (Barcelona: Editorial Planeta, 1972).
17 Federico García Lorca, *Sonetos del amor oscuro. Poemas de amor y erotismo. Inéditos de madurez* (Barcelona: Ediciones Áltera S.L., 1995), p. 30. Poem: *El poeta pide a su amor que le escribe [The poet begs his beloved to write to him]*. First published in 1941.
18 Translation by Paul Archer. http://www.paularcher.net/translations/fede rico_garcia_lorca/sonnets_of_dark_love/the_poet_begs_his_beloved_to_ write_to_him.html.
19 Ghyka, *El número de oro*, p. 192.
20 Luis Moya, *Arquitectura* no. 28, 1961, p. 2.
21 María Isabel Navarro Segura, *Basa* no. 24, 2001. p. 12.
22 Santiago Amón, *Picasso* (Madrid: VISOR Distribuciones S.A., 1989), p. 122.
23 Moya, *Arquitectura*, p. 2.
24 *Diccionario de la lengua española*, 1992.
25 María Lejarraga, *El amor brujo*, libretto for the work of the same name by Manuel de Falla (signed with her husband's pseudonym Gregorio Martínez Sierra). Madrid, 1915. Translation: www.scribd.com/document/356923397/ Cancion-Del-Fuego-Fatuo-English-Translation.
26 Thomas Mann, *La montaña mágica. Volumen I* (Madrid: Unidad Editorial, 1999), p. 272.
27 Hermann Bahr, *Expresionismo* (Murcia: Colegio oficial de aparejadores y arquitectos técnicos de Murcia, 1998), p. 95.

Bibliography

Amón, Santiago, *Picasso* (Madrid: VISOR Distribuciones S.A., 1989).
Arnheim, Rudolf, *Arte y percepción visual* (Madrid: Alianza Editorial, 1979). Original edition: Arnheim, Rudolf, *Art and Visual Perception. A Psychology of the Creative Eye* (Berkeley: The University of California Press, 1954).
Arquitectura n°28, abril 1961. pp. 6–9.
Bahr, Hermann, *Expresionismo* (Murcia: Colegio Oficial de Aparejadores y Arquitectos técnicos de Murcia, 1998). Original edition: 1916.
Basa n°24, 1° semestre 2001. pp. 4–35.
Diccionario de la lengua española [Dictionary of the Spanish Language]. Real Academia Española (21st ed. 1992).
Eco, Umberto, *Historia de la belleza a cargo de Umberto Eco* (Barcelona: Editorial Lumen S.A., 2004).
Gallego, Antonio, *Manuel de Falla y El amor brujo* (Madrid: Alianza D.L., 1990).
García Lorca, Federico, *Sonetos del amor oscuro. Poemas de amor y erotismo. Inéditos de madurez* (Barcelona: Ediciones Áltera S.L., 1995).
Ghyka, Matila C., *El número de oro: los ritmos. Ritos y ritmos pitagóricos en el desarrollo de la civilización occidental* (Buenos Aires: Editorial Poseidon, 1968). Original edition: 1931.
Hanse, Olivier, *Rythme et civilisation Dans la pensée allemande autour de 1900*, Tesis doctoral en la disciplina de estudios germánicos por la universidad Rennes 2, Haute Bretagne, 2007.
Hogar y arquitectura n°42, septiembre-octubre 1962, pp. 17–50.
Larousse, Enciclopedia (Barcelona: Editorial Planeta, 1972).

Lejarraga, María, *El amor brujo*, libretto for the work of the same name by Manuel de Falla (signed with her husband's pseudonym Gregorio Martínez Sierra) (Madrid: R. Velasco. Imp., 1915).

Mann, Thomas, *La montaña mágica. Volumen I* (Madrid: Unidad Editorial, 1999).

Meyer, Leonard B., *Emoción y significado en la música* (Madrid: Alianza Editorial, 2001). Original edition: Meyer, Leonard B., *Emotion and Meaning in Music* (Chicago, IL: University of Chicago, 1956).

V.V.A.A., *La fotografía del siglo XX* (Museum Ludwig Colonia, Colonia: Taschen, 2002).

3 The Varieties of Mood Intentionality

Jonathan Mitchell

Introduction

In this chapter, I provide a philosophical account of the different ways moods—as personal-level experiential states—are intentional, where intentionality can be understood, minimally at first, as the way in which such a state is directed towards or 'about' something.[1] Drawing on work in affective psychology, I distinguish between two levels of mood experience: a first-order level (FOL) of phenomenal experience, and a second-order level (SOL), which consists in attention to aspects of the first-order experience. Using this distinction, I argue that the intentionality present at the FOL of mood experience is an immersed, non-propositional awareness of 'the world'—as what I call the subject's 'universal horizon' presented under specific evaluative aspects—and it is only at the SOL that moods can also become explicitly (a) self-focused and (b) bodily-focused. So, my fundamental claim in what follows is that, while there are varieties of mood intentionality, I argue that we should recognise the primacy of their world-directed aspect.

Before the analysis begins, some housekeeping is necessary. My focus in the chapter will be on moods as personal-level occurrent experiences, that is, personally and temporally indexed conscious episodes of varying duration, which are a familiar feature of most people's affective psychology and which have a distinctive phenomenal character. Folk psychology latches onto moods in this sense when we report of ourselves, and others, that we are 'in a mood.' Moreover, we have at our disposal a relatively extensive mood-typology which reflects this usage, when we talk of being currently depressed, happy, sad, joyous, elated, listless, melancholic, anxious, morose, irritable, calm, etc. When thought of in these terms there is undeniably 'something-it-is-like' to be in a mood—moods have a first-person phenomenology.

Conceptual and phenomenological analysis substantiates the thesis, adumbrated in the above folk psychology, that moods are distinct kinds of personal-level occurrent (affective) experiences, not simply emotional dispositions or temperaments, or emotions masquerading under mood-terms. Here I take this understanding of moods—as occurrent personal-level experiences with a distinct phenomenal character—for granted in order to focus substantively on their intentional content, and specifically on the variety of that content.[2] Moreover, while I will have something to say about pathological moods (or moods disorders)—since confusion about the intentionality of moods is often the result of unwarranted generalisations from pathological cases—I will not be concerned with computational or functional accounts which are framed at the subpersonal level.[3] Neither will I be concerned to attempt a reduction of the manifest phenomenal intentional content of mood experience to the kinds of causal-nomological or teleosemantic relations which often figure in those computational and functional accounts.[4] As such, my aim is limited to elucidating the personal-level intentional content of moods as experientially present in phenomenal consciousness.

The discussion proceeds as follows: the 'Different Levels of Experience and Mood Experience' section explains an important distinction in conscious experience between first-order and second-order levels, and then provides a basic conception of personal-level intentionality; the 'World, Self and Body' section considers in more detail the different aspects of mood intentionality, namely that of 'the world,' 'the body,' and 'the self,' and finally, the chapter closes with a summation of the analysis.

Different Levels of Experience and Mood Experience

FOL and SOL

To understand the varied intentionality of moods, it is helpful to make a distinction in conscious experience between what I will call, following affective psychologists Anthony Marcel and John Lambie, first-order phenomenal experience (FOL) and second-order attention, as awareness of (or to) aspects of first-order phenomenal experience (SOL). The nature of the distinction can be clarified with some characterisations of contrasting features:

> Def of FOL: (i) immersed, no distinction between is and seems (ii) not cognitively mediated (iii) non-propositional, an experience *of* not *that*, (iv) detects, rather than describes, (vi) self is implicit and recessive (as an ecological self-awareness), (vii) basic phenomenal presence of an attitudinal relation between self and world.
>
> Def of SOL, as attention to FOL experience: (i) detached, distinction between is and seems (ii) typically cognitively mediated, (iii) typically propositional, can be both an experience of *and* that (iv) self-awareness is explicit and so can be taken as an object, (v) can be categorical, awareness of experience *as a* particular experience (when so is conceptual).[5]

It should be clear that there are important differences between FOL and SOL, where the latter is understood, broadly, as attention to aspects of that first-order phenomenal experience. Talk of mood experience in what follows is taken to encompass both FOL and SOL. Yet before analysing the kind of intentionality that arguably operates at these different levels, I want to say more about the relation between the levels.

First, it is important not to confuse the SOL with separate acts of reflection about mood experience, say a detached non-affective reflection about a particular mood I was in, which takes a particular mood experience as an object. As already noted, mood experience should be taken to include both FOL and SOL. Consider the difference between an experience of depression which includes SOL thoughts about worthlessness and hopelessness (the precise nature of which, in their relation to FOL phenomenal experience, I will explain in what follows), and a non-affective reflection about a depressed mood. Clearly the former thoughts, as grounded in SOL attention, are part of the experience.

Second, a central claim, made by Marcel and Lambie, about the relation between FOL and SOL is that in typical cases, unless there is attention (of some kind), one will not be able to report the phenomenal character of FOL, or be able to recall it in episodic memory. Yet, at the same time, the kind of attention that SOL brings to features of FOL modifies their character, and more broadly, the experience as a whole, according to the precise mode of attention in question. For example, analytic focal attention to specific aspects of the phenomenal character of a pain experience might diminish its felt unpleasant quality. This result in the less than ideal situation that reports of FOL are typically only possible on the basis of SOL attention, but in many cases such attention modifies one's overall experience. This is especially evident in the case of the categorical dimension of SOL, which is likely to involve schematising effects. For example, if a joyful mood was to involve a categorisation of it *as an experience of joy*—perhaps mediated through a cognition of some sort—we might, in SOL attention, simply distort or overlook the fine-grained or rich phenomenology of the mood as experientially manifest at the FOL.

Given this, folk psychological reports—while they may be an instructive source of data for philosophical investigation—need careful analysis. We should resist the naïve idea that complex structural or constitutive features of FOL—say its intentional nature or the character of any intentional content—can simply be 'read off' from first-personal reports.

Intentionality and Mood Experience

Before attempting to theorise the intentionality of moods, and examine mood experience, it helps to have a characterisation of intentionality. We can provide the following definition of personal-level intentionality:

Def of PLI (personal-level intentionality):

   (a) The occurrent experience must be directed toward 'something' (directedness)

   (b) That 'something' must be presented under a determinate aspect (aspectual shape), 'as thus and so'

   (c) That 'something' must be presented under a determinate aspect, to the subject of experience in phenomenal consciousness (indexicality)[6]

If conditions (a), (b), and (c) are met, then we have a personal-level intentional experience. The definition adds to the basic idea of directedness, that the 'something' presented through an intentional experience must be presented under a determinate aspect. For example, a paradigmatic visual perceptual experience would not just present a table, but present that table under determinate aspects, as having certain properties and not others—say as being of a certain size, or coloured red all over. Moreover, it is a necessary condition of personal-level intentionality that the 'something' presented, under a determinate aspect, is presented to a subject of experience, through phenomenal consciousness, securing that the what-it-is-likeness of the experience is a what-it-is-like-*for-me*. From this definition, we also get a minimal conception of manifest intentional content, specified as 'the something as it is so determinately presented to the subject of experience through phenomenal consciousness.'

To mark out the different kinds of intentional content of moods, and where they fit in to a two-tier account of conscious experience, we need some phenomenological data to probe. We can begin with a rich description of the mood of joy:

> I feel like smiling...I'm loose relaxed, there's sense of well-being...
> I'm completely free from worry...I'm in tune with the world...the
> world seems basically good and beautiful...there is an inner warm
> glow, a radiant sensation...a sense of being very integrated and at
> ease with myself...I'm at peace with the world...there's a particu-
> larly acute awareness of pleasurable things, their sounds, their co-
> lours, and textures – everything seems more beautiful, natural, and
> desirable...there is an intense awareness of everything...there is a
> sense of lightness, buoyancy and upsurge of the body...I'm experi-
> encing everything fully, completely, thoroughly; I'm feeling all the
> way...I'm less aware of time...the feeling seems to be all over, no-
> where special, just not localized...the feeling fills me completely.[7]

The least controversial claim that can be made on the basis of the above description is that we are dealing with an occurrent, experiential state with a first-personal phenomenology; consider the extensive use of the terms 'feel' and 'feeling,' and relatedly, 'seems,' 'experience,' and 'aware.'

In addition, we can identify the following three recurrent features as present: (a) 'the world,' or 'everything,' under specific determinations ('as beautiful' or 'as good'); (b) the self, under specific determinations (e.g., 'as free from worry,' 'at ease'); and (c) the body, under specific determinations ('as buoyant' or 'upsurging'). Consider another rich mood description, this time (non-pathological) depression:

> I feel empty, drained, hollow...there is a sense of being dead inside...
> my body seems to slow down...there is a sense of uncertainty about
> the future....a sense of being totally unable to cope with the situa-
> tion...everything seems out of proportion....I'm completely uncer-
> tain of everything...everything seems useless, absurd, meaningless...
> there is a lack of involvement and not caring about anything that
> goes on around me...there is an inner ache you can't locate...there is
> a lump in my throat...it seems nothing I do is right...I keep search-
> ing for an explanation, for some understanding; I keep thinking
> 'why'...my body wants to contract, so as to draw closer to myself...
> it's a bottomless feeling.[8]

Again, aside from the fact such a report details an occurrent experiential state with a first-personal phenomenology, we can identify the
same three recurrent features as present: (a) 'the world' or 'everything,'
under specific determinations ('as out of proportion,' 'as useless, absurd,
meaningless'); (b) the self, under specific determinations ('nothing I do is
right,' 'unable to cope with the situation'); and (c) the body, under specific determinations (as 'slowed down, an 'inner ache,' as 'contracting').
For sake of brevity, I will not detail every mood in this way, and will use
joy and depression as paradigmatic. It is plausible that, if we were to do
so we would find these three dimensions recurring.

One view suggested by the above reports is that moods, as occurrent
experiential states, are directed to, or about, the world, self, and body
synchronously—all under specific aspects, and all presented in and to
phenomenal consciousness (thus satisfying the conditions of PLI). However, such a view is problematic. If in joy I am experiencing 'an intense
awareness of everything' (world-focus), can I synchronously be explicitly
aware of 'an inner warm glow' or 'radiant sensation' (bodily-focus), or
indeed of myself as 'free from worry' or 'at ease' (self-focus)? Likewise,
in depression, if I am aware of a 'sense of being totally unable to cope
with the situation' (self-focus), can I also be synchronously explicitly
aware of 'an inner ache' or 'a lump in the throat' (body-focus), or that
'everything seems out of proposition...', 'useless, absurd, meaningless'
(world-focus)?

Arguably, it is part of the nature of explicit 'awareness of' in the intentional sense, and so as a necessary dimension of a criterion of intentionality, that it is in any given moment (at time t) directed towards one

object, or one 'something.' In other words, intentional directedness, at least as manifest in personal-level experience, seems monadic (about 'X'), rather than conjunctive (about 'X, Y, and Z'). Note that this point should not be confused with the different, and incorrect, claim that intentional directedness needs to pick out only one feature of its object. Rather, the claim is that it can only have only one intentional object at a time, although that intentional object could be complex, and admit of a conjunctive specification, e.g., as square and black all over, or a full state of affairs, say, an entire visual scene as perceptually presented. In any case, it seems intuitive to say I do not typically, in one and the same moment, have a conscious experience as exteroceptively directed towards my spatio-temporal environment and synchronously towards myself or my body. Notwithstanding this, intentional directedness may oscillate, of course, between these different objects fairly rapidly, and when it does so, one or the other will fall into the background or come into the foreground.

However, one problem with rejecting the above synchronous account—that moods could be, at the same time directed towards world, body, and self—is that the reports of joy or depression above attest to the presence of all these features, as that towards which the mood is putatively directed. To accommodate them all within a theory of moods' intentionality we need to deploy the distinction between FOL and SOL in conscious experience.

World, Self, and Body

The World

The first substantive claims I want to make about the intentionality of moods are as follows: (i) paradigmatic mood experience involves an experience of 'the world' as affectively presented under determinate evaluative aspects, and (ii) this experience of 'the world,' as evaluatively qualified, is the fundamental level of mood intentionality, as present in FOL (first-order phenomenal experience). However, we need to say more about what this evaluative presentation of 'the world' amounts to.[9]

The first point to note is that the sense of the 'world' as presented in a mood is not to be equated with any perceptually present spatio-temporal particular, or indeed in general with the world of perceptually present spatio-temporal particulars (although it may include the latter). While it is difficult to pin down this sense of 'the world' as involving 'everything' and 'nothing in particular,' the sense deployed in folk reports seems close to what the phenomenologists, and specifically Edmund Husserl, call the life-world (*Lebenswelt*) of the world as the 'universal horizon' for the subject,[10] which will include modal, temporal, agentive relations. Modal and temporal relations are explicit in the report of depression which highlights that 'there is a sense of uncertainty about the future.' But this aspect is also found in a mood like joy, as involving a sense of optimism about the future. Note here that it would be too restrictive to think of these modal and temporal relations exclusively in terms of opportunities for specific action, or lack thereof. While such agentive aspects are clearly present, we might say, in more general terms, that 'the world' is given in a depressed mood as not affording a broader sense of meaningful engagement.

Given this, 'the world' as presented in a mood is not a neutral presentation but rather is given under a specific evaluative aspect, *as depressing, as joyous, as offensive*—in that sense the intentional object is 'the world' as the universal *evaluative* horizon for the subject (as including my projects, values, and desires). That 'the world' is so evaluatively presented is reflected in the above mood descriptions: in joy 'everything seems more beautiful, natural, and desirable ... the world seems basically good'; in depression 'everything seems out of proportion ... useless, absurd, meaningless.' And it is because in depression 'everything seems useless, absurd or meaningless,' that 'the world,' so presented does not afford opportunity for meaningful engagement; or contrastingly in joy because 'everything seems more beautiful, natural, and desirable', that 'the world,' so presented, affords opportunity for meaningful engagement. Finally, it should be clear that 'the world,' as the subject's universal evaluative horizon, is presented to the subject of a mood through phenomenal consciousness; there is something 'the world' is like for them (as we shall see below, however, the affective dimension of moods complicates this picture somewhat).

So, if mood experience involves being directed at 'the world' in the above sense—as directed towards the subject's universal evaluative horizon—what is the motivation for locating this kind of intentionality at Marcel and Lambie's FOL of phenomenal experience? In answering this question, further features of mood experience and this world-focused aspect of their intentionality can now be elucidated.

Following the definition of FOL provided in the 'Different Levels of Experience and Mood Experience' section, a mood in which 'the world,' is experienced as having a specific evaluative character, plausibly is (i) an immersive state, in which the distinction between 'the world' seeming a certain way and being that way does not arise. For example, when experiencing a joyous mood, it seems phenomenologically correct to say the subject does not immediately question whether 'the world' is indeed joyous; rather, it just seems it is, and is taken at face value (likewise for non-pathological depression). Second, (ii) this kind of 'world-directed' mood experience seems intuitively described as instantiating a basic kind of intentionality, akin to perceptual experiences and emotions, which are not typically cognitively mediated or thought-involving. Non-reflective or pre-reflective experience of a joyous mood, need not, and typically will not involve entertaining thoughts approximating to 'the world is a joyous place' (although as we shall see in the '"World focus" in SOL' section FOL mood experience might ground them). Third, and relatedly, (iii) mood experience of this kind is non-propositional, in that it does not involve entertaining thoughts with the content 'that the world is depressing' or 'that the world is joyous,' but rather is constituted by an experiential evaluative presentation of the world: it detects rather than describes, as so is an experience *of*, not *that*. And fourth, (iv) insofar as 'the self' that figures at this level is not an explicit object of awareness, but rather is 'implicit and recessive,' the self is minimally present as the subject undergoing the experiencing.

Furthermore, a complex and distinctive feature of moods—along with other affective experiences—is that they are felt responses, such that being in a mood is experienced as being responsive to something. Given that we are focusing on the world-directed aspect of mood experience, we can plug in this aspect, and say moods are experienced as felt responses to 'the world,' as the subject's universal evaluative horizon. In this sense, the world-directed dimension of mood experience not only satisfies the final FOL criterion of involving 'basic phenomenal presence of an attitudinal relation between self and world,' but also indicates that, in mood experience, this attitudinal relation is an affective one, as a felt response to 'the world,' so evaluatively presented.

On the basis of the above analysis, we have the following picture: moods, at the FOL, are experienced as immersive, non-cognitively mediated, non-propositional, affective attitudes towards 'the world,' as evaluatively presented under a specific aspect. The basic phenomenology of moods is one of directedness towards a subject's universal evaluative horizon ('the world'), through an affective attitude. The basic attitude component here can be thought of as a favour or disfavour with the characteristic of globality, as a negatively or positively charged intentional attitude, which picks up on, and so is a response to, that universal evaluative horizon.[11]

It should be clear that the world-focused intentionality of moods is apt to be placed at the FOL. Not only does it satisfy all the defining features of that level, but it should be clear that 'self-focused' and 'body-focused' intentionality would in various ways fall short of those criteria. For example, if the self, under specific determinations, was the main object of awareness at the FOL, then it would cease to be implicit or recessive, and it would therefore be puzzling how it could constitute one part of the attitudinal relation between self and world. Likewise, if the body, under specific determinations, were considered to be the main object of awareness at the FOL, then again it seems that the basic phenomenal presence of an attitudinal relation between self and world would be significantly complicated (see the section titled 'The Body' for more on this).

Relatedly, it is more difficult to make sense of moods as an affective phenomenon—that is as felt responses—if they are principally a response to the self or the body. On such a picture, moods would be, at the FOL, primarily reflexive or inward-looking states. Aside from any other considerations this seems to be phenomenologically inapt. Consider the following competing explanations. (1) In a depressed mood, there is a first-order phenomenal experience of 'the world' as *depressing*, on the basis on which subjects may come—in second-order attention to aspects of that phenomenal experience—to explicitly focus on their body or self, under specific determinations. (2) In a depressed mood, there is a first-order phenomenal experience of one's self or one's body, under specific determinations (say, in the first case as 'worthless' or in the second as 'sluggish, heavy'), on the basis of which subjects may come—as a matter of second-order attention to that phenomenal experience—to explicitly focus on the world 'as depressing.' I expect it will strike most readers that (1) is a more phenomenologically apt description of non-pathological mood experience.

Further, on the second picture—of 'the world' as an object of second-order attention—we would no longer strictly have an affective attitude, as a felt response, but a thought involving a propositional attitude *that the world is thus and so.* As such, this picture overlooks the phenomenological datum, reflected in folk reports, that there is a phenomenal experience of 'the world,' in paradigmatic mood experience, which is different from any cognitively mediated thoughts or representations about 'the world.' The world being affectively presented as joyous or depressing is phenomenologically distinct from the entertaining of thoughts to the effect *that* 'the world' is joyous or depressing. And while such thoughts may come to be part of the overall mood experience, in SOL, it seems the FOL of moods is best thought of as constituted by a non-propositional experience of 'the world' affectively presented under a specific evaluative aspect. Accordingly, it makes more sense to say moods can become 'inward-looking' or reflexive, rather than essentially beginning as inward-looking or reflexive.

So, on the basis of this discussion, we have sufficient motivation for thinking of the intentionality of mood experience, at the FOL, as a matter of 'the world' being affectively presented under a specific evaluative aspect. In what follows, I concentrate on the way the body and then the self can come to be the explicit object of awareness in mood experience at the SOL, and explain how this relates to FOL mood experience.

The Body

It is an undeniable feature that bodily states figure in mood experience, and those folk psychological reports of depression and joy testify to their presence.[12] Nonetheless, positing bodily states as the intentional object in FOL phenomenal experience of moods is problematic for a number of reasons.

One immediate problem with that proposal is that it would be insufficient to distinguish FOL mood experience from the phenomenal experience of a range of other affective states, say pains, somatoform disorders, and arguably some emotions (in a somatic feeling theory). Consider the case of depression in which the relevant bodily states are those of feeling drained, heavy, and sluggish. If the FOL phenomenal experience of depression was directed towards such bodily states, it would be indistinguishable from somatoform disorders described in similar terms. Absent some distinguishing criteria at the FOL, we would be forced into the counter-intuitive position of saying mood experience is distinguishable from analogous states only at the SOL of explicit attention to features of FOL, say in virtue of the way we attend to phenomenal experience. Second, reports of different moods highlight the same somatic aspects as consciously present, for example, sluggish or heavy body in depression, boredom, and apathy, and a tense body in irritable mood, anxiety, and nervousness.[13] If we take this at face value, then the bodily states present to which FOL phenomenal experience is putatively directed would not provide the resources to be taken up in SOL type-identification (of categorical experience, of awareness of depression *as depression*). There would be no immediate phenomenological difference between being in a mood of irritability, anxiety, or nervousness, or depression, boredom, and apathy which could then serve as the basis for a distinguishing criterion for being in these different moods.

Given these considerations, there is sufficient motivation for not positing bodily states as intentional objects in FOL mood experience. Rather, it seems more plausible to claim that bodily states can become intentional objects of mood experience at the SOL, in which certain implicit features of FOL can become explicitly thematised.

However, one immediate problem with positing bodily states as objects of second-order attention in mood experience is that we need a story about the presence of bodily states prior to that explicit thematic attention to them. It cannot be the case that an act of attention to a bodily sensation in a mood—say in depression the feeling of being 'empty, drained, hollow'—brings that bodily state into existence; rather it just brings it to explicit (intentional) awareness. As such, we are led to the following important claim about bodily feelings in FOL mood experience: the first-order phenomenology of moods includes, as part of its overall phenomenal character, bodily states as non-intentional accompaniments (or 'raw feels' akin to Reidian sensations). Without such bodily states as non-intentional accompaniments in FOL mood experience it would be mysterious how SOL mood experience could subsequently become explicitly 'about the body.'

However, we need to say more about how the body figures in FOL in contrast to its being explicitly thematised as an intentional object at the SOL. Marcel and Lambie make a number of important claims about this issue. They say that due to the holistic character of FOL affective-evaluative experience, it is not the case that separable bodily states or changes, for example specifically feeling a high temperature, or a lump in the throat, are salient as such—that is under those specific determinations. As they put it, 'bodily changes are not available in experience as separate components [...] unless analytically attended to in second-order awareness.'[14] In this sense, the bodily states which figure in FOL mood experience as non-intentional accompaniments will be of a holistic kind, say that of a general 'sluggish feeling' (depression) or a general sense of relaxation of 'well-being' (joy). Note though, at this level the subject will not be entertaining descriptive thoughts of the form 'my body is relaxed,' but rather there will typically be a holistic non-intentional state of the body which accompanies the world-directed phenomenology.

It is a complex question why, for certain subjects at least, mood experience typically tends towards analytic focus on specific bodily states or changes. One distinguishing criterion might be the intensity of the bodily states in FOL. While it might be the case that all FOL mood experience has somatic accompaniments, these will be stronger in certain cases. For example, the non-intentional somatic accompaniments, if there are any, in a mood of serenity or listlessness are likely to be of a sufficiently low level of intensity that it would be atypical for a subject to come to focus on bodily states in SOL. Contrastingly, 'hot' moods, and especially those which are more towards the spectrum of pathology, such as clinical depression, intense anxiety, and mania, will typically involve a much higher intensity of bodily feeling as present in the FOL, such that analytic attention to specific bodily changes is much more likely, happens much more quickly, and in certain cases might be almost inevitable. The transformative power of such explicit bodily attention is often deleterious for the subject; for example, analytic attention to specific bodily states in anxiety can snowball into hyper-analytic attention to breathing rhythms and heart rate, leading to anxiety attacks.[15] Such a pathological mood experience, as including this kind of SOL hyper-analytic focus on bodily states, is significantly different from a non-pathological FOL mood experience of 'the world' as hostile (as generally anxiety inducing). So, the temptation to think of moods as fundamentally about 'the body,' likely stems from an over-generalisation from 'hot' moods, and unwarranted generalisations from pathological cases.

Moreover, understanding the role of the body in mood experience is an instance in which we need to be careful when examining folk reports as a means to elucidate the nature of those experiences. Asked to describe their moods, subjects may readily and repeatedly pick out bodily states, and while this means that any account of mood experience will have to account for their somatic phenomenology, it should not lead theorists to jump to the implausible and problematic claim that FOL mood experience takes the body as its intentional object, or that mood experience is first and foremost about the body. As we have seen, there are ways of accommodating holistic bodily states within the FOL, and one which makes sense of how they can be taken up as explicit objects of attention in SOL, without committing to such a somatic view of FOL mood experience.

Moreover, as a final point, we might note that in cases when somatic states become the focus of attention, arguably the bodily feelings are experienced as caused by—as apparent effects of—that prior affective representation of 'the world' as being a certain way at the FOL.[16] For example, it might be on the basis of a felt disfavour towards 'the world' as depressing that I then come to explicitly experience my body as drained, therefore explaining the switch of intentional focus from FOL to SOL.

The Self

In the 'The World' section, we saw that 'the self' is a poor candidate for the intentional object of FOL mood experience, largely due to features of FOL which seem to place 'the self' in a different role, namely as implicit and recessive, rather than explicit. However, as with body states, folk reports of moods often highlight an awareness of the self under specific determinations; in joy, the subject putatively experiences 'themselves' 'as free from worry' and 'at ease,' or in depression, that 'nothing I do is right' or that I am unable to 'cope with the situation.' Such statements reflect a directed experience of oneself under specific determinations, as present to phenomenal consciousness, and so meet the basic criterion for personal-level intentionality.

To understand the role of the self in mood experience, we should first distinguish what I will call self-presentations from any more obviously detached, cognitively mediated categorical self-ascriptions. The latter more obviously operate at the SOL of mood experience, in the form of representing myself as being in a *joyous* or *depressed* mood. There is an intuitive and important phenomenological distinction between representing myself as joyous and pre-reflectively being in a joyous mood,[17] and it is not difficult to see how on the basis of FOL mood experience of 'the world' as depressing or joyous a subject might come, in thematic attention to aspects of that FOL phenomenal experience, to reflectively deploy such categorical self-ascriptions.

Contrastingly, the non-categorical self-presentations described above—of myself as 'free from worry' in joy, or as 'unable to cope' in depression—have a more complex genesis. As with bodily states and changes, it cannot be the case that SOL attention creates such self-presentations from nothing; there must be some aspects of FOL phenomenal experience that involve 'the self' which allow for the self, under specific determinations, to be taken as an explicit object of thematic attention.

The answer to this question has in fact already been adumbrated in the section on 'the world' (the 'The World' section), where we discussed directedness towards the subject's universal evaluative horizon, as including modal, temporal, and agentive relations. Consider the following explanation: in non-pathological depression, it is because 'the world' seems bleak and hostile to its subject that it does not afford opportunities for meaningful engagement. In such an account, 'the self' that figures in FOL phenomenal experience is a recessive and implicit one, which is dependent, for its general comportment, on the world-directed intentional content of mood experience. Those explicit self-presentations—that is those involving explicit attention to 'the self' as an intentional object, under determinate aspects (oneself as useless or unable to act)—are therefore dependent on that more basic phenomenal presence of attitudinal relation between 'self' and 'world' in FOL mood experience. At the SOL, it is one term of that attitudinal relation, namely the implicit and recessive self, that can be taken as an explicit object of attention, switching from content of the form 'the world does not afford opportunities for meaningful engagement' to 'I am not capable of meaningful engagement' (i.e., I am useless). In this kind of SOL attention, such self-presentations will typically take the form of determinate thoughts about oneself, or judgements, with a propositional structure, for example, 'that I am useless or 'that I am at ease,' or 'that I am able to cope with everything.'

It is interesting to note, however, that the tendency towards a switch of focus specifically to 'the self' in SOL attention might be more prevalent in negative cases, in which FOL mood experience involves significant limitations on the possibility of meaningful engagement. An FOL experience in depression of the world as not affording opportunities for meaningful action seems more likely to give rise to (at the SOL) self-presentations, and self-ascriptions of worthlessness, uselessness, and so on. Pathological negative moods, like clinical depression, might be especially susceptible to this form of thematic attention to the self under negative determinations. However, even in these cases it seems right to say that we can make sense of the way 'the self' can become an explicit object of attention in mood experience only on the basis of a more basic or minimal, recessive self which is, in FOL mood experience, given in terms of a relation between the self and 'the world.'

As a final point about the role of 'the self' in mood experience, we should also be careful not to confuse the above analysis with the claim that subjects can come to gain a certain kind of self-knowledge on the basis of their mood experience—that moods might 'reveal something about the subject' (say that I am of a melancholic disposition). Reflective assessments of moods, and what they tell us about ourselves, are clearly neither part of the pre-reflective phenomenology of mood experience, nor to be built into SOL thematic attention to that first-order level.

As a final point, we should note that explanations of why subjects, in SOL, come to focus attention on the self, rather than the body, or vice versa, are most likely highly dependent on the precise character of the FOL mood experience combined with complex dimensions of the subject's prior affective psychology (including affective dispositions, and dispositions to attend in certain ways, e.g., melancholic subjects may be more disposed to self-focus in SOL, whereas anxious subjects may tend more towards body-focus in SOL). Understanding in general terms why SOL attention takes the specific direction it does in particular cases, rather than a different one, will therefore be suggestive rather than definite, proceeding on a case-by-case basis.

'World Focus' in SOL

As a final dimension to the analysis, I want to say something about the way immersed, non-propositional directedness towards 'the world' (as the subject's universal evaluative horizon), in FOL phenomenal experience, is transformed in SOL. As we have seen SOL can be characterised by an explicit thematic attention to the body, or the self. However, SOL can also take 'the world,' as providing the intentional content of FOL phenomenal mood experience, as an object of second-order thematic attention. This will be manifest in specific thoughts or judgements about 'the world,' under determinate aspects, say 'that the world is joyous' or 'that the world is depressing.' Note the distinction here between 'the world' as presented in FOL mood experience and 'the world' as represented in SOL attention, is that we switch from a non-propositional intentional presentation, to a propositional cognitively mediated mental state.

With this switch, we also establish a distinction between 'is' and 'seems.' In FOL mood experience I said, following Marcel and Lambie, that this distinction does not typically arise; rather, 'the world' being a certain evaluative way is taken at face value. Yet in SOL attention, with its propositional form, we get a variable mood-of-verb, such that we are no longer 'immersed' but 'detached,' and so the distinction between 'is' and 'seems' is established. In other words, the content of FOL mood experience, as taken up in SOL cognitive attitudes, is no longer pre-reflectively taken at face value. I may assent to the belief 'that the world is depressing,' say, but I might also 'wonder whether it is,' or 'doubt whether it is.' The propositional content 'that the world is depressing' may be taken up as the content of various different intentional attitudes, at least some of which involve withholding assent to whether that experiential content (re)presents things as they really are.

Summation of Analysis and Conclusion

In this chapter, I have provided an account of the varieties of mood intentionality. Making use of a distinction in conscious experience between FOL and SOL, I argued that we do best to locate moods' 'world-directed' intentionality at the FOL. The way moods can be explicitly about 'the self' and about 'the body' were shown to figure as SOL thematic attention to aspects of that FOL phenomenal affective experience of 'the world' (which provides the materials for SOL attention). The view articulated here is relatively parsimonious, insofar as it attempts to reconcile folk intuitions that moods are about 'the world,' 'the body,' and 'the self,' without committing to an unrealistically complex, and philosophically problematic idea, of pre-reflective mood experience as involving synchronous intentional directedness towards all three aspects. Rather, by recognising the 'world-directed' aspect as primary in FOL, we can better understand how SOL thematic attention to moods can come to take 'the body' and 'the self' as intentional objects. In this sense, recognising the varieties of mood intentionality is compatible with arguing for the primacy of the 'world-directed' aspect as I have done here. It is the latter aspects which ground any further intentionality that moods may enjoy in SOL attention.

While the analysis provided here 'demystifies' mood experience by providing a schematic and hierarchical understanding of its intentionality and phenomenology, the hope is that it rings true to experience. No doubt more could be said about all the aspects of mood intentionality discussed here, and the analysis was not intended to be exhaustive. In particular, more work is required to clarify the evaluative dimension of FOL mood experience. Nevertheless, on the basis of the analysis provided, philosophers and affective psychologists, in particular, will have a more precise theoretical framework for thinking about mood experience than has previously been on offer.

Notes

1 For contrasting, non-intentional views of moods in philosophy, see Deonna and Teroni 2012: 4; Mulligan 1998: 162; De Sousa 1987: 7, 68, 285; Lormard 1985: 385–407.
2 See Mitchell 2018, the 'Different Levels of Experience and Mood Experience' section for the arguments.
3 See Lormard 1985: 385–407; Davidson 1994: 51–55; Sizer 2000: 743–769; 2006: 108–135; Price 2006: 49–68; Wong 2016: 179–197. Among these accounts, opinion is divided about whether moods are intentional states (on the positive side see Price 2006; on the negative Lormard 1985; Sizer 2000: 742–769).
4 See, for example, Dretske 1980.
5 Marcel and Lambie 2002: 219–259. Other features are highlighted, but these definitions will suffice for my purposes.
6 See Searle 1983: Chapter 1 for more on these conditions, and Crane 1998 for broader discussion.
7 This description is an assemblage of descriptions of joy given in Joel Davitz's 1969 study (see Davitz 1969: 68–70).
8 Again, this description is an assemblage of descriptions of depression given in Davitz's 1969 study (see Davitz 1969: 45–47).
9 A number of philosophers claim that moods are in some sense about 'the world,' but this claim is rarely developed in detail. See Ryle 1949: 96; Solomon 1993: 17; Lyons 1980: 104; Lazarus 1994: 79–85; Crane 1998: 229–251; Goldie 2000: 141–151; Frijda 1987. In psychology, see Reisenzein and Schonpflug 1992: 34–45.

10 See Husserl 1970: §37.
11 For similar views of emotions, see Mitchell 2017: 1–28; Poellner 2016: 1–28; Montague 2009: 171–192.
12 For accounts of moods that make bodily awareness central, see Tye 1995: 130. Bodily states also figure as a constitutive part of Matthew Ratcliffe's 'existential feelings' (Ratcliffe 2008).
13 See Davitz 1969: 32–84.
14 Marcel and Lambie 2002: 238.
15 For discussion of mood pathologies, see Power 1994.
16 See Soldati 2008: 257–280 for this claim for emotions.
17 See Mendelovici 2013: 147.

References

Crane, Tim, 'Intentionality as the Mark of the Mental', in *Contemporary Issues in the Philosophy of Mind*, ed. by Anthony O'Hear (Cambridge: Cambridge University Press, 1998), pp. 229–51.

Davidson, Richard J., 'On Emotion, Mood, and Related Affective Constructs', in *The Nature of Emotion*, ed. by Paul Ekman and Richard J. Davidson (Oxford: Oxford University Press, 1994), pp. 51–5.

Davitz, Joel R., *The Language of Emotion* (New York: Academic Press, 1969).

De Sousa, Ronald, *The Rationality of Emotion* (Cambridge, MA: MIT Press, 1987).

Deonna, Julien, and Fabrice Teroni, *An Introduction to the Philosophy of the Emotions* (London: Routledge, 2012).

Dretske, Fred, 'The Intentionality of Cognitive States', in *The Nature of Mind*, ed. by David Rosenthal (Oxford: Oxford University Press, 1980), pp. 354–62.

Frijda, Nico, *The Emotions* (Cambridge: Cambridge University Press, 1987).

Goldie, Peter, *The Emotions: A Philosophical Exploration* (Oxford: Oxford University Press, 2000).

Husserl, Edmund, *The Crisis of European Science and Transcendental Phenomenology*, trans. by David Carr (Evanston: Northwestern University Press, 1970).

Lazarus, Richard, 'The Stable and the Unstable in Emotion', in *The Nature of Emotion*, ed. by Paul Ekman and Richard J. Davidson (Oxford: Oxford University Press, 1994), pp. 79–85.

Lormard, Eric, 'Towards a Theory of Moods', *Philosophical Studies*, 47 (1985), 385–407.

Lyons, William, *Emotions* (Cambridge: Cambridge University Press, 1980).

Marcel, Anthony J., and John A. Lambie, 'Consciousness and the Varieties of Emotion Experience: A Theoretical Framework', *Psychological Review*, 109, 2 (2002), 219–59.

Mendelovici, Angela, 'Pure Intentionalism about Moods and Emotions', in *Current Controversies in Philosophy of Mind*, ed. by Uriah Kriegel (London: Routledge, 2013), pp. 135–57.

Mitchell, Jonathan, 'The Epistemology of Emotional Experience', *Dialectica*, 71, 1 (2017), 1–28.

———, 'The Intentionality and Intelligibility of Moods', *European Journal of Philosophy*, Online Early View, https://doi.org/10.1111/ejop.12385, 1–18.

Montague, Michelle, 'The Logic, Intentionality, and Phenomenology of Emotion', *Philosophical Studies*, 145, 2 (2009), 171–92.

Mulligan, Kevin, 'From Appropriate Emotions to Values', *The Monist*, 81, 1 (1998), 161–88.

Poellner, Peter, 'Phenomenology and the Perceptual Model of Emotion', *Proceedings of the Aristotelian Society*, CXVI, Part 3 (2016), 1–28.

Power, Mick, *Mood Disorders: A Guidebook of Science and Practice* (Sussex: Wiley, 1994).

Price, Carolyn, 'Affect Without Object: Moods and Objectless Emotions', *European Journal of Analytic Philosophy*, 2, 1 (2006), 49–68.

Ratcliffe, Matthew, *Feelings of Being* (Oxford: Oxford University Press, 2008).

Reisenzein, Rainer, and Wolfgang Schönpflug, 'Stumpf's Cognitive-Evaluative Theory of Emotion', *American Psychologist*, 47 (1992), 34–45.

Ryle, Gilbert, *The Concept of Mind* (Paris: Hutchinson, 1949).

Searle, John, *Intentionality: An Essay in the Philosophy of Mind* (New York: Cambridge University Press, 1983).

Sizer, Laura, 'Towards a Computational Theory of Mood', *British Journal of the Philosophy of Science*, 51 (2000), 743–69.

——, 'What Feelings Can't Do', *Mind and Language*, 21, 1 (2006), 108–35.

Soldati, Gianfranco, 'Transparenz der Gefühle', in *Emotionen Interdisziplinär*, ed. by Björn Merker (Paderborn: Mentis, 2008), pp. 257–80.

Solomon, Robert, *The Passions: Emotions and the Meaning of Life* (Indianapolis: Hackett, 1993).

Tye, Michael, *Ten Problems of Consciousness* (Cambridge, MA: MIT Press, 1995).

Wong, Muk Yan, 'Towards a Theory of Mood Function', *Philosophical Psychology*, 29, 2 (2016), 179–97.

4 Against the Grain
Heidegger and Musical Attunement

Erik Wallrup

'Stimmung ist eine Weise.' So Martin Heidegger says or—for once—even sings in his lecture course *The Fundamental Concepts of Metaphysics*, held in 1929/1930. Mood (*Stimmung*) is a melody (*Weise*), which tunes the human existence (*Dasein*). Heidegger does so in a moment of the course when he is about to say what kind of phenomenon mood is, and the musical formulation is the first positive one after a long series of negations: moods are not inside or outside us; they do not appear 'in the soul as an experience'; they are not at hand, a circumstance that invalidates answers from the 'psychology of feelings, experiences, and consciousness.' But understood in terms of music, when the double sense of *Weise*—both 'melody' and 'manner'—is used as hinge between 'manner of being' and 'being in tune,' Heidegger is able to articulate what ordinary meanings cannot allow him to say.[1]

The double entendre of both *Weise* and *Stimmung* (the latter term being the German word for not only the affective state of mood, but also in its original meaning the tuning of an instrument), have not been lost on philosophers and theorists of a musical bent. The philosopher Andrew Bowie has suggested that Heidegger in another series of lectures—on logic and truth, held in Marburg four years earlier—hinted at the ambiguity of *Weise* without making anything of it. However, Bowie holds that a young student of Heidegger, the musicologist Heinrich Besseler, took advantage of this potential usage when writing that music 'becomes accessible to us as a *manner/melody [Weise] of human existence.*'[2] Another contemporary philosopher, Giorgio Agamben, alludes to the double sense of *Stimmung*, when he draws on the etymological roots of the affective term, which go back to *Stimme* (voice). Responding to the question of what philosophy is today, he says that the answer lies in a reform of music or in the experience of the Muse: 'in a certain society and in a certain time, music expresses and governs the relation that men have to the event of word,'[3] and this event cannot be articulated within language. He concludes: 'The Muse—the music—marks the split between man and his language, between voice and *logos*. The opening up to the world is not logical, it is musical.'[4] (It should be noted that Agamben here translates *Stimmung* with *tonalità emotiva*, 'emotional tonality,' usually a quite awkward expression when Heidegger's philosophy is rendered in Italian, but here related to the acoustical-musical sphere of voice.)

Bowie is very well aware of the fact that he needs Besseler in order to musicalise Heidegger since he has disregarded the extremely rare formulation in *The Fundamental Concepts of Metaphysics*. The phrase is indeed an exception in Heidegger's works. Heidegger had not at all taken advantage of music in his first thematic treatment of *Stimmung*, in *Being and Time*, from 1927. Yet, this suppression was nothing compared with the hostility that was to come. We find a fierce criticism of music as an art during the 1930s, a tendency that was still valid as late as 1955, when Heidegger in his lecture 'What is Philosophy?' is eager to point out that *Stimmung* must not be misunderstood as a 'music of accidentally emerging feelings.'[5] Is it not odd that Heidegger's and Agamben's judgements on music are opposed to each other when they try to answer the same question (the question of what philosophy is), and when they both give *Stimmung* a prominent position in their answers? Heidegger distances himself from music; Agamben says that philosophy today can only take place as a reformation of music (understood in relation to the Muse).

I am not going to deal with their question, having no ambition to say what contemporary philosophy is or should be. The topic here is music and attunement, the latter term an alternative to 'mood,' more apt as a translation of Heidegger's later *Stimmung* concept, having less bearing on existential circumstances than the earlier concept (the difference is vital for our understanding of the development of Heidegger's thought and political engagement). In music, we know what mood is from prepacked mood music and the emotional response to sentimental music of any genre, a gorging activity that Heidegger contemptuously would have termed *Erlebnis*. My main question is instead: how can we better understand the phenomenon of musical attunement in relation to Heidegger's thinking, that is, both through and against him? In order to answer that question we must try to figure out what Heidegger actually thought about music during the period when attunement was a keyword in his philosophy.

Some of this work has already been done, since Heidegger's comments on Wagner's *Gesamtkunstwerk* in his Nietzsche lectures, later published in the two-volume work *Nietzsche*, are well known and thoroughly expounded. Here we will only mention two commentators. Philippe Lacoue-Labarthe is as critical about music's presumed cultural dominance as Heidegger in *Musica Ficta (Figures of Wagner)*, but the French philosopher also outlines the 'national aestheticism' of Heidegger's thought during the 1930s.[6] Yet, as is often the case with Heidegger, the grand gestures of dismissal can sometimes hide secret correspondences. In a valuable book on Wagner's philosophical thinking, Julian Young suggests that Heidegger read and took advantage of several of Wagner's works written directly after the revolution of 1848: Young finds traces of Wagner's particular version of Hegel's 'death of art' thesis as well as the composer's notion of 'great art' in 'The Origin of the Work of Art,'[7] but Young does not comment on Heidegger's outright hostility against the composer. When writing about the philosophy of tragedy through history in another book, Young comments on Heidegger's treatment of the *Gesamtkunstwerk*, finding that the German thinker actually agrees with the Wagner of the revolutionary years (when the composer saw drama, not music, as the end of the music-drama) and attacks a stance that Wagner would take after reading Schopenhauer in 1854.[8]

Anyone interested in Heidegger's thinking concerning music has been restricted to some minor, rather unqualified references.[9] With the recent publishing of the Black Notebooks from the 1930s and early 1940s, we may learn in greater detail how Heidegger interpreted music and along the way, what attunement meant to him in relation to music. In the wake of the heated political discussion on the notebooks, the philosophical understanding of what Heidegger writes there has been put within brackets, and it comes as no surprise that the passages on music have hardly been observed at all. However, just as Young suggests, Wagner's writings may have influenced Heidegger in his understanding of the role of the work of art, and it is even possible to assume that Heidegger saw music as the most modern of the arts during this period of time. That was, though, not a sign of his appreciation.

*

I have already suggested that 'attunement' is a keyword in Heidegger's thinking during the 1930s.[10] In *Being and Time*, he had written: 'Mood has always already disclosed being-in-the-world as a whole and first makes possible directing oneself toward something.'[11] That means that we always relate to the world in a mood, and that every world-disclosure is attuned. This conception is radicalised in the 1930s, when Heidegger develops the central notion of a history of Being (*Seinsgeschichte*[12]), where Being is given or refused in different ways through history—and where 'attunement,' with its less obvious bonds to emotionality, starts to be a more convenient translation of *Stimmung* than 'mood.' Something extraordinary happens, according to Heidegger, in the early years of that decade: Being is suddenly given in a totally new way. One reason for this is that he himself starts to think about Being in a new manner; another reason, or at least a sign of change, is that Germany rises. Heidegger presumes that the national revolution of 1933 is attuned to Being's call. When we read the Black Notebooks, it becomes clear in a horrifying way how Heidegger identifies the turn of Being with the political turn that takes place. Before long, he shall be disillusioned concerning

National Socialism, but even then he thinks that something fundamental has changed and that he himself is able to respond accordingly to that change. *Stimmung* is decisive in this change, where the existential-ontological concept of 'mood' is replaced by the Being-historical concept of 'attunement,' even if the word in German still is—*Stimmung*.

The notebooks are at this stage full of diatribes. Heidegger attacks colleagues and politicians, authors and poets, cultural business and cultural politics. He attacks all leading nations including the German one. He attacks the Christian faith. And, yes, there are also formulations on Judaism and Jewishness, some of them best characterised as mere prejudices, awkward for a philosopher of Heidegger's rank, but some of them most disturbing and disreputable for his thought. Until now, the reception of the Black Notebooks has been totally dominated by the political aspects,[13] but here I want to focus on the passages where music is discussed and on his denunciation of the culture of his day. That is not apolitical, but the perspective will be dislocated.

We know from Heidegger's treatise 'The Origin of the Work of Art' that a main target of his criticism during these years is the shallowness of the experience, *Erlebnis*, of art. His is an early version of the concept of 'experience society.' In the Black Notebooks, his reflections on shallow art experiences are more detailed and also related to the cultural life he finds around himself: he scorns unchained subjectivism, limitless emotionality, thoughtless experiencing, at first associated with bourgeois culture, and later with Nazi culture. The Wagner cult is especially threatening to him, since it seems to place music, not the poetic word, at the centre of culture.

Heidegger has during this period begun his great confrontation, his *Auseinandersetzung*, with Nietzsche. He stands on Nietzsche's side when it comes to the dramatic breakup between the composer and his young prophet after a long friendship, a friendship which had produced, as at least one of its consequences, *The Birth of Tragedy*. Nietzsche could not stand the milieu of Bayreuth, even if Wagner there tried to accomplish in Germany what the great tragedians had done in ancient Greece—to make the drama festival into the heart of the *polis*. If Heidegger in his Nietzsche lectures from 1936 thought of Wagner's *Gesamtkunstwerk* as something that had to fail since music could not bring about a determinative 'formation and preservation of the beings as a whole' (*das Seiende im Ganzen*),[14] he could in his notebooks from 1938/1939 only establish how well the notion of Bayreuth as a holy ground for the German *Volk* suited the cultural politics of the Nazi state.

There is another reason why Heidegger's reaction is vehement. Wagner challenges Heidegger's convictions at their most vulnerable point. The composer's urge to find a renewal of the German nation is nothing but a counter-offer to the prospects that Heidegger had found in Hölderlin's promises to the German people.[15] The music-dramas by Wagner made people gather and share experiences, the works told the old German sagas once again but with a modern accent, they persuaded the spectators that they had a common fate, they assaulted the willing listeners with an emotional turmoil. Heidegger's musings concerning 'the domain in which poetry unfolds its power'[16] when reading Hölderlin did not stand against the prepossessing powers of Wagner's music. Wagner offered endless pleasures, stirring excitement, and overwhelming experiences. Poetry seemed to be at a disadvantage in the contest with the music-drama.

This is also how we should understand Heidegger's criticism directed at Wagner in his Nietzsche lectures. Music is there said to make the poetic saying (*Sage*) secondary in a biased way. But we should also take a closer look at a reference that Heidegger affords the reader in this context, where Nietzsche's relation to Wagner is dealt with, namely to Kurt Hildebrandt's *Wagner und Nietzsche: Ihr Kampf gegen das neunzehnte Jahrhundert* (1924). Heidegger scarcely refers to secondary literature, so why does he do so on this occasion? Hildebrandt had been a part of the circle around Stefan George since his collaboration in the *Jahrbuch für die geistige Bewegung* (1910–1912). This fact draws us near to a milieu in which the interest in Hölderlin's poetry rose in the beginning of the twentieth century: Norbert von Hellingrath, who had discovered late hymns by Hölderlin and his Pindar translations, was—due to these findings—introduced to the extremely influential George circle. Heidegger had given his support to Kurt Hildebrandt, when the latter became professor in philosophy at Kiel University without being qualified through the normal *Habilitation*.[17] It was hardly Hildebrandt's writings on eugenics that had made an impression on Heidegger, but rather the book on Plato (1933) in which Hildebrandt expounds a political system led by a philosophic and creative elite, a book to which Hans-Georg Gadamer gave an appreciative review the same year as it was printed.[18]

In Hildebrandt's book *Wagner und Nietzsche*, a history is told where a movement through German art and thinking starts with Wagner, is deepened with the interaction between Wagner and Nietzsche during the years of friendship and cooperation, and then purified through Nietzsche's break with the composer. However, in congruity with many other works originating in the George circle, the historical development points at the emergence of Stefan George himself as the saviour and reviver of German culture. Under such circumstances, a composer of music can only choose the wrong path. Hildebrandt suggests that Wagner's project was doomed to failure since it had its origin in music—that 'Dionysian-barbaric' art.[19] Wagner is seen as the 'battlefield' between music and poetry,[20] with two torrents going in different directions:

> The higher leads to the sun, to an intuition of the world, to order, to light and domination. The lower remains flowing feeling, desire, darkness of death, chaos. The higher way leads to a poetry, which

does not need the orchestral lyricism—the lower to a music, which remains only a specific musical element to poetry, despite Wagner's all quibbles.[21]

The opposition between music and poetry is stressed again and again, with a final declaration close to the end of the book:

> The poet is the maker of existence, the musician—at best!—only the transfigurer, otherwise the dissolver. The eye of the poet looks into the future, the eye of the musician into the past. Music is the most forceful of presences, its flutes and trombones never allow a verse to appear, but even if it may beautify the vision of the player, that is wiped out only minutes later. Homer and Dante create unceasingly the human beings through their images, whereas the music from earlier ages remains incomprehensible to us.[22]

The programme behind these lines is very close to that of Heidegger. That is not tantamount to suggesting that there is a dependence on Hildebrandt here from Heidegger's side, but it is nonetheless plausible that he found endorsement for his scepticism concerning Wagner, impulses to a historical understanding of the relation between Wagner and Nietzsche, and some useful reflections about the relation between music and word. Even more crucial: Heidegger and Hildebrandt have linguicentrism in common.

Yet, if Hildebrandt identifies a psychological weakness in Wagner, it was of course Nietzsche himself who had made Wagner into a case in the first place: the composer's works are supposed to be sick. In the music-dramas, Wagner is said to fill the stage with problems of hysteria, due to his own hypersensitive sensibility, his instability, and taste for always stronger flavouring. '*Wagner est une névrose.*'[23] That is also Heidegger's verdict, when he in his *Nietzsche I* attacks the composer, saying that his music-dramas aim at 'the tumult and delirium of the senses.'[24] In this work, Heidegger confers upon Wagner's endeavour the position as one of the six essential moments in the history of the philosophy of art. Since this history, like almost every history told by Heidegger, is a history of decay, the distinction is not to be taken as an honour, at least not only. Heidegger's judgement is of even greater dimension in another context: in an additional note to the lecture 'The Age of the World Picture,' he says that

> [o]nly when we succeed in grasping Nietzsche's thought independently of value-representation, do we achieve a standpoint from which the work of the last thinker of metaphysics can be comprehended as an exercise in questioning, and his antagonism to Wagner as a necessity of our history.[25]

Lacoue-Labarthe has paid attention to this formulation in his considerations on the figure of Wagner in a French-German debate, which he
follows from Baudelaire to Adorno in the work referred to in my introduction above, *Musica Ficta*. Heidegger's phrase must be seen from the
perspective of the history of Being: it becomes clear that Nietzsche's re-
valuation of all values is still part of the philosophy of values and therefore within an earlier stage of metaphysics. Lacoue-Labarthe writes: 'the
rupture with Wagner is not a minor or anecdotal incident; it translates
Nietzsche's fundamental metaphysical position, under whose horizon
the historical destiny of Europe is played out.'[26] It is the thinker of the
will to power and the eternal return that reaches outside the position of
Wagner and of the philosophy of values. Yet, the sixth and last moment
in Heidegger's history of aesthetics is Nietzsche's notion of a 'physiology
of art,' bringing aesthetics to an end: 'The state of feeling is to be traced
back to excitations of the nervous system, to bodily conditions.'[27]

But was Heidegger right about Wagner's paradigmatic position during
the Third Reich? He was right concerning Nazi propaganda, which drew
on Wagner's anti-Semitism, the nationalistic traits of his music-dramas
and Bayreuth as a centre of German culture. Thomas Mann famously
wrote that the opera house in Bayreuth became Hitler's court theatre.[28]
However, the musicologist Erik Levi has shown that even if Wagner belonged to the most performed opera composers in Germany, his operas
were actually staged less and less often during the period 1933–1938.
For the season 1932/1933, 1,837 performances are recorded with four
Wagner operas among the ten most popular ones. In 1939/1940, the
number of performances had been lowered to 1,154 performances, and
no Wagner work belonged to the ten most popular operas.[29] Instead,
Italian opera (Verdi and Puccini, of course, but also Leoncavallo's and
Mascagni's pair of operas *I Pagliacci* and *Cavelleria Rusticana*) rose to
the top positions, and the composer of comic operas, Albert Lortzing,
became more and more popular. References were indeed made to the nationalistic scenes of Wagner's operas in the political propaganda: Hans
Sach's praise of the German art in *Die Meistersinger von Nürnberg* and
King Heinrich's call 'German swords for German land' in *Lohengrin*
are two such moments taken from his operas. However, studies made on
Wagner and the National Socialistic Party show that in the party leader-
ship, Hitler was quite alone in his reverence for the German composer.[30]

Yet, it is true that Wagner became a symbolic figure from the very
start of the Third Reich. Just by chance, the fiftieth anniversary of Wagner's death happened to fall on 13 February 1933 and Hitler set out to
organise a memorial ceremony in Leipzig on that date, less than two
weeks after having been appointed chancellor by President Hindenburg.
In his history of the Bayreuth festival, Frederic Spotts says that the Wagner festival became a Hitler festival. He almost echoes the journalistic
impressions from an English report from 1933:

It would have been a pardonable error on the part of any casual visitor to Bayreuth to have mistaken this year's Wagner festival for a Hitler festival. For previous festivals every shop, no matter what its wares, managed by hook or by crook to display a photograph or at least some reproduction of Wagner's face. From the windows of china shops dozens of ceramic Wagners used to gaze into space. Booksellers displayed Wagner's Autography. This year the china shops are full of Hitler plaques, and 'Mein Kampf' has displaced 'Mein Leben'. From every flagstaff and nearly every window a Swastika flag is flying. Brown shirts are almost de rigueur, and passing 'Café Tannhäuser' and 'Gasthof Rheingold' one hears nothing but the Horst Wessel Lied.[31]

This scene from Bayreuth 1933 tells us something important about Wagner in the Third Reich. His musical works and opera house were usurped by the Nazis, who could only refer to specific passages with nationalistic tendencies in the music-dramas. Then, there are of course the anti-Semitic essays, from *Judaism in Music* to the biological racism of the regeneration papers of the late Wagner, all of them inspiring the propaganda. But this was without interest to Heidegger, who saw another essential problem with Wagner: he composed music.

*

Music, almost absent in the earlier notebooks, becomes more and more frequent in Heidegger's reflections in the middle of the decade, leading to a massive attack:

The highest form of explanation and thus still remaining explanation [*Erklärung*] is transfiguration [*Verklärung*]. For this a-historical but thoroughly historiological human is by no means a temperate calculating being; in him romanticism celebrates its supreme triumph. Music, wordless and truthless yet thoroughly calculated and indeed touching 'life' and the body, is becoming 'the' art which gathers all arts in itself and around itself. That is to say, art is becoming τέχνη in the sense of technology, politically ordered up and politically calculable, one means among others for making manageable what is present-at-hand and for doing so indeed in the mode of transfiguration.[32]

But Heidegger does not stop there. Soon his pursuit continues, now in relation to his treatise 'The Origin of the Work of Art' (first held as lectures in 1935). Music entices and seduces, it leads man away from the 'plight of Being [*Not des Seyns*]' due to its misleading liveliness: 'With the help of beings (the abundance of "lived experience") an evasion of

Being [*des Seyns*]?'[33] He writes that he wanted to reach the point of decisive decision with his treatise, a point in time where it would be possible to leave the domain of metaphysics:

> Yet here it is still possible that art will no longer find any resonance and that then all the more constantly, cleverly, and calculatively will artistic activity become something ordinary. Then the *sheltering of the truth of Being* [des Seyns] *in beings* will designate a process whose future configuration will remain just as obstinately hidden to us as self-refusal (qua the essential occurrence of Being [*des Seyns*]) illuminates itself to us and *unsettles* us from lostness in beings and through this unsettling tunes the attunement of Dasein.[34]

We can now see that music has a definitive role in the history of Being. It is the art both of subjectivity and of manipulation, thereby illustrating the most destructive tendencies of the state that Heidegger calls 'machination,' *Machenschaft*. Music is modern, it is the art form of the times, it is, in short, up-to-date—in the worst of senses. In one of the most central passages on the arts and modernity in the Black Notebooks, Heidegger deals with that question in a text with the heading 'Philosophy,' covering more than ten pages. There he describes how boundless calculation makes everything open for manipulation, leaving nothing spared. But man is no mere calculating machine, no, as a consummate subject man can unfold that which is hailed as *Erlebnis*, experience. These components are brought together in a quotation that needs to be long in order to illustrate the complex argument:

> 'Art' undertakes the management and the corresponding organization of lived experience (as a feeling of the feelings), whereby the conviction must arise that now for the first time the tasks of calculation and planning are uncovered and established, and thus so is the essence of art. Since, however, the enjoyment of the feelings becomes all the more desultory and agreeable as the feelings become more indeterminate and contentless, and since music most immediately excites such feelings, music thus becomes the prescriptive type of art (cf. romanticism, Wagner, and—Nietzsche). Music bears in itself a proper lawfulness and also a calculability of the highest kind, yet that does not at all contravene—but merely manifests—how decisively it is that pure number and the sheer feeling of the feelings are compatible and require each other. All types of art are apprehended musically, in the manner of music, i.e., as expressions and occasions of the enjoyment of the feelings (feelings of achievement, glory, power, communion). Poetry, in case such ever arises beyond mere ink spilling, becomes 'song' and the word merely a supplement to the sound and to its flow and rhythm. 'Thoughts,' especially if

they disturb meditationlessness, are prohibited; moreover, one disposes of the genuine thoughts (λόγοι) in the calculation and planning that can 'effect' something. The interpretation of art in terms of lived experience is elevated to the role of the measure for all active and productive human comportment (τέχνη); comportment is most highly honored when judged to be 'artistic' (the state as a 'work of art'). In the manner of art is also configured the apprehension of culture and of cultural politics—these are organizations of lived experience as expressions of the 'life' of the organizers. Culture, pursued in that way as political culture, becomes the basic form of the planning and of the management of the lived experience of consummate subjectivity.[35]

The quotation clarifies why one can say that music was actually the most modern of all arts according to Heidegger's analysis of modernity. Music is here characterised by the two prominent features of modern culture: calculability and subjectivity; it is both number and feeling.

Then another question is necessary to ask: why is feeling such a problem in a philosophy which made mood or attunement essential in any relation to the world? Heidegger answers that question four pages later. He says that, in *Being and Time*, he did not just replace the word 'feeling' with 'mood'; he did it under pressure from the question of Being [*des Seyns*] and from the perspective of Dasein. And he concludes: 'Being attuned does not mean to wallow in moods qua feelings and to feel these feelings; instead, it means: in appertaining to Being [*Seyn*], to be the 'there' qua the clearing of concealment as such'.[36] To many readers who are not used to the Heideggerian way of philosophising, these words are likely to be just gibberish. But what he writes has to do with the possibility of being attuned to Being and the partaking in the event of the truth of Being. Truth happens, according to Heidegger, and it happens to us when we are attuned to Being. Here, language is essential to Heidegger. Language is the house of Being, as the phrase goes, music is not.

But let us approach the problem in another way than by just saying that music is not language (that is partly true, but not a good starting point). Let us start with Heidegger's notion of music. What he does is to reproduce two standard conceptions of music: (1) music is sounding mathematics, and (2) music is the language of feeling. These two conceptions are often held to be opposites or mutually exclusive, but Heidegger is indeed not the first to try to combine them: Kant did so, as did Nietzsche. This double-faced appearance of music goes all the way back to Ancient Greece, to Pythagorean speculation and Plato's discussion on music and virtue respectively. For once, Heidegger accepts such conventional and traditional notions.

However, even if Heidegger seems to be something of a music hater in the 1930s, he does not leave music outside his treatise 'The Origin of the Work of Art.' No, the musical work is to be found in that treatise, grounded upon its earthy aspects, but never described in terms of its 'worlding' despite the fact that it must allow a world to world in order to be a work of art. This is the crux. If music should be sheer mathematics, no world can be expected to rise. If music is sheer feeling, the order necessary for a world to appear is out of reach. That is Heidegger's position in the Black Notebooks.

I have elsewhere suggested another way of entering the problem, instead of reproducing conventional ideas of the essence of music.[37] In a musical work of art, the world is constituted by temporality, mobility, and spatiality, all of them grounded upon a materiality which they let come forth. Music does not merely have a tempo, it also sets up a temporality. It has not only rhythm, but it sets up a mobility. It has not only ambitus, a pitch set, harmonies, but it sets up a spatiality. The world that is opened up is of course a musical world, but that does not lead to a separation from the world around it. Music changes our understanding of time and history. It affects our idea of motion. It does not only take place in the space of a concert hall or a church, where that space is changed by it, but it also transforms our notion of space.

Furthermore, music does not only accompany the great moments of our lives—from baptism to funeral—as well as the great moments of a nation—from victory to defeat, from moments of joy to moments of sorrow; it celebrates these moments, letting them be what they are to us. Any reader of Heidegger's treatise on the work of art will surely recognise echoes from that text in my formulations here.

*

So, am I blaming Heidegger for being tone-deaf? Perhaps he just put too much trust in the two main branches of musical understanding, two traditions that still today say that music should be viewed as the art of combination and calculation (i.e., musical analysis) or the art of feelings (i.e., certain kinds of music psychology and philosophy of music).

At the same time, Heidegger did identify a pitfall for any discussion on music and mood/attunement, indeed any discussion on mood/attunement itself: we are always running the risk of reducing the phenomenon of mood and even attunement into a special kind of feeling. His statement can even be turned against him: he himself mistook the collective emotional turmoil of the revolutionary turn of 1933 for an attunemental turn in the history of Being; it was something that had to do with mood, not attunement. Music, then, can of course be seen as a tranquilliser and energiser. It can create auditory atmospheres for splendid film experiences, romantic dinners, and delightful shopping. It can be a pastime and a soundtrack to our lives. With magnetic resonance imaging, we can study how music activates the limbic areas of the brain, associated with emotions. If we do all that, and nothing more, then Heidegger was perfectly right in his criticism. But music is also something else. It may change our being in the world. Being attuned, being musically attuned, means being radically open to what *was* not us but what *is becoming* us. In order to understand this assertion, we need to ask two questions: is it possible to reach beyond not only the thrownness of the human being, but also the givenness of the world? If that is the case, is then the word and nothing but the word constitutive for world-disclosure?

The Canadian philosopher Nikolas Kompridis has devoted a book to world-disclosure and the possibility of comprising the philosophical insights in Heidegger within critical theory. We can, though, look at his attempt from a different angle, namely as a way of bringing a critical perspective into the notion of world-disclosure. Already the former Heidegger student Otto Friedrich Bollnow was unsatisfied with the exposure to the forces of moods when he wrote his book *Das Wesen der Stimmungen* (first edition 1941): he saw it as a necessity to balance mood with composure, or, to put it succinctly, he saw that *Stimmung* must be tempered by *Haltung*.[38] Kompridis identifies the same problem as Bollnow, but his solution is instead to underscore the activity in the disclosive event. Instead of passivity, a more active perception of how that which is given is actually given should be achieved. The tendency in Heidegger's thinking during the 1930s to a submission to the historical forces is counteracted:

> What is being proposed is therefore nothing like blind submission to fate, but rather, a way by which we might become more attuned to our pre-reflective understanding of the world, to our inherited ontologies and to our historical circumstances, and thereby open up a freer relation to them.[39]

Kompridis does not strive for an authentic relation to the world in contrast to inauthenticity (to use Heidegger's parlance in *Being and Time*), but instead seeks a reflective relation to that which has been inherited. It is an act of not internal critique, but 'intimate critique.'[40]

Kompridis comes from a critical theory built upon the ground of Habermas's thinking, and it is therefore relevant here to bring in Habermas's own critical account of Heidegger's notion of world-disclosure, which takes place in a series of lectures on the philosophic discourse on modernity, dealing with the critique of modern reason. Here, in the lecture on Heidegger, Habermas reconstructs both the internal problem-solving traits of Heidegger's philosophical turn during the 1930s and the political function of the same solution. In doing so, Habermas can point at a turn, where Heidegger through the concept of enframing (*Gestell*) can subordinate fascism, communism, and Americanism (liberalism) under the metaphysical power of technique:

> It is only after this turn that fascism, like Nietzsche's philosophy, belongs to the objectively ambiguous phase of the overcoming of metaphysics. With this shift in meaning, the activism and decision-ism of self-assertive Dasein, in both its versions, the existentialist and the national revolutionary, also lose their meaning-disclosing function; only now does the pathos of self-assertion become a basic trait of the subjectivity that holds sway over modernity. In the later philosophy, the pathos of letting be and of readiness to listen takes its place.[41]

However, both Habermas's and Kompridis's discussions stay within the linguistic field. It comes as no surprise that Heidegger finds that language, be it the philosophical, be it the poetic word, is primordial. But Habermas's criticism is a consequence of his own linguistic subjectivity, and Kompridis never tries to question exactly that. Here, we should remember Agamben's words, quoted on the first pages of the present essay: 'in a certain society and in a certain time, music expresses and governs the relation that men have to the event of word.' Even Heidegger's notion of listening, stressed by Habermas in the quotation above as a solution to the acute problem of how to leave activism and decisionism behind, is related to language. To listen (*hören*) is also to belong (*zu gehören*) to Being in the later Heidegger, but in this act of listening, language is always present or present through its absence in silence (*Stille*).

Music allows a different route, just as Agamben says, but Heidegger never notices that path. Later in the Black Notebooks as well as in his published works, he sometimes seems to musicalise his concept of *Stimmung*, but even if he minimises linguistic meanings and turns to a pause that only has a counterpart in the general pause of a musical work, he always turns back to language: 'Silence's voice—the *tuning* as preparation of the ability to let the destined tone re-verberate. The tuning as enowning in the ability to listen, re-verberation, the ability to answer—letting-oneself-be-said—poetize.'[42]

It is in the polarised conceptions of music as either mathematical form or the language of feeling that the world-disclosive capability of music is lost. It is true that the sheer formal aspects of music have little to contribute to any world-disclosure. The same holds for the blatantly emotional response to music. But as already suggested, music is capable of creating temporality, or, as Federico Nicalaci formulates it: 'the temporality of music and our being-there share the same temporal structure.'[43] This temporal structure is decisive for our situatedness, and therefore for how we feel and behave. The musical way of moving makes us understand movement in a new manner, and motion is never far from emotion.

Our perception of space is changed by music, and the spatiality of music forces us to conceive of space in a new manner.

In this way, the conception of music as either a kind of mathematical manipulation or an emotionality characterised by total passivity is changed into a perspective where music allows us to encounter the world-disclosure itself. Composition means now not the compilation of different components, but the transgressive interplay between given elements and practices, bringing about new meanings and new possibilities. We are coming into the open, listening. This act of listening is not a discriminating one, it does not rely on the assumption of a steady ground upon which reflection can begin to unfold. The open space is not an empty space separated from that which is to be reflected upon. Instead, reflection takes place in the midst of things, bringing about a contrapuntal act of combining and transgressing. That would be a musical thinking and being.

Notes

1 Martin Heidegger, *The Fundamental Concepts of Metaphysics: World, Finitude, Solitude*, trans. by William McNeill and Nicholas Walker (Bloomington and Indianapolis: Indiana University Press, 1995), p. 67. The translators do not use 'mood,' but 'attunement.' I comment on the difference in the main text here shortly.

2 Besseler's essay 'Grundfragen des musikalischen Hörens' quoted by Andrew Bowie in *Music, Philosophy, and Modernity* (Cambridge: Cambridge University Press, 2007), p. 294 (Bowie's own comment on the double meaning of *Weise* has been removed from the quotation). Even if I myself doubt that we really find the double meaning of *Weise* in Besseler, Bowie takes advantage of this potential in a very interesting way. For a discussion, see Erik Wallrup, *Being Musically Attuned: The Act of Listening to Music* (Farnham: Ashgate, 2015), p. 78. The Heidegger lectures commented on by Bowie are *Logic: The Question of Truth*, trans. by Thomas Sheehan (Bloomington and Indianapolis: Indiana University Press, 2010).

3 Giorgio Agamben, *Che cos'è la filosofia?* (Macerata: Quodlibet, 2016), p. 135 (my trans.).

4 Agamben, *Che cos'è la filosofia?*, p. 138 (my trans.).

5 Martin Heidegger, *What is Philosophy?*, trans. by William Kluback and Jean T. Wilde (London: Vision Press, 1958), pp. 77–9.

6 Philippe Lacoue-Labarthe, *Musica Ficta (Figures of Wagner)*, trans. by Felicia McCarren (Stanford, CA: Stanford University Press, 1994).

7 Cf. Julian Young, *The Philosophies of Richard Wagner* (London: Lexington Books, 2014), p. 59, ft. 1.

8 Cf. Julian Young, *The Philosophy of Tragedy* (Cambridge: Cambridge University Press, 2013), pp. 213–17.

9 Despite the scarcity of sources, there are some texts on Heidegger and music of interest, such as Joseph J. Kockelmans, 'On the Meaning of Music and Its Place in Our World,' in *Kunst und Technik: Gedächtnisschrift zum 100. Geburtstag von Martin Heidegger*, ed. by Walter Biemel and Wilhelm-Friedrich von Herrmann (Frankfurt: Klostermann, 1989), pp. 351–76; Eduardo Marx, *Heidegger und der Ort der Musik* (Würzburg: Königshausen & Neumann, 1998); Augusto Mazzoni, *Il dono delle muse: Heidegger e la*

musica (Genoa: Il nuovo melangolo, 2009); Günther Pöltner, 'Mozart und Heidegger: Die Musik und der Ursprung des Kunstwerkes,' *Heidegger Studies*, 8, 1992, pp. 123–44, Federico Nicolaci, *Esserci e musica: Heidegger e l'ermeneutica musicale* (Saonara: Il prato, 2012) and the Heidegger parts of Wesley Philips, *Metaphysics and Music in Adorno and Heidegger* (Houndmills, Basingstoke, Hampshire: Palgrave Macmillan, 2015). In my *Being Musically Attuned* and in the article 'Music, Truth and Belonging: Listening with Heidegger,' published in *Philosophy of Music Education Challenged: Heideggerian Inspirations*, ed. by Frederik Pio and Øivind Varkøy (Dordrecht: Springer, 2015), I was only able to hint at Heidegger's position in the Black Notebooks. The present article is an attempt to grasp the implications of the stance taken by him.

10 On Heidegger and *Stimmung*, see prominent works, such as Paola-Ludovika Coriando, *Affektenlehre und Phänomenologie der Stimmungen: Wege einer Ontologie und Ethik des Emotionalen* (Frankfurt: Klostermann, 2002); Boris Ferreira, *Stimmung bei Heidegger: Das Phänomen der Stimmung im Kontext von Heideggers Existenzialanalyse des Daseins* (Dordrecht: Kluwer, 2002); Byung-Chul Han, *Heideggers Herz: Zum Begriff der Stimmung bei Martin Heidegger* (Munich: Fink, 1996); Romano Pocai, *Heideggers Theorie der Befindlichkeit: Sein Denken zwischen 1927 und 1933* (Freiburg and Munich: Alber, 1996) and Peter Trawny, *Martin Heideggers Phänomenologie der Welt* (Freiburg and Munich: Alber, 1997).

11 Martin Heidegger, *Being and Time: A Translation of Sein und Zeit*, trans. Joan Stambaugh (Albany: State University of New York Press, 1996), p. 129.

12 *Seins-* in *Seinsgeschichte* is by Heidegger (most often) spelled with 'y,' *Seynsgeschichte*, indicating that he understands Being in a non-metaphysical way. Translators of Heidegger's later texts have begun to use the term 'beyng,' which may be functional but looks very strange if you move between Heidegger's thought and other philosophers. In order to avoid such formation of words, I will instead use the normalised 'history of Being' and add *Seyn* within brackets to 'Being,' when Heidegger's spells the term with 'y.' That includes quotations from translations of Heidegger's texts, too.

13 It all started in late November 2013, when some sinister Heidegger quotations were related to by Stéphane Zagdanski on his blog 'Paroles des Jour.' A heated discussion in France followed, months before the actual publication of the German edition of the first volume of the Black Notebooks on 13 March 2014. The editor of the notebooks in Heidegger's *Gesamtausgabe*, Peter Trawny, published contemporaneously his small volume *Heidegger und der Mythos der Jüdischen Weltverschwörung*, translated into English as *Heidegger and the Myth of a Jewish World Conspiracy* (Chicago, IL: The University of Chicago Press, 2016). It has been followed by volumes, such as Donatella Di Cesare, *Heidegger e gli ebrei: I 'Quaderni neri'* (Turin: Bollati Boringhieri, 2014); *Heidegger, die Juden, noch einmal*, ed. by Peter Trawny and Andrew J. Mitchell (Frankfurt: Klostermann, 2015); Jean-Luc Nancy, *Banalité de Heidegger* (Paris: Gallilée, 2015, in English 2017) and *Reading Heidegger's Black Notebooks 1931–1941*, ed. by Ingo Farin and Jeff Malpas (Cambridge, MA: MIT Press, 2016). A bibliography covering publications on the Black Notebooks, compiled in connection with a conference on Heidegger and National Socialism at the University of Siegen in Germany, comprised no less than 53 pages, reaching to June 2016 (see https://www.uni-siegen.de/phil/philosophie/tagung/bibliographie_zu_den_schwarzen_heften.pdf).

14 Cf. Martin Heidegger, *Nietzsche*, vol. 1, *The Will to Power as Art*, trans. by David Farrell Krell (San Fransisco, CA: Harper & Row, 1979), p. 89.

15 See for instance Martin Heidegger, *Hölderlin's Hymns 'Germania' and 'The Rhine,'* trans. by William McNeill and Julia Ireland (Bloomington and Indianapolis: Indiana University Press, 2016).

16 Ibid., p. 21.

17 Cf. Rainer Kolk, *Literarische Gruppenbildung: Am Beispiel des George-Kreises 1890–1945* (Berlin: De Gruyter, 1998), p. 529, n. 192. See also the letter of 28 January 1934 from the rector of the Kiel university Karl Lothar Wolf to the 'Minister für Wissenschaft, Kunst und Volksbildung,' reprinted in *Literarische Gruppenbildung*, p. 621.

18 The Plato book by Hildebrandt is *Platon. Der Kampf des Geistes um die Macht* (Berlin: Bondi, 1933). Hans-Georg Gadamer's review is reprinted in *Gesammelte Werke* (Tübingen: Mohr Siebeck, 1999), vol. 5, pp. 331–8. Eugenics plays a certain role in Hildebrandt's Plato book, too, but Gadamer does not give any attention to it.

19 Kurt Hildebrandt, *Wagner und Nietzsche: Ihr Kampf gegen das neunzehnte Jahrhundert* (Breslau: Hirt, 1924), p. 30 (my trans.).

20 Ibid., p. 29 (my trans.).

21 Ibid., pp. 29–30 (my trans.).

22 Ibid., pp. 470–71 (my trans.).

23 Friedrich Nietzsche, *Der Fall Wagner*, in *Kritische Studienausgabe* (Munich: DTV, 1988), vol. 6, p. 22.

24 Martin Heidegger, *Nietzsche*, p. 86.

25 Martin Heidegger, 'The Age of the World Picture,' in *Off the Beaten Track*, trans. by Julian Young (Cambridge: Cambridge University Press, 2002), pp. 57–85 (p. 77).

26 Lacoue-Labarthe, *Musica Ficta*, p. 90.

27 Heidegger, *Nietzsche*, p. 91.

28 Thomas Mann, *Im Schatten Wagners: Thomas Mann über Richard Wagner: Texte und Zeugnisse 1895–1955*, ed. by Hans Rudolf Vaget (Frankfurt: Fischer, 2005), p. 211.

29 Cf. Erik Levi, *Music in the Third Reich* (London: MacMillan, 1994), pp. 192–3.

30 Frederic Spotts describes a situation in which the party ideologist Alfred Rosenberg criticised not only *Parsifal* but also the *Ring* tetralogy, the propaganda minister Joseph Goebbels only used Wagner's works in an instrumentalised way, and the rest of the party found Wagner a boring necessity due to Hitler's enthusiasm. Cf. Frederic Spotts, *Bayreuth: A History of the Wagner Festival* (New Haven: Yale University Press, 1994), pp. 165–66. Of a similar opinion is Reinhold Brinkmann, even if he identifies a more appreciative attitude in Goebbels, cf. 'Wagners Aktualität für den Nationalsozialismus: Fragmente einer Bestandaufnahme,' in *Richard Wagner im Dritten Reich: Ein Schloss Elmau-Symposion*, ed. by Saul Friedländer & Jörn Rüsen (Munich: Beck, 2000), pp. 109–41. More recently, Anders Carlberg discusses the same questions, finding many examples of Goebbels's positive reaction to Wagner, cf. *Hitlers lojala musiker* (Stockholm: Santérus, 2016).

31 Walter Legge, 'The Bayreuth Festival—"Featuring" Herr Hitler,' *Manchester Guardian*, August 15, 1983. Reprinted in *Bayreuth im Dritten Reich: Richard Wagners politische Erben*, ed. by Berndt W. Wessling (Weinheim and Basel: Beltz Verlag, 1983), pp. 189–92 (pp. 189–90).

32 Martin Heidegger, *Ponderings VII–XI: Black Notebooks 1938–1939*, trans. Richard Rojcewicz (Bloomington & Indianapolis, IN: Indiana University Press, 2017), p. 102.

33 Ibid., p. 105.

34 Ibid., pp. 105–106. (Translation slightly revised.)

35 Ibid., pp. 115–16.

36 Ibid., p. 120. (Translation slightly revised.)

37 Wallrup, *Being Musically Attuned*, esp. pp. 113–31.
38 Otto Friedrich Bollnow, *Das Wesen der Stimmungen* (Frankfurt: Klostermann, 1995[1941], 8th ed.), pp. 154–61.
39 Nikolas Kompridis, *Critique and Disclosure: Critical Theory between Past and Future* (Cambridge, MA: MIT Press, 2006), pp. 201–2.
40 He describes it as 'a mode of criticism based on reciprocal recognition, on re-knowing one another in terms different from those on which we previously relied.' Kompridis, *Critique and Disclosure*, p. 260.
41 Jürgen Habermas, *The Philosophical Discourse of Modernity*, trans. by Frederick Lawrence (Cambridge, MA: MIT Press, 1987), p. 160.
42 Martin Heidegger, *Anmerkungen I–V (Schwarze Hefte 1942–1948)*, in *Gesamtausgabe*, vol. 97 (Frankfurt: Klostermann, 2015), p. 73 (my trans.). These two sentences must be quoted in German, too, due to the complexity of the language: 'Die Stimme der Stille—das *Stimmen* als Bereiten auf das Wieder-geben-können des schicklichen Tones. Das Stimmen als Ereignen in das Hörenkönnen, Wieder-geben, Ant-worten-können—Sich-sagen-lassen—Dichten.'
43 Federico Nicolaci, *Esserci e musica*, p. 25 (my trans.).

5 Modelling the Spread of Mood

Edward M. Hill and Thomas House

Introduction and Philosophical Considerations

In his seminal work *The Structure of Scientific Revolutions*, Thomas Kuhn made a strong argument that science does not proceed according to an idealised process of steady accumulation of truths, but rather through long periods of 'normal science' focused on solving problems, interspersed with 'paradigm shifts' (Kuhn 1962). Though much has changed in science and society in the decades since Kuhn formulated his ideas, the fundamental insights remain pertinent.

We are professional mathematical scientists who, together with collaborators, have authored two papers on the spread of mood in adolescent social networks (Hill et al. 2015; Eyre et al. 2017). These studies were carried out in a 'normal science' framework—we sought evidence for and against certain hypotheses—and to do so we developed novel methodology within existing conceptual frameworks. Most of this chapter is devoted to a non-technical explanation of the aforementioned work, which we are enthusiastic to present to an interdisciplinary academic audience because we believe that attempts to study mood quantitatively could significantly benefit from new concepts, i.e., the kind of thinking that scientists typically call 'speculative.' Concretely, we are using a modelling framework modified from that used to capture spreading of literal viral diseases on networks. Clearly, a mood is not a virus, although we will explain how they can be analogous in some contexts, but it would be preferable to work in a theoretical framework that was much more general.

A standard approach to looking for causation assumes that there are no 'loops' in the network describing causal relationships (Pearl 2000). For example, the rain causes Fred to put up his umbrella, but Fred's umbrella does not cause the rain. But even for such a simple example, the famous 'butterfly effect' of extreme sensitivity of outcome to initial conditions means that a causal link between an umbrella and rain cannot be ruled out on principle, although such remote possibilities may have little practical relevance. When considering social systems, *complex systems theory* is a methodological approach that allows for the absence of a simple reductionist explanation (Byrne 2002). Being *complexity scientists* (Ball et al. 2013), we (loosely speaking) recognise the absence of a simple linear chain of causation. Yet, in order to make progress we attempt to find regimes in which we can find *approximate* chains of explanation. Indeed, even in non-complex contexts, much of the power of the scientific method is that it divides large problems into smaller ones, allowing incremental progress to be made.

Epistemologically speaking, this puts our approach within the broad tradition of pragmatism (McDermid 2018). We are not committed to thinking that moods are literally viral, or even that an analogy between social contagion and viruses is a particularly good one. Rather, if using and extending methodology developed for diseases caused by germs *works* in the sense of delivering evidence for hypotheses that meets the expectations of the scientific community, and is *useful* in the development of evidence-based policy, then we are happy from the point of view of 'normal science.'

Despite the importance of making steady progress, we believe (as do many other scientists who take the time to reflect more broadly) that it is important not to neglect the insights that can arise from ethnography and the broader social sciences and humanities, as well as from all other fields of enquiry. Consider, for example, the Nobel Prize-winning physicists Richard Feynman and Murray Gell-Mann: the former was inspired by watching a spinning plate (Feynman 2018); the latter was one of the founders of modern complexity science and drew inspiration for nomenclature from Buddhism and Joycean literature (Gell-Mann 1995). It is unlikely that we will be able to understand a phenomenon as complex as mood using existing theoretical frameworks, and as such we are grateful to the editors of this volume for the opportunity to reach out to other intellectual communities interested in mood, and to offer this present work in a genuinely interdisciplinary context, seeking the new models of work that lie hidden between the constraining formats of currently existing disciplines.

Our Motivation for Studying Social Contagion

Social contagion is the name given to the spread of behaviours, memes, rumours, etc. from person to person. We see this in everyday phenomena such as the spread of fashions, but can the effects of social contagion be seen in mental health? Social factors such as living alone or experiencing abuse in childhood play a large role in the development of depression. There is evidence that social support is important for the mental wellbeing of adolescents and that befriending can have a positive effect on mental health (Ueno 2005; Mead et al. 2010; Rueger et al. 2010).

Our principal questions for investigation were therefore, informally speaking, as follows: can the social impact of being friends with people who are depressed drag you down as well? And does having a positive mood keep those around you in high spirits?

By unravelling the posed questions, we may glean an improved understanding of the social processes that drive the epidemiology of mood disorders, supporting efforts to reduce the overall strain of these medical conditions upon public health.

Depression and other mood disorders are a growing affliction upon modern society, with considerable losses in global health and functioning (Moussavi et al. 2007). In 2015, an estimated 322 million people worldwide were living with depression, a staggering 4.4% of the global population. Depressive disorders are ranked as the single largest contributor to non-fatal health loss worldwide, with a predicted total of over 50 million years lived with disability in 2015 (Vos et al. 2016; World Health Organisation 2017a).

The overall growth of the global population adds further pressure, reflected by the total number of people living with depressive conditions increasing by approximately 18.4% between 2005 and 2015. Health systems are yet to adequately respond, with there being a stark gap between the need for treatment of depressive disorders and its provision. In low- and middle-income countries, where more than 80% of the depressive disorder burden occurs (Vos et al. 2016; World Health Organisation 2017a), between 76% and 85% of people with mental disorders receive no treatment. In high-income countries, between 35% and 50% of individuals living with mental disorders are in the same situation (World Health Organisation 2017b).

Adjoined to these economic costs and human health issues, depressive disorders can, in the worst cases, result in attempted suicide. It is recognised that depression is the major contributor towards suicide deaths, which number close to 800,000 people every year, with secondary consequences of many millions of people being affected or experiencing suicide bereavement. Of particular concern is suicide being the second leading cause of death among individuals aged 15 to 29 globally (World Health Organisation 2017c).

Therefore, there is a particular focus on the burden of depression among adolescents. In certain instances, the prevalence of depressive disorders among young people has been found to exceed the global average. For example, the National Survey on Drug Use and Health in the United States estimated three million adolescents aged 12 to 17 had at least one major depressive episode in 2015, representing 12.5% of the population within that age group (National Institute of Mental Health 2016).

The Mathematical Modelling Cycle

To quantify the extent to which such mood factors are influenced by one another, we adopt methods similar to those used to track the spread of infectious diseases. As we noted in our introduction, such borrowing of concepts may not be ideal, but allows practical progress to be made.

In general, a significant component of such epidemiological work is analytical studies involving the use of mathematical models, which comprises a real-world epidemiological problem being observed and studied via the application of the mathematical modelling cycle.

The procedure to analyse real-world epidemiological problems via a modelling approach can be broken down into four constituent parts. *Stage one*—Following recognition of the issue, a precise, qualitative description of the problem is made through simplifying information and eliminating what is deemed unnecessary. *Stage two*—Formulation of a mathematical model to describe the simplified problem. *Stage three*—Obtain solutions to the mathematical problem by fitting the model to applicable data and inferring model parameter values. *Stage four*—Verify through computer simulation that the model can capably produce outputs that have reasonable correspondence with what has been observed. Following the completion of one cycle, outputs can be interpreted, with proposed models undergoing refinement if required.

Concretely, the cycle proceeds in the ensuing manner (Figure 5.1).

Following the recognition of the issue, the first step is to make the problem as precise as possible, identifying and selecting those concepts to be considered as basic in the study and to define them carefully. In other words, this step involves simplifying the information as much as possible and eliminating what is deemed unnecessary, typically through making certain idealisations and approximations.

Having established a qualitative description of the problem of interest, the formulation of a mathematical model can then take place. Mathematical models provide a mechanistic representation through mathematical equations of how the number of a given entity changes over time. The models are comprised of parameters, a set of measurable factors that define the system.

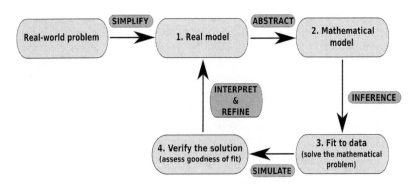

Figure 5.1 Schematic diagram of the mathematical modelling cycle.

Subsequent to establishing the mathematical model, the model parameters may then be estimated from available data, enabling us to better understand the original situation. In an epidemiological context, the typical motivation behind estimating mathematical model parameters is to check whether the mathematical framework includes all necessary mechanistic features, and to enable the prediction of spreading dynamics in the future given what has already occurred.

To complete the cycle, as a form of verification, we must check whether the model can capably produce outputs that have reasonable correspondence with what has been observed. The process usually proceeds through several iterations, with multiple models and/or scenarios being evaluated (and undergoing refinement) to determine which provides the best correspondence with the empirical data available.

Data Requirements

We embrace the above series of actions in attempting to address the question of whether there is any evidence for mood spreading in a form akin to social contagion. Integral to the modelling cycle concept is having access to a dataset that would be amenable to examining the problem under consideration. Data permit the estimation of model parameters and facilitate comparisons between candidate models.

Knowing the mood of individuals within a cohort and how that changed over time would not be sufficient. This mood-specific data needed to be combined with information on how many friends everyone initially had and their personal mood status. To be precise, the following three features had to be present within the data:

i   Information on who was friends with whom—the friendship network;
ii   For each individual, a codified representation of mood;
iii   Longitudinal data for the quantifiable measure of mood (consisting of repeated observations of the attribute over a designated period of time).

These criteria were met by in-home interview surveys carried out as part of the National Longitudinal Study of Adolescent to Adult Health, henceforth referred to as Add Health (Harris et al. 2009). Add Health is a school-based longitudinal study, exploring health-related behaviour of a nationally representative sample of United States adolescents that were in grades 7 through 12 (ages 12–18) when the study began in 1994–1995. To date, Add Health has collected data from five sampling points, referred to as *waves*.

At its inception, Add Health involved students from roughly 130 schools. However, when amassing data, sometimes information is only collected from a sample of the target population. With the target population for the Add Health study being adolescent students, if the method of choosing the sample of students was biased in any way, not proportionally representing a specific age group as one example, then these biases would conceivably affect our results.

But one of the strengths of the Add Health study was being designed to purposefully enable the analysis of friendship networks. For 16 schools, all enrolled students were selected for in-home interviews, thus eliminating selection bias. These schools are hereby referred to as saturated schools. Another appeal of the Add Health dataset was that it was the adolescents themselves who provided the responses. Had they instead been contributed by a third party on their behalf, our confidence in the accuracy of the information would be diminished.

The data of interest to us were taken from the in-home survey component in wave I (first sampling point), which took place during the 1994–1995 academic year, and wave II (second sampling point), which took place in 1996. For both time points, the required information was drawn from two distinct sections.

The first section related to constructing the friendship networks within the saturated schools at the initial time point. The in-home survey asked each respondent who attended a saturated school to nominate up to five male and five female friends. In detail, the friend nomination procedure saw each participant given a roster of names for their own school, with every individual assigned an ID number. If a name was chosen from the roster, the corresponding ID number for the nominated individual was recorded.

We are keen to stress that a common issue when working with data is that not all the reported data can necessarily be made use of. In this case, if a respondent had a friend from their own school but could not find them on the roster, possibly due to them having only recently joined school and/or only knowing them by a nickname, a generic ID code was recorded instead. Only being able to record a generic ID code in such instances meant that a connection for the friendship network within that school was lost. A similar concept was adhered to for recording friends that did not attend the same school as the participant. Nonetheless, we built a complete a friendship network as allowed by the nominated friends' data.

Now that we had the friendship network, we needed a way of determining the mood status of the participants from the saturated schools. A suitable measure of mood was obtained via a separate portion of the in-home survey, containing questions from the Centre for Epidemiologic Studies Depression Scale (CES-D scale) (Radloff 1977).

The CES-D scale is a 20-item self-assessment measure that asks the respondent to rate how often over the past week they experienced symptoms associated with depression, such as restless sleep, poor appetite, and feeling lonely.

Each item had four identical response options with an associated score from 0 to 3. The majority of the questions are negatively worded with the following score designations: 0—rarely or none of the time, 1—some or little of the time, 2—moderately or much of the time, and 3—most or almost all the time. For the subset of questions that are positively worded, the scores are reversed.

As the in-home interview component of the Add Health survey includes 18 of the 20 questions that constitute the CES-D scale, scores could range from 0 to 54. Higher scores indicate greater depressive symptoms. While the CES-D scale merely indicates depressive symptoms and does not represent a medical diagnosis, work has been undertaken to identify a score cut-off that correlates with a clinical diagnosis of depression. According to this score cut-off, we may use the CES-D scores to classify individuals as either having depressive symptoms (low mood) or not being depressed (healthy mood).

For the original 20-item CES-D scale, it has been discerned that the score cut-off to provide the best agreement with clinical assessments for depression should be gender-specific. These gender-based threshold values are 24 for females and 22 for males (Roberts et al. 1991). Due to the in-home interview component of the Add Health study including 18 of the 20 questions that constitute the CES-D scale, we amended the thresholds to 22 for females and 20 for males. The thresholds were used to create a binary indicator of emotional state (depression status). Respondents matching or exceeding the threshold were classified as having 'depressive symptoms' (labelled as having mood state value D). They were otherwise classified as 'not depressive,' denoted by mood state value N.

To be included in our study sample, at both sampling points the student participant must have provided complete answers to all the CES-D survey-related questions. This sifting resulted in our study sample comprising 2,194 participants. Overall, for each student we now had a CES-D score at each time point, a classification as being 'not depressed' or having 'depressive symptoms' at each time point, plus who they were friends with at the first time point.

The Initial Research Question

With the data in place, the journey on the mathematical modelling cycle could commence. To inform the broader question of whether mood spreads socially in a contagion-like way, our first venture was to establish if there was evidence of recovering from depression and/or becoming depressed based on the mood status of your friends.

Our Modelling Framework and Avoiding Confounding

Having determined the exact issue of interest, we moved onto the next step in the modelling cycle, formulating the problem within a mathematical framework. However, before devising a methodology to address the problem, we had to be aware of any potential pitfalls that may influence the analysis. Doing so ensured that the chosen approach was robust and minimised the likelihood of acquiring misleading conclusions.

Previous work relating to spreading of depression on social networks has generally made at least one of the following key assumptions: (i) low mood and/or depression spreads like an infectious agent; (ii) healthy mood (non-depression) does not spread like an infectious agent; and (iii) the information to distinguish between transmission and no-transmission models can be found in differences in static network measures such as clustering of disease (Joiner and Katz 2006; Hill et al. 2010; Christakis and Fowler 2013), or in coarse population-level measures such as web-search over time (Bentley and Ormerod 2010).

Each of these assumptions presents possible issues. The first couple of points potentially restricts the amount of attainable outcomes. To ensure our model framework allows more flexibility, we made no prior assumption as to whether it is low mood or healthy mood that spreads.

Another difficulty when aiming to discern the presence or absence of social contagion is being able to distinguish a 'contagion' mechanism (the spread of a behaviour from one person to another) from other possible phenomena that can lead us to observing groups of individuals having the same behaviour, which may confound any positive findings of contagion. The work outlined in the third point has come under criticism for these reasons (Cohen-Cole and Fletcher 2008; Aral et al. 2009; Lyons 2011; Thomas 2013).

We next describe the two simplest confounding phenomena that can generate 'false-positive' conclusions, where we may assert the presence of a contagion-like mechanism as the explanatory reason behind the empirical data, whereas in actual fact the observed effect was produced by other actions. The two processes are homophily and shared context. Homophily is the tendency for people to have friends who are like themselves. For example, if a group of friends all drink large amounts of alcohol and several become depressed, it may be the alcohol rather than the friendships that cause the depression. Shared context refers to individuals tending towards the same behaviour, whether they are friends or not, due to some outside influence (Lyons 2011). The differences between the homophily, shared context, and contagion-like mechanisms are visualised in Figure 5.2.

If there is homophily or shared context at work in the friendship network, either in terms of depressive symptoms, or a variable that is not

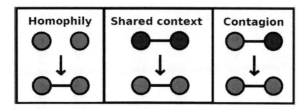

Figure 5.2 Illustration of phenomena that can lead us to observe groups of individuals having the same state/behaviour. In these examples, individuals are represented by filled circles. Lines connecting circles correspond to a friendship link. There are two possible states an individual can have: light grey and dark grey. **(Left)** Homophily—Tendency for people to have friends who are like themselves. In the above example, there are two individuals with the same state (light grey). Due to having matching states they become friends. **(Centre)** Shared context—individuals tend towards the same behaviour whether they are friends or not due to some outside influence. Here, a pair of individuals who are friends both change state at the same time, from dark grey to light grey. **(Right)** Contagion—spread of a behaviour from one person to another. The light grey state behaviour spreads from one individual to their friend whose state was originally dark grey.

directly observed but that is correlated with depressive symptoms, these phenomena will tend to increase the number of D to D or N to N pairs in the absence of any transmission effect. Deducing the presence of a social contagion effect, because we observe groups of friends having the same mood state, can therefore be an erroneous conclusion.

Our solution to this confounding dilemma was supplied through utilising longitudinal data on mood state. But why would such an approach mitigate the potential for confounding? To provide intuitive insight, Figure 5.3 illustrates the model schematically. When working with two waves of data, the presence of homophily and shared context mechanisms will simply lead to more instances of individuals having the same mood state as their friends. Referring to our schematic of model events (Figure 5.3), additional instances of individuals having the same mood state as their friends equates to more individuals in the initial states associated with events (2) and (6) than events (3) and (5), respectively. But using longitudinal data allows us to directly model changes in mood by noting each individual's mood state at one time point and whether or not their mood state had changed at a second time point. Crucially, by working with data from multiple time points, the other characteristics of the study's participants do not matter. If there is sufficient data to find a statistically significant effect in favour of a contagion-like mechanism, then homophily and shared context cannot confound those results.

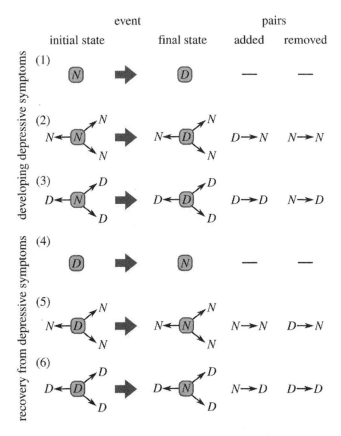

Figure 5.3 Pictorial representation of the possible events in our model. Develop-
ing or recovering from depressive symptoms; in the absence of friends
(no-transmission model), with friends with healthy mood (N-transmits
model), or with friends with depressive symptoms (D-transmits model).
The changes in pairs produced are also shown. Figure reproduced from
Hill, E.M., F.E. Griffiths, and T. House. 2015. 'Spreading of Healthy
Mood in Adolescent Social Networks,' *Proceedings. Biological
Sciences / The Royal Society*, 282.1813: 20151180.

Model Descriptions

Aware of the potential complications and how they could be avoided, we
set about completing the second phase of the modelling cycle, developing
the mathematical model. Expressly, we constructed a suite of mathematical models with differing dynamical assumptions regarding how mood
may spread among friends.

Throughout we model mood in a 'memoryless' manner. The memoryless property means the mood state at the next time step depends only

on the current state, with the sequence of events that preceded it having no influence. Recall that we are currently treating mood as a binary measure, meaning at each time point each individual is classified as either having depressive symptoms (value *D*) or not depressed (value *N*). These collection of models were consequently specified by two events, each associated with a probability of that event occurring. The first relates to the chances of developing depressive symptoms by the next time point, moving from state *N* to state *D*. The second is associated with the likelihood of mood improving, moving from state *D* to state *N*, resembling the process of recovering from the condition of having depression.

For each type of event, we specified three model variations. One we name the no-transmission model, in which the event probabilities are fixed constants; the probabilities do not depend on the moods of an individual's friends. Visually, change in mood state not being dependent upon the number of friends of a particular state is conveyed via a flat line (Figure 5.4(a)). The second we label the *D*-transmits model; the chances of an individual changing state by the next time point are altered by the number of named friends of state *D* they have. The third, and final, model variant we call *N*-transmits; an equivalent formulation to *D*-transmits, except now the chance of an individual changing state by the next time point depends on the number of named friends of state *N* they have.

For both flavours of transmission model, *D*-transmits and *N*-transmits, the relationship between the chances of changing mood state by the next time point and the number of named friends of a given mood state had a non-linear, S-shaped (sigmoidal) form (Figure 5.4(b)). Choosing a sigmoidal dependence was motivated by their prior use in the complex contagion literature (Centola 2010; Centola and Macy 2007).

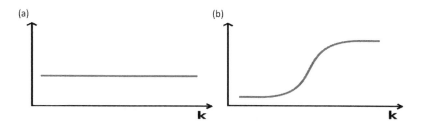

Figure 5.4 Pictorial representation of event dependency on the number of friends of a given mood state, *k*. (a) No-transmission model. Event probabilities are fixed, irrespective of the number of friends of a given mood state, *k*. (b) Transmission model. Event probabilities vary non-linearly with the number of friends of a given mood state, *k*.

Model Fitting and Selection

With the models established, we proceeded onto the third stage of the modelling cycle, estimating model parameter values from available data.

Our data sample could be partitioned into four groups, listing the number of participants who were (i) state N at both time points; (ii) state N at the first time point, and state D at the second time point; (iii) state D at both time points; and (iv) state D at the first time point, and state N at the second time point. The first two groupings are associated with the recovery event type, while the latter two are associated with the deterioration event type.

For each model, we aim to acquire parameter estimates that make that particular model explain the data at hand as much as possible. But how can we find the set of parameters that explain the data the best (i.e., maximise the probability of replicating the observed data)?

We applied a statistical technique known as maximum likelihood estimation. By employing computational algorithms, a maximum likelihood estimation approach efficiently samples plausible parameter sets, subject to user-defined constraints on allowable parameter ranges.

We fit each of our three proposed models to the Add Health data moving from the first time point to the second time point, once for the deterioration in mood event (corresponding to developing depressive symptoms), and then again for the recovery event type.

At this juncture, we needed to be aware that our candidate models had differing amounts of complexity. Given the options, we want to select the model that provides the best approximation to the true model for the entire population. The selected model should not only fit the current sample, but new samples too.

In general, the larger the amount of parameters in the model, the easier it is for the model to fit the data. In these circumstances, the model may 'overfit.' An overfit model is one that is too complicated for the dataset. When overfitting occurs, the model becomes tailored to fit the quirks and random noise in the data rather than reflecting the overall trends. If we were to obtain another data sample, it would have its own quirks, and the original overfit model would not likely fit the new data.

Therefore, when comparing models with disparities in the level of complexity, more complex models typically do a better job at explaining the data at hand, yet may lack the capability to explain a new set of similarly formatted data. Within our setting, our transmission models had more parameters to fit to the data, three to be exact, than the no-transmission model, which was just a single parameter (corresponding to a straight line). The extra relative complexity within the transmission models equates to them likely being preferred to the no-transmission models for the specific set of data we had, but would that be the case for another set of data?

To compensate, when selecting between models, two factors are taken into account: first, the ability to explain the available data as much as possible; second, the level of model complexity, with the magnitude of the penalisation scaling up with the amount of parameters in the model. By incorporating a penalisation term linked to model complexity within the model comparison process, we mitigate the likelihood of an overfitted model being selected.

For our work, between-model comparisons were performed by employing standard statistical methods, principally Akaike information criterion (AIC) (Akaike 1974).

Initial Study Outcomes

Unravelling whether there was any evidence for the recovery and/or deterioration of an individual's mood being dependent on the number of friends they had with depressive symptoms (no-transmission model against D-transmits model), we found the no-transmission model was the preferred choice. On the other hand, when considering the no-transmission model against the N-transmits model, the N-transmits model was the preferred choice for both event types.

The above-mentioned outcomes equate to depression not 'spreading' between friends, but healthy mood among friends being associated with significantly reduced risk of developing and increased chance of recovering from depression.

By adopting a mathematical approach, we are also able to quantify the relative chances of these events. For example, we discerned that having five or more friends with a healthy mood can halve the probability of developing depression over a six- to twelve-month period, while having ten healthy-mood friends doubles the probability of recovering from depression compared to those who have just three such friends.

Introducing Subclinical Depression

Thus far, we have treated a complex set of mood states in a binary manner, defining individuals' mood state as either being 'not depressed' ('not ill') or having 'depressive symptoms' ('ill').

However, this binary mood state assumption can be an oversimplification. The main drawback is an inability to consider individuals with subthreshold levels of depressive symptoms, a condition in which a person has depressive symptoms but does not meet the criteria for a depressive disorder. Not only are subthreshold levels of depression a condition recognised as carrying notable public health importance (Das-Munshi et al. 2008), among adolescents they are a particular issue of great current concern. They have been found to be very common, to cause a reduced quality of life and to lead to greater risk of depression later on in life than having no symptoms at all (Bertha and Balázs 2013; Klein et al. 2013; McLeod et al. 2016).

Refining the Method

In light of these limitations concerning handling mood state in a binary manner, we next wanted to discern if there was evidence of overall mood improving and/or worsening based on the mood status of one's friends. With our issue of interest having altered, we had now begun a new iteration of the modelling cycle.

Exploring our amended objective would require us to study the increases and decreases in the CES-D raw scores (corresponding to worsening and improving mood respectively) between the two time points, relative to the CES-D raw scores held by their named friends at the initial time point.

However, due to the previously developed methodology using a binary measure of mood status, and therefore being unable to account for the possibility of different numerical scores for the CES-D components, our confounding-robust model had to undergo refinement. Chiefly, we had to generalise it to accommodate non-binary states.

To relax the binary mood status assumption, we let an individual's mood state now be an integer value between 0 and 54 (taken from their CES-D score). Whereas before our models were specified by two event types, developing depressive symptoms (moving from state N to D) and recovering (transitioning from state D to N), the revised model was specified by three event probabilities: the probability of increasing state score (worsening in mood), the probability of decreasing state score (improving in mood), and the probability of remaining in the same mood state.

In similar fashion to when we treated mood as having a binary form, two functional constructs were considered for improving/worsening in mood. The first was conditioned on the number of friends of an individual who had better/worse mood at the first time point. Carrying forward an assumption from the initial work, the dependence on the number of friends with a given mood state again took the form of a discrete, S-shape (sigmoidal). The second functional form was independent of the states of the friends.

With separate model variants conditioned either on higher-scoring friends or on lower-scoring friends, using each possible combination of the two functional forms (one dependent on friend mood states, and the other independent of friend mood states) gave four models for comparison:

Model 1 had both increasing and decreasing states being dependent on friend states.

Model 2 had neither increasing nor decreasing state being dependent on friend states.

Model 3 had increasing state alone being dependent on friend states.

Model 4 had decreasing state alone being dependent on friend states.

In parallel with the model modifications, the data we were using had to be correspondingly transformed. Our study sample was partitioned into three groups, listing the number of participants whose CES-D scores between the two time points had (i) decreased (corresponding to an improvement in mood), (ii) increased (worsened in mood), and (iii) stayed the same (no change in mood).

The model fitting and selection procedure was analogous to the initial study.

Second Study Outcomes

The principal finding was that out of the four models, model 1 was determined to be the preferred choice. Accordingly, having more friends who suffer worse moods was associated with a higher probability of an individual experiencing low moods and a decreased probability of improving. The opposite applied to adolescents who had a more positive social circle.

Do these conclusions not superficially contradict the earlier work finding that healthy mood spreads while depression does not? While warranting being thoroughly scrutinised, addressing this question would require a different modelling set-up. The previously described models deal with the probability of an individual undergoing a change in mood state in the next six to twelve months, given the number of friends they have at the initial time point of a given mood state.

However, one may instead assume that the initial state and the state at the next time point are known, while treating the number of friends they have (with either a better or a worse mood state) as the variable to be modelled. In effect, given the mood score at the two time points, how many friends with a worse mood state and how many friends with a better mood state would we expect them to have?

The estimates acquired for the aforementioned question are portrayed in Figure 5.5, with striking conclusions garnered from this assessment. In Figure 5.5(a), we see that individuals who had more friends with worse mood (corresponding to higher-scoring friends) are contained

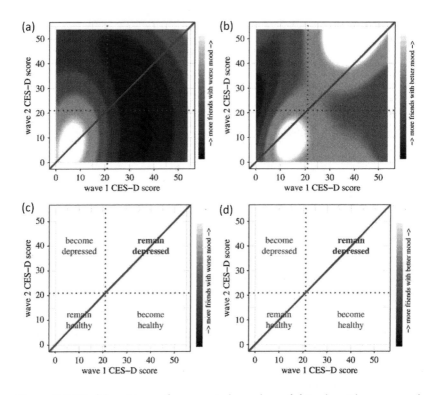

Figure 5.5 Model estimates for expected number of friends with worse and better mood for each wave 1 and wave 2 Centre for Epidemiological Studies depression scale (CES-D) score combination. Column (**a,c**) is coloured by expected number of friends with worse mood. Column (**b,d**) is coloured by expected number of friends with better mood, Panels (**c,d**) show how to interpret the delineated quadrants. The light regions in plots (**a,b**) show where individuals with greater numbers of worse or better mood friends, and therefore those we expect to experience a stronger contagion effect, are concentrated. The set of states for those who have not changed in state is shown by the diagonal solid line. The gender-averaged threshold boundary between the states of depressed and not depressed for each wave are shown by the dashed lines. Reproduced from Eyre, Robert W., Thomas House, Edward M. Hill, and Frances E. Griffiths. 2017. 'Spreading of Components of Mood in Adolescent Social Networks,' *Royal Society Open Science*, 4.9: 170336.

in the bottom left quadrant. These individuals remain below the depression threshold at both time points, with any negative shift in mood caused by contagion seldom enough for the individual to transition to being classified as having depressive symptoms. In contrast, inspecting Figure 5.5(b), we notice that individuals with more better mood friends (corresponding to lower-scoring friends) are spread out over the bottom two quadrants, meaning that they relatively often improve in mood to such an extent that they cross from being classed as depressed to being healthy at the second time point.

The findings suggest that both better and worse moods are contagious, but while better mood is contagious enough to push individuals over the boundary from depressed to not depressed, worse mood is not contagious enough to push individuals into becoming depressed. This explanation elucidates why we would not expect to find contagion-like characteristics for depression when applying the models from our initial investigation (where mood state was treated in a binary manner). Additionally, and pertinent to the design of public health interventions, bringing to light the apparent spread of worse mood among adolescent friendship groups in partnership with the none spread of depression emphasises the need to consider those who exhibit levels of depressive symptoms just below those needed for a diagnosis of actual depression.

Evidence to Support Our Collective Findings

In short, the implication is that both good and bad moods can be 'picked up' from friends, giving support to the claims that there exists a social contagion of mood, but depression cannot. The distinction in spreading behaviours supports the view that there is more to clinical depression than simply low mood (although the latter may be indicative of the former).

But do our findings make sense in a biological context? Is there evidence for the existence of psychological processes that may stimulate the transmission of mood between people?

The psychology literature offers support in both cases. Automatic transmission of mood between people has been demonstrated (Neumann and Strack 2000). Another avenue of research has shown that people who are, or tend to be, depressed are less able to maintain a positive outlook from moment to moment (Höhn et al. 2013). It is also in keeping with a tendency for a reduction in the normal social interactions that lead to spreading of mood during an episode of depression (Cruwys et al. 2014).

For those individuals who are, or who tend to be, depressed, having sufficient exposure and interaction with healthy friends could address the issue of low mood, with this assertion supported by the finding that unconscious mimicry enhances social rapport (Lakin and Chartrand 2003). Consequently, those feeling positive towards the person with whom they are interacting socially are more likely to mimic, and so build rapport (Leighton et al. 2010), and thus the opportunity for the transmission of healthy mood.

Concluding Remarks

In this work, we have provided an exposition of two studies that we were involved in that considered the spread of mood in adolescent social networks (Hill et al. 2015; Eyre et al. 2017). We have also been involved in the study of other kinds of social contagion (Sprague and House 2017) alongside our main research interests in infectious diseases and mathematical epidemiology. There are, however, many questions that remain unanswered by our work and that of others in the field. These are detailed in the original publications, with one of the most salient being that we are not yet able to formulate from first principles a fully general model for the changes in components of mood as a function of friends' mood components.

We have posited that while it is possible to use existing theoretical concepts to make progress, it may be that a phenomenon as complex as mood will require an entirely novel approach to allow us to continue to gain knowledge—but what might such an approach involve? One possibility is that one's moods represent beliefs about likelihood of positive outcomes from one's actions (Clark et al. 2018). If such an approach were correct, then we would explain social contagion via information flow between individuals in contact with each other, which would be more mathematically complex than the analogy with viral spread, but arguably more realistic. An idea in the current volume (Mitchell, Chapter 3) is that we should distinguish between the first-order level of experience of mood, which is the direct phenomenological experience, and the second-order level that is attention to the first-order. Since we do not have access to each other's phenomenology, the modelling implications for this framework would be that social contagion happens at the second-order level, and CES-D scores reflect the first-order level. Resembling this two-level system would mean that our mathematical approach should include interactions between both levels within the individual, which is conceptually similar to the concept of 'within-host' modelling of infectious diseases (Gog et al. 2015).

Still more generally, there are questions raised by studies of culture within the other chapters in the current volume that are undoubtedly relevant for the scientific study of mood, but where broad issues rather than detailed implications are suggested. Ferguson (Chapter 10) considers how mood is communicated in written text, discussing the Heideggerian view that moods are 'important precisely because they are not within our ultimate control and yet are also not solely grounded in the external world.' Our methodological approach is not to reduce mood either to individual biology or a social phenomenon, but rather to attempt to quantify the size of different interactions in a complex system. As such there is a parallel between attempts to understand the communication of mood aesthetically and its social contagion, since both must balance processes internal and external to the individual. Richardson (Chapter 8) discusses the subtleties of translation between French and English, providing a window into the myriad ways in which even two geographically close countries with much shared history can differ. Turning to the question of variability of epidemiological outcomes across countries, suicide rates are highly variable internationally (World Health Organisation 2017c). A pressing question is whether such 'ecological' data can be used to improve our understanding of public health questions. However, it is notoriously difficult to adjust for all possible differences between areas when considering such data.

In conclusion, we hope to have explained both the limitations and the usefulness of mathematical modelling in understanding social contagion of mood, including the benefits that may be possible from interactions across disciplines.

Acknowledgements

We would like to thank Rob Eyre, Frances Griffiths, and Dan Sprague for discussions and collaboration relevant to this work; in particular, Rob Eyre produced Figures 5.2 and 5.4.

Bibliography

Akaike, Hirotugu, 'A New Look at the Statistical Model Identification', *IEEE Transactions on Automatic Control*, 19, 6 (1974), 716–23.

Aral, Sinan, Lev Muchnik, and Arun Sundararajan, 'Distinguishing Influence-Based Contagion from Homophily-Driven Diffusion in Dynamic Networks', *Proceedings of the National Academy of Sciences of the United States of America*, 106, 51 (2009), 21544–49.

Ball, Robin, Vassili Kolokoltsov, and Robert S. MacKay, *Complexity Science: The Warwick Master's Course* (Cambridge: Cambridge University Press, 2013).

Bentley, R. Alexander, and Paul Ormerod, 'A Rapid Method for Assessing Social versus Independent Interest in Health Issues: A Case Study of "Bird Flu" and "Swine Flu"', *Social Science & Medicine*, 71, 3 (2010), 482–5.

Bertha, Eszter A., and Judit Balázs, 'Subthreshold Depression in Adolescence: A Systematic Review', *European Child & Adolescent Psychiatry*, 22, 10 (2013), 589–603.

Byrne, David, *Complexity Theory and the Social Sciences: An Introduction* (London: Routledge, 2002).

Centola, Damon, 'The Spread of Behavior in an Online Social Network Experiment', *Science*, 329, 5996 (2010), 1194–97.

Centola, Damon, and Michael Macy, 'Complex Contagions and the Weakness of Long Ties', *The American Journal of Sociology*, 113, 3 (2007), 702–34.

Christakis, Nicholas A., and James H. Fowler, 'Social Contagion Theory: Examining Dynamic Social Networks and Human Behavior', *Statistics in Medicine*, 32, 4 (2013), 556–77.

Clark, James E., Stuart Watson, and Karl J. Friston, 'What Is Mood? A Computational Perspective', *Psychological Medicine*, 48, 14 (2018), 1–8.

Cohen-Cole, Ethan, and Jason M. Fletcher, 'Detecting Implausible Social Network Effects in Acne, Height, and Headaches: Longitudinal Analysis', *BMJ*, 337 (2008), a2533.

Cruwys, Tegan, S. Alexander Haslam, Genevieve A. Dingle, Catherine Haslam, and Jolanda Jetten, 'Depression and Social Identity: An Integrative Review', *Personality and Social Psychology Review: An Official Journal of the Society for Personality and Social Psychology, Inc*, 18, 3 (2014), 215–38.

Das-Munshi, Jayati, David Goldberg, Paul E. Bebbington, Dinesh K. Bhugra, Traolach S. Brugha, et al., 'Public Health Significance of Mixed Anxiety and Depression: Beyond Current Classification', *The British Journal of Psychiatry: The Journal of Mental Science*, 192, 3 (2008), 171–7.

Eyre, Robert W., Thomas House, Edward M. Hill, and Frances E. Griffiths, 'Spreading of Components of Mood in Adolescent Social Networks', *Royal Society Open Science*, 4, 9 (2017), 170336.

Feynman, Richard P., *'Surely You're Joking, Mr. Feynman!': Adventures of a Curious Character* (New York: W. W. Norton, 2018).

Gell-Mann, Murray, 'What Is Complexity? Remarks on Simplicity and Complexity by the Nobel Prize-Winning Author of the Quark and the Jaguar', *Complexity*, 1, 1 (1995), 16–19.

Gog, Julia R., Lorenzo Pellis, James L. N. Wood, Angela R. McLean, Nimalan Arinaminpathy, et al., 'Seven Challenges in Modeling Pathogen Dynamics within-Host and across Scales', *Epidemics*, 10 (2015), 45–8.

Harris, Kathleen Mullan, Carolyn Tucker Halpern, Eric Whitsel, Jon Hussey, Jeffrey Tabor, et al., 'The National Longitudinal Study of Adolescent to Adult Health: Research Design', (2009). www.cpc.unc.edu/projects/addhealth/de sign [accessed 9 February 2018].

Hill, Alison L., David G. Rand, Martin A. Nowak, and Nicholas A. Christakis, 'Emotions as Infectious Diseases in a Large Social Network: The SISa Model', *Proceedings. Biological Sciences / The Royal Society*, 277, 1701 (2010), 3827–35.

Hill, Elizabeth M., Frances E. Griffiths, and Thomas House, 'Spreading of Healthy Mood in Adolescent Social Networks', *Proceedings. Biological Sciences / The Royal Society*, 282, 1813 (2015), 20151180.

Höhn, Petra, Claudia Menne-Lothmann, Frenk Peeters, Nancy A. Nicolson, Nele Jacobs, et al., 'Moment-to-Moment Transfer of Positive Emotions in Daily Life Predicts Future Course of Depression in Both General Population and Patient Samples', *PloS One*, 8, 9 (2013), e75655.

Joiner, Thomas E., Jr., and Jennifer Katz, 'Contagion of Depressive Symptoms and Mood: Meta-Analytic Review and Explanations from Cognitive, Behavioral, and Interpersonal Viewpoints', *Clinical Psychology: Science and Practice*, 6, 2 (2006), 149–64.

Klein, Daniel N., Catherine R. Glenn, Derek B. Kosty, John R. Seeley, Paul Rohde, et al., 'Predictors of First Lifetime Onset of Major Depressive Disorder in Young Adulthood', *Journal of Abnormal Psychology*, 122, 1 (2013), 1–6.

Kuhn, Thomas S., *The Structure of Scientific Revolutions* (Chicago, IL: University of Chicago Press, 1962).

Lakin, Jessica L., and Tanya L. Chartrand, 'Using Nonconscious Behavioral Mimicry to Create Affiliation and Rapport', *Psychological Science*, 14, 4 (2003), 334–9.

Leighton, Jane, Geoffrey Bird, Caitlin Orsini, and Cecilia Heyes, 'Social Attitudes Modulate Automatic Imitation', *Journal of Experimental Social Psychology*, 46, 6 (2010), 905–10.

Lyons, Russell, 'The Spread of Evidence-Poor Medicine via Flawed Social-Network Analysis', *Statistics, Politics, and Policy*, 2, 1 (2011), 124.

McDermid, Douglas, 'Pragmatism', *The Internet Encyclopedia of Philosophy*, (2018). www.iep.utm.edu/.

McLeod, Geraldine F. H., L. John Horwood, and David M. Fergusson, 'Adolescent Depression, Adult Mental Health and Psychosocial Outcomes at 30 and 35 Years', *Psychological Medicine*, 46, 7 (2016), 1401–12.

Mead, Nicola, Helen Lester, Carolyn Chew-Graham, Linda Gask, and Peter Bower, 'Effects of Befriending on Depressive Symptoms and Distress: Systematic Review and Meta-Analysis', *The British Journal of Psychiatry: The Journal of Mental Science*, 196, 2 (2010), 96–101.

Moussavi, Saba, Somnath Chatterji, Emese Verdes, Ajay Tandon, Vikram Patel, et al., 'Depression, Chronic Diseases, and Decrements in Health: Results from the World Health Surveys', *The Lancet*, 370, 9590 (2007), 851–8.

National Institute of Mental Health, 'Major Depression among Adolescents', (2016). www.nimh.nih.gov/health/statistics/prevalence/major-depression-among-adolescents.shtml [accessed 15 February 2018].

Neumann, Roland, and Fritz Strack, '"Mood Contagion": The Automatic Transfer of Mood between Persons', *Journal of Personality and Social Psychology*, 79, 2 (2000), 211–23.

Pearl, Judea, *Causality: Models, Reasoning, and Inference* (New York: Cambridge University Press, 2000).

Radloff, Lenore Sawyer, 'The CES-D Scale: A Self-Report Depression Scale for Research in the General Population', *Applied Psychological Measurement*, 1, 3 (1977), 385–401.

Roberts, Robert E., Peter M. Lewinsohn, and John R. Seeley, 'Screening for Adolescent Depression: A Comparison of Depression Scales', *Journal of the American Academy of Child and Adolescent Psychiatry*, 30, 1 (1991), 58–66.

Rueger, Sandra Yu, Christine Kerres Malecki, and Michelle Kilpatrick Demaray, 'Relationship between Multiple Sources of Perceived Social Support and Psychological and Academic Adjustment in Early Adolescence: Comparisons across Gender', *Journal of Youth and Adolescence*, 39, 1 (2010), 47–61.

Sprague, Daniel A., and Thomas House, 'Evidence for Complex Contagion Models of Social Contagion from Observational Data', *PloS One*, 12, 7 (2017), e0180802.

Thomas, Andrew C., 'The Social Contagion Hypothesis: Comment on "Social Contagion Theory: Examining Dynamic Social Networks and Human Behavior"', *Statistics in Medicine*, 32, 4 (2013), 581–90.

Ueno, Koji, 'The Effects of Friendship Networks on Adolescent Depressive Symptoms', *Social Science Research*, 34, 3 (2005), 484–510.

Vos, Theo, Christine Allen, Megha Arora, Ryan M. Barber, Zulfiqar A. Bhutta, et al., 'Global, Regional, and National Incidence, Prevalence, and Years Lived with Disability for 310 Diseases and Injuries, 1990–2015: A Systematic

Analysis for the Global Burden of Disease Study 2015', *The Lancet*, 388, 10053 (2016), 1545–1602.

World Health Organisation, 'Depression and Other Common Mental Disorders: Global Health Estimates', (2017a). http://apps.who.int/iris/bitstream/10 665/254610/1/WHO-MSD-MER-2017.2-eng.pdf [accessed 15 February 2018].

——, 'Mental Disorders – Fact Sheet No.396', (2017b). www.who.int/media centre/factsheets/fs396/en/ [accessed 9 February 2018].

——, 'Mental Health – Suicide Data', (2017c). www.who.int/mental_health/ prevention/suicide/suicideprevent/en/ [accessed 15 February 2018].

6   From 'Hard Rock Hallelujah' to 'Ukonhauta' in Nokialand—A Socionomic Perspective on the Mood Shift in Finland's Popular Music from 2006 to 2009

Mikko Ketovuori and Matt Lampert

Introduction

Pop music is an integral part of Finland's society and culture. Finns' taste in pop music includes both home-grown artists and imported genres. More than any other country, metal music has achieved a cultural prominence in Finland's popular music. Since the 1990s, Finland has boasted the highest concentration of metal bands per capita in the world (Makkonen 2014: 1586). Bands such as Nightwish, Apocalyptica, Children of Bodom, and HIM have boosted Finnish music exports and contributed to international interest in Finnish culture (Hjelm 2013). Other Finnish pop genres, such as 'Suomi-rock,' share many of metal's features. Mäkelä (2009: 372) suggests that pop music in Finland today has a similar role to that of composer Jean Sibelius' work in the early twentieth century: the music is a symbol of Finland's status as a modern Western state and a high civilisation.

Finnish pop music might sound sad, dolorous, or even bizarre, at least to foreign ears. Indeed, it is often characterised as melancholic and dark. Yet is it persistently dark, or does the aggregate mood of Finnish pop music fluctuate over time? In this chapter, we compare the levels of optimism and pessimism in a random sample of songs from the pop chart in Finland in 2006 to a comparable sample from 2009. We find that the 2009 sample is significantly more pessimistic than the 2006 sample. We employ socionomic theory to understand this change in mood within the context of a broader trend towards negative social mood in Finland, which also manifested in a rise in radical politics, an increase in unemployment, a plunge in measures of economic confidence, a financial and economic crisis both domestically and internationally, and a fall in the fortunes of Nokia, one of the most successful firms in the country's history. We also contribute to the literature at the methodological level by introducing a technique to assess optimism and pessimism in music.

Our results suggest that researchers could gauge important elements of a nation's social psychology by examining the mood of its popular music. The study also serves to enrich our understanding of how popular music is embedded within the broader human social experience and is influenced by the same waves of social psychology that also influence the tenor and character of politics, financial markets, the economy, and other domains of popular culture. The study thus helps researchers to better understand the linkages between popular music and other fields of study to reach a deeper, interdisciplinary understanding of social behaviour.

Theory

Robert Prechter's socionomic theory (1985, 1999, 2003, 2016) proposed that social mood—the unconscious, aggregate levels of optimism and pessimism in a society—influences the tenor and character of social actions. One of Prechter's (1985) earliest empirical applications of the theory was to popular entertainment and the stock market. He proposed that both popular entertainment and the stock market reflect underlying social mood trends, as each is an arena where participants express optimism and pessimism. He found that rising trends in the Dow Jones Industrial Average during the twentieth century were associated with a greater quantity and intensity of frisky fashion trends, bright colours and positive, optimistic themes in popular entertainment in the USA, whereas falling trends in the Dow Jones were associated with a greater quantity and intensity of sombre fashion trends, dark colours and negative, pessimistic themes in popular entertainment in the USA.

Prechter (1985: 5) also surveyed more than 60 years of American popular music and concluded that the music had 'been virtually in lock-step with the Dow Jones Industrial Average as well.' He examined the hyper-fast dance music and jazz of the 1920s bull market; the folk music laments and mellow ballroom music that proliferated after the 1929 stock market crash; the vibrant swing music that gained popularity during the post-1932 bull market; the crooners who sang down-tempo love songs as the market slowed and eventually corrected in the late 1940s; the upbeat rock 'n' roll music that emerged as the market soared from the 1950s to mid-1960s; and the depressed, angry, or psychedelic rock, heavy metal and punk music that flourished as the market corrected from 1966 to 1982. Prechter updated his analysis of American popular music and the stock market in 1999 and 2006 (Prechter 1999; Moore 2006), and Lampert and Wilson (2009) carried the analysis up to 2009. Prechter (2010) showed how social mood trends can also drive the careers of pop stars in a pair of case studies on the Beatles and John Denver.

Socionomic theory recognises that there is always a mix of popular music styles. The theory proposes that in the aggregate, the ratio of the quantity and intensity of positive expressions to those of negative expressions will fluctuate with the social mood trend: more joyous, optimistic, up-tempo, major-key songs gain popularity during positive mood periods and more sad, pessimistic, down-tempo, minor-key songs gain popularity during negative mood periods. To be clear, the theory does not propose that the stock market regulates popular entertainment trends or that popular entertainment trends regulate the stock market. Rather, the theory proposes that social mood regulates popular entertainment trends and stock market trends concurrently.

Most studies that address mood and popular music, such as that by Rea, McDonald, and Carnes (2010), seek to understand how popular music influences the mood of listeners. Socionomic studies, however, seek to understand how the moods of listeners influence the types of music that become popular. Scheel and Westefeld's (1999) findings are compatible with this positioning. The authors found that though a disproportionate percentage of metal fans entertain thoughts of suicide, this may be because the pessimism of metal is likely to attract listeners who are already unhappy, alienated, and at greater suicide risk. Thus, they proposed that metal music does not produce suicides but rather *reflects* its listeners' unhappy feelings. Indeed, Swaminathan and Schellenberg (2015) find in a thorough review of the literature that music's cultural universality is associated with its connection to feelings and affective states. Socionomic theory proposes that the moods of popular music and moods of society are related, as the popular music of an era is so because it resonates with the social mood.

Of course, any theoretical or methodological framework has limitations to what it can disclose. The socionomic framework, though, is especially well-suited to provide stability and coherence for our study and conclusions. At the metatheoretical level, socionomics recognises that the reductionist mechanics paradigm of exogenous causality and rational reaction does not work well in describing and predicting aggregate human behaviour in contexts of uncertainty. Instead, socionomics combines the worldviews of organicism and contextualism (Pepper 1942) in a holistic model of endogenous causality and pre-rational action (Prechter 2016). Its metatheoretical construction sets it in diametrical opposition to the reigning mechanics paradigm in finance and macroeconomics, under which the efficient market hypothesis (Fama 1970) and dynamic stochastic general equilibrium models (Kydland and Prescott 1982) fall. A detailed presentation of socionomics' metatheory and a thorough comparative treatment of it against mechanistic analytical approaches are available in Parker's contributions to Prechter (2016: 621–666, 691–729). Parker cited C.S. Peirce's argument that *usefulness* should be employed as a criterion to arbitrate debates between incommensurable metatheoretical worldviews that aim to explain the same domain, with *predictive accuracy* serving as the benchmark against which usefulness can be judged. The socionomically generated hypothesis that we test in this paper is one sign of the theory's usefulness, as the results described below serve to bolster the case for that hypothesis' predictive accuracy.

Methods

The primary aim of our study was to assess whether the aggregate mood of popular music in Finland in the spring of 2006 was significantly different from that of the spring of 2009. We applied socionomic theory (Prechter 1985, 1999, 2003, 2016) to hypothesise that the aggregate mood of the 2009 sample would be substantially darker and more pessimistic than the 2006 sample, owing to a broader shift towards negative social mood in Finland, as revealed by its stock market decline and other manifestations described in more detail below. In the following section, we evaluate the social mood context of the time periods we studied, explain the tool we used to assess the mood of Finland's popular music, and describe the two phases of testing we conducted.

Study Period: Spring of 2006 vs. Spring of 2009

The year 2006 was the year before major peaks in many major stock market indexes around the globe, a time when socionomic theory would expect social mood to be relatively positive in the countries associated with those indexes. In contrast, 2009 was the year of the corresponding lows in many of those indexes, and thus a time when socionomic theory would expect social mood to be relatively negative in the countries associated with those indexes. We suspected, then, that the global shift in social mood would be evident not only in Finland's stock market but also in the mood of its popular music. We chose to examine the spring because global stock market lows generally occurred in March 2009, a time when mood would be especially depressed. We then also decided to examine the spring of 2006 to control for seasonal factors.

Finland's Social Mood Context: Spring of 2006 vs. Spring of 2009

Here we evaluate and contrast the social mood in Finland in the spring of 2006 to that of the spring of 2009. We begin by plotting four social mood indicators in Figure 6.1. We describe the data series below and use them to evaluate the social mood during the periods of our study. We then consider additional social mood indicators to provide an even deeper context for our analysis.

Stock Market Performance

We follow Prechter's (1985) method by first examining the trends in Finland's primary stock market index, the OMX Helsinki 25 Index. The index consists of the prices of the 25 most-traded stocks on the Helsinki Stock Exchange, weighted by market capitalisation with a maximum

Figure 6.1 Social mood indicators in Finland.

weighting of 10% per stock (Bloomberg 2015). We plotted the daily closing values in the OMX Helsinki 25 Index from its 8 October 2002 low to February 2011. We note that the spring of 2006 occurred in the middle of the 212% rise in the index from October 2002 to November 2007, whereas the spring of 2009 followed the 66% decline in the index from November 2007 to March 2009. These data, therefore, indicate that social mood was relatively positive in the spring of 2006 and relatively negative in the spring of 2009.

The Rise and Fall of Nokia

Nokia, a high-profile brand with global reach, is one of the most successful firms in Finland's history. Its importance as an iconic Finnish brand can be traced to a period of economic catastrophe in Finland, which followed the collapse of the Soviet Union. The entire economic structure of bilateral trade with the USSR in lumber, iron, and other raw materials suddenly ended, and the unemployment rate in Finland skyrocketed from 3.5% to 16.5% (Gorodnichenko, Mendoza, and Tesar 2012). In the 1990s, Finns began searching for new economic resources and opportunities. Nokia, a local producer of black rubber boots, tyres, and toilet paper, transformed itself into a global leader in the development of mobile phones. The company rose in prominence as Finland emerged from a deep depression and began to experience widespread prosperity. In its heyday in 2000, Nokia's stock shares accounted for more than 70% of the Helsinki stock market's capitalisation (Kelly 2013). Finland became 'Nokialand.' However, Nokia lost its status as a global mobile phones market leader in 2007, when Apple and Samsung smartphones emerged. In 2011, CEO Stephen Elop famously compared Nokia with a burning oil platform (Ziegler 2011). Rapidly losing its share of the market, the company sold its mobile phones business to Microsoft in 2013. Even though the firm's network division survived, for many Finns the collapse of the most tangible part of the company was seen as a sad symbolic loss (Euronews 2013). Interestingly, in 2016, after a multi-year rally in the Finnish stock market, a Finland-based firm consisting of ex-Nokia employees acquired from Microsoft the rights to use the Nokia brand on a new range of smartphones and tablets (BBC News 2016). Thus, Nokia phones went back into the hands of a Finnish corporation and back on the market at a time of heightened social optimism in the country, as reflected by the trend of the nation's primary stock index.

We plotted the daily closing stock price of Nokia, adjusted for dividends and splits, from October 2002 to February 2011 as a proxy for Nokia's performance. Figure 6.1 shows the firm's dramatic rise into 2007 followed by a precipitous fall. Like the OMX Helsinki 25 Index, the trends in this data series also reflect relatively positive mood in the spring of 2006 and relatively negative mood in the spring of 2009.

Economic Sentiment

Indexes of consumer confidence and economic sentiment can also serve as indicators of social mood (Prechter 2016). In Figure 6.1, we also plotted the European Commission's Eurostat Economic Sentiment Indicator for Finland, an index that consists of weighted values from surveys of industrial confidence, services confidence, consumer confidence, construction confidence, and retail trade confidence (Eurostat 2015). The surveys used in the construction of the index are conducted under the Joint Harmonised EU Programme of Business and Consumer Surveys. While the advance into 2007 is not as steep as it is in the other social mood indicators we have considered so far, the general pattern remains the same: this indicator shows that social mood in Finland was relatively positive in the spring of 2006 and relatively negative in the spring of 2009.

Global Financial Crisis

Of course, the shift from positive to negative social mood did not occur only in Finland. A worldwide mood shift ultimately resulted in the global financial crisis. Figure 6.1 plots the Dow Jones Global Stock Index, a 150-stock index that tracks leading companies from around the world. This measure indicates that global social mood was relatively positive in the spring of 2006 and relatively negative in the spring of 2009.

Macroeconomic Trends in Finland

In addition to the four data series in Figure 6.1, we also consider other variables in order to provide a richer context for our understanding of the social mood in Finland during the springs of 2006 and 2009. Prechter (2004) explained that changes in macroeconomic indicators such as GDP and unemployment levels can also serve as measures of social mood, although mood-motivated actions that lead to fluctuations in GDP and unemployment take longer to execute than stock trades and therefore tend to lag the overall trends of stock market indexes. From 2006 to 2009, the unemployment rate in Finland grew from 7.6% to 8.2%. GDP data tell a similar story. The nation's annual GDP growth rate plunged from 4.1% in 2006 to −8.3% in 2009. These indicators confirm that social mood in the nation was relatively positive in the spring of 2006 and relatively negative in the spring of 2009.

Radical Politics

Socionomic theory proposes that social mood manifests not only in popular music, financial market indexes, and economic indicators but also across the full spectrum of human social behaviour, including cultural and political activity (Prechter 1999: 237). Prechter (1999: 233) proposed that positive mood breeds political consensus, whereas negative mood engenders political polarisation and a growing popularity for radical parties and proposals. In Europe, these political dynamics manifested in the rise of 'Non-Inscrits,' or non-affiliated members, in the European Parliament; their numbers increased from 8 in 1999 to 52 in 2014 (Whitmer 2015). In Finland, the rise of the Finns Party (previously the 'True Finns') has mirrored the success of the Non-Inscrits in broader Europe. The Finns Party—espousing 'a brand of Finnish nationalism that targets refugees, immigrants and the Swedish population in Finland' (Sundberg 2015)—became the third-biggest party in Finland in 2011 when it won 39 of the 200 seats in parliament. Other parties in Finland have condemned the Finns Party's 'hate speech' and attacks on multiculturalism (Crouch 2015). The rise of this radical party in Finland reflected the shift towards negative social mood in the nation.

Life Satisfaction

There is one potential mood indicator of which we are aware that differs from all of the above. The Eurobarometer Life Satisfaction Survey reveals that slightly more people in Finland were satisfied with their lives in the spring of 2009 than in the spring of 2006. In April 2006, 33% of survey takers reported they were very satisfied with the lives they led, whereas 5% of people reported they were not very satisfied with the lives they led. In June 2009, 38% of people reported they were very satisfied with the lives they led, whereas 3% of people reported they were not very satisfied with the lives they led. We cannot say definitively why this indicator differs from the others we have considered. It could be that this survey fails to capture social mood, or it could be that the survey date in June 2009 was too late to capture the depressed mood that coalesced in early spring. The dynamic nature of social mood guarantees that it rarely will be uniformly positive or negative, so we evaluate the social mood trend in the context of the basket of indicators that we have presented in this section rather than on the output of any particular indicator.

Conclusion

While social mood was not uniformly positive in 2006 and uniformly negative in 2009, on the whole the evidence overwhelmingly suggests that social mood in Finland was substantially more positive in the spring of 2006 than in the spring of 2009.

Musical Mood Measurement Scale

Next, we propose and validate a tool to quantitatively evaluate the mood of popular music. According to Rentfrow and Gosling (2003), individuals can reliably assess musical attributes. They report high inter-rater reliability of *qualitative* musical 'attributes' or moods—such as depressing, sad, uplifting, optimistic, or enthusiastic—despite raters' heterogeneous personal musical preferences.

We contribute to this established practice in the field of music research by developing a tool for the *quantitative* measurement of mood in music. Moisi (2009) discussed three classes of mood: hope, fear, and humiliation. Casti (2010) mapped Prechter's socionomic theory onto this classification scheme and replaced the word 'humiliation' with 'despair' to develop the 'Taxonomy of Moods' depicted in Figure 6.2. The taxonomy simply illustrates Prechter's observation that aggregate feelings of optimism and hope generally become more common and intense as social mood trends positively, and aggregate feelings of pessimism and fear generally become more common and intense as social mood trends negatively. Hubris characterises a positive social mood extreme and thus an extreme in optimism, and despair characterises a negative social mood extreme and thus an extreme in pessimism. Mood fluctuates across these categories.

In order to measure moods in music quantitatively, we adapted the Taxonomy of Moods to a scale that is used frequently in healthcare. Health workers often employ the Visual Analogue Scale (VAS) to measure patients' subjective experiences of pain, where different diagnoses and types of pain have unique categories of words and their equivalents on the VAS. The two extremes of the scale are 'no pain' and 'worst pain' (see Figure 6.3).

The concept was originally developed in the USA (Melzack and Torgerson 1971), yet the scale has been adapted for clinical use in Finland (Ketovuori and Pöntinen 1981). We adapted this scale of pain measurement to fit the Taxonomy of Moods by changing its two extremes to 'despair' and 'hubris.' Our completed musical mood measurement scale appears in Figure 6.4.

+ Mood trending positively + Positive mood extreme – Mood trending negatively – Negative mood extreme

| Hope | Hubris | Fear | Despair |

Figure 6.2 Taxonomy of moods, adapted from Casti (2010: 25).

Figure 6.3 Pain measurement (VAS—Visual Analogue Scale).

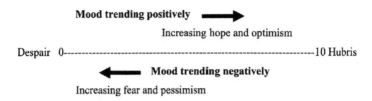

Figure 6.4 Scale for measuring moods in music.

Phase 1: Pilot Study

To determine the reliability and validity of our musical mood measurement scale, we conducted a pilot study. Test groups of students from the University of Helsinki (four test groups, $n = 72$) and the University of Turku (one test group, $n = 10$) used the scale to evaluate the moods of four songs. We selected four songs that, in our view, clearly express either a positive or negative mood. University of Helsinki students came from the Faculty of Education and had no specific training in music, whereas University of Turku students specialised in music studies in the Department of Teacher Education. University lecturer Sara Sintonen directed the pilot study in Helsinki, and university lecturer Mikko Ketovuori directed the pilot study in Turku. The proctors in both locations employed the same instructions and procedures.

Each of the sessions took 45 minutes. At the beginning of each session, the proctors played the four songs and instructed the students to evaluate the levels of pessimism or optimism in each song using the musical mood measurement scale. The proctors did not give the students any other information about the research study, including why or how the four songs were selected. The proctors also collected additional information about the students' personal music tastes and preferences (heavy, classical, jazz, or pop), as well as their gender and years of musical experience (for example, whether the student had ever played an instrument or sung in the choir).

We expected the first two songs in the pilot study to be rated as generally optimistic and the final two songs to be rated as generally pessimistic.

SONG 1

Spice Girls, 'Wannabe' (*Spice*, 1996). Average Rating: 8.6.

'Wannabe' is one of the highest-selling singles by a female group in the world. The song is an up-tempo dance-pop song with a hint of rap and hip-hop music. The song presents an optimistic, future-oriented, hopeful attitude. The song's average student rating was 8.6.

SONG 2

Queen, 'We Are the Champions' (*News of the World*, 1977). Average Rating: 8.2.

'We Are the Champions' is one of Queen's most famous songs. It is often used as an anthem in sports events. Though many people can recite the catchy chorus of this ballad, fewer are familiar with the beginning of the song, a segment that is much more retrospective rather than triumphant in tone. Thus, the song contains some elements of mixed mood before it ultimately capitulates to a positive tone. The students rated the song as 8.2, slightly lower than 'Wannabe' but still strongly optimistic.

SONG 3

Nirvana, 'Smells Like Teen Spirit' (*Nevermind*, 1991). Average Rating: 3.8.

'Smells Like Teen Spirit' represents alternative rock, also defined as post-punk, grunge, or indie. The lyrics are cynical and pessimistic. The song is at the very least one of the best-known songs in its genre, if not an anthem of a generation. The students rated the song as 3.8, moderately pessimistic.

We were surprised that the song was not rated lower on the musical mood measurement scale. We discovered the following explanation for the students' rating: according to the students, many of them liked the song very much and felt that it was unfair to give Nirvana a low rating. For them, differentiating between personal fondness and the mood of the song was a difficult task. However, in discussions, many of the students admitted, 'To be honest, the song is really not optimistic at all.' We took these factors into account when evaluating the paper's main study, as discussed in a subsequent section.

SONG 4

Slipknot, 'Psychosocial' (*All Hope Is Gone*, 2008). Average Rating: 2.9.

The final song in the pilot study is from the American heavy metal band Slipknot, which falls into the nu metal, thrash metal, or death metal genre. Slipknot is known for its energetic, chaotic, and even violent live performances. The band's songs often feature aggressive tones, profanity and themes of nihilism, anger, disaffection, and psychosis. The music video for 'Psychosocial' includes a burning barn and purgatory masks. In sum, the tone of the song is deeply pessimistic and fulfils the promise of the title of the album: *All Hope Is Gone*.

To evaluate the results of the pilot study, we first considered whether the aggregate average rating for each song generally aligned with our expectations. Since, indeed, the first two songs were rated as substantially more optimistic than the final two, we then performed a paired two-sample *t*-test in which each student's average rating for the first two songs in the sample was paired with his or her average rating for the final two songs in the sample. The test results confirm that the first two songs were rated as significantly more optimistic than the final two (t = 18.9604, d.f. = 81, one-tailed p < 0.0001). We determined that the musical mood measurement scale worked well enough to be used in our main study.

Phase 2: Test Music Samples

Once we confirmed the accuracy of the musical mood measurement scale, the proctors then repeated the evaluation process with the same test groups of students for a larger sample of songs.

The proctors collected the music samples for this phase of the study from IFPI Finland's monthly statistics (lists of the highest-selling pop albums) for the spring of 2006 and the spring of 2009. IFPI Finland is a national non-profit trade association representing 23 record companies, including major international firms (EMI, Sony, Universal, and Warner) and small, independent record producers in Finland. The proctors randomly selected ten songs for the students to evaluate—six songs from the spring of 2006 and four songs from the spring of 2009. The songs came from the ten most-popular albums during those months. The styles of the songs vary and include ballads, Suomi-rock, and heavy rock. The songs are detailed below.

From 2006:

Lordi, 'Hard Rock Hallelujah.' Average rating: 6.0.

This is the winning song from the 2006 Eurovision Song Contest. Finland had taken part in the annual contest since 1961 but had achieved relatively little success, finishing last ten times, including three entries that earned zero points. Thus Lordi's unexpected triumph was widely celebrated throughout the country. Interestingly, 2006 marked a peak in Finnish pop music exports. From 1999 to 2006, Finnish music exports increased from €3.8 million to €28.9 million before trending lower in subsequent years (Mäkelä 2009: 370).

Egotrippi, 'Nämä ajat eivät ole meitä varten' ('These Are Not Times for Us'). Average rating: 6.2.

The song's album, *Vielä koittaa uusi aika* (*There Will Come a New Era*), went gold within a week of its release. Anecdotally, we observe that the album title stands in contrast to the group's subsequent 2008 release, *Maailmanloppua odottamassa* (*Waiting for the End of the World*). This song, the album's lead single, features a protagonist who attempts to console a sad and desolated companion, promising better times ahead. The band evinced an admittedly muted but nevertheless hopeful outlook for the future with this spring of 2006 hit, declaring in the chorus 'toivoasi et saa menettää' ('you can't lose your hope'), before succumbing to a pessimistic outlook once mood had turned negative in 2008.

Scandinavian Music Group, 'Hölmö rakkaus' ('Stupid Love'). Average rating: 7.5.

The song can be described as a happy, breezy hit. The group consists of former members of the band Ultra Bra, which released an array of successful songs beginning in 1994. Ultra Bra started its career by competing in a political song contest held by the Finnish Democratic Youth League, and many of their songs deal with politically conscious issues such as the environment and equal rights. The 2006 hit, 'Stupid Love,' on the other hand, sounds light and casual without any political connotations or reservations.

Pink, 'Stupid Girls.' Average rating: 5.4.

The song was recorded in the USA in 2005 and released in 2006. It reached the top 10 in 15 countries, including Finland. The song is upbeat instrumentally, and lyrically it carries a message of female empowerment, decrying female objectification and promoting positive decision-making.

Andrea Bocelli, 'Ama Credi e Vai' ('Because We Believe'). Average rating: 5.0.

The song is from the album titled *Per Amore* (*For Love*). Andrea Bocelli is a crossover artist who brought classical music to the top of international pop charts. The music is from the closing ceremony of the 2006 Winter Olympics in Turin and features a sentimental Italian *bel canto* melody.

Shapeshifters, 'Incredible.' Average rating: 6.9.

This is an energetic dance song from a UK house music duo. The lyrics describe the 'amazing' feeling the protagonist experiences when she engages in 'incredible' actions. The joyful chorus entreats listeners to partake likewise, 'Let's all do something incredible/Make it happen when we come together/Just stay in here, it's so wonderful/Incredible.'

From 2009:

Apulanta, 'Ravistettava ennen käyttöä' ('Shake Before Use'). Average rating: 3.8.

Originally a punk band, Apulanta's style also has characteristics of alternative rock and nu metal. The lyrics of the song deal with the problem of being, noting that there is an error in the protagonist's internal programming that includes unpredictability, pessimism, and dissatisfaction.

Kotiteollisuus, 'Ukonhauta' ('Man's Grave'). Average rating: 2.0.

This heavy metal song deals with the shame and unlived life of a man. The songs of the band usually deal negatively with themes of the nation, religion, and mankind. The band's leader, guitarist-vocalist Jouni Hynynen, is known for insulting his audience during live shows.

Waldo's People, 'Lose Control.' Average rating: 6.9.

This electronic dance song was the Finnish entry in the 2009 Eurovision Song Contest. *Nomen est omen,* the song went to the final round but then dribbled to last place among the remaining songs. Despite its upbeat musicality, the lyrics convey the sentiments of an emotionally volatile protagonist who is losing control while experiencing 'a panic emotion that I cannot describe to you' as the 'world is tumbling down.'

Happoradio, 'Puhu äänellä jonka kuulen' ('Speak with a Voice I Can Hear'). Average rating: 3.7.

This typical Suomi-rock song features a simple form and chord structure. The almost laconic melody places more emphasis on the lyrics. The protagonist sings about the problem of communication with a loved one, inquiring 'Miksi sä itket/kun radiossa joku rakkaudesta laulaa?' ('Why do you cry/when someone on the radio sings about love?')

To avoid objections that we chose these songs strategically, we segmented the selection process: Sara Sintonen identified the IFPI lists for the study, and Mikko Ketovuori randomly chose the samples of songs from those lists.

Results

The paired two-sample (each student's average rating for the songs in the 2006 sample *vs.* each student's average rating for the songs in the 2009 sample) *t*-test showed a statistically significant difference of 2.0764 (t = 13.9369, d.f. = 81, one-tailed $p < 0.0001$), which was surprisingly clear: the songs from the spring of 2006 were significantly more optimistic than the songs from the spring of 2009.

We recognise that universally agreed upon classifications of 'optimistic' and 'pessimistic' do not exist; personal sentiments, opinions, and preferences affect the evaluation. This observation is apparent in Scheel and Westefeld's (1999) study on metal music: some of the listeners in their study associated even the darkest music with positive moods. We counteract potential individual idiosyncrasies by using a large group of independent student evaluators, as the aggregate evaluation should be accurate (Lorenz *et al.* 2011).

In the pilot study, we found that some students appeared to have difficulty distinguishing their personal affinity for a song and its associated rating on the musical mood measurement scale. To assess whether personal musical preferences and other factors unduly influenced our results, we collected data on several background variables for each student including gender, personal musical tastes, and years of musical experience. We found that these background variables had no influence on the results. In addition, the results from students at the University of Turku did not differ significantly from those from the University of Helsinki.

Discussion

We suggest that the generally optimistic mood of the highest-selling pop music in Finland in the spring of 2006 reflected a generally positive Finnish social mood during that period. Similarly, the generally pessimistic mood of the highest-selling pop music in Finland in the spring of 2009 reflected a generally negative Finnish social mood during that period.

Our results are consistent with Prechter's socionomic theory (1985, 1999, 2003, 2016), which proposes that social mood influences social actions, including the tenor and character of popular music. A positive social mood trend in Finland impelled the increased popularity of optimistic music in the spring of 2006. The positive mood trend also manifested in advances in the country's primary stock market index, good times for Nokia, lower unemployment, and a rise in measures of consumer confidence. Similarly, a negative mood trend impelled the increased popularity of pessimistic music in the spring of 2009 and also manifested in declines in Finland's primary stock market index, bad times for Nokia, higher unemployment, a drop in measures of consumer confidence, a financial and economic crisis domestically and abroad, and a surge in radical politics.

Limitations and Opportunities for Further Research

Limitations of our study highlight opportunities for further research. We note several of them.

Our test music samples were relatively few in number. Future studies could examine a greater number of songs to increase the robustness of our findings.

Our study was limited geographically to Finland and temporally to the springs of 2006 and 2009. To the extent that comparable data series exist for other countries, similar analyses could be performed to determine the cross-national robustness of our findings. The study also could be extended temporally within Finland to consider earlier and subsequent years.

We analysed songs from the highest-selling pop albums during the spring of 2006, when social mood in Finland was in the middle of a long-term positive trend. Yet Finland's primary stock market index did not peak until more than one year later in late 2007, and it underwent a brief correction in the spring (see Figure 6.1). That could be why the average rating for the songs from the 2006 sample, while generally positive, did not reach the elevated levels we would expect to see had we considered a sample closer to the positive mood extreme. Likewise, Finland's primary stock market index bottomed in early March 2009. Examining the mood of popular music more precisely at these stock market turns could yield interesting, and possibly more extreme, results.

We used our musical mood measurement scale to evaluate the mood of Finland's popular music, yet there are many other tools that researchers could employ to measure musical mood. Scholars in the field of sentiment analysis could assess the mood of songs through the automated analysis of the lyrics. Researchers could also employ technologies to conduct automated analysis of other song traits, such as tempo, key, and timbre.

Finally, several—but not all—of our social mood indicators are financial in nature. One may wonder whether our indicators suffer from a representative bias, as stock market participation is far from universal. Allaying these concerns, socionomic studies have found that stock market indexes function as accurate social mood indicators even in historical periods when few people invested in the stock market (Prechter *et al.* 2012; Hall, Lampert, and Hayden 2016), and the twenty-first century is a period of historic levels of elevated stock market participation. Furthermore, we did consider non-financial mood indicators, which in all but one case confirmed the message in the stock market data that the spring of 2006 was a period of relatively positive social mood and the spring of 2009 was a period of relatively negative social mood. Nevertheless, future researchers could consider and perhaps even apply statistics to other social mood indicators to further evaluate the robustness of the findings.

Conclusion

Popular music in Finland shifted from relatively positive in the spring of 2006 to relatively negative in the spring of 2009. We link this shift to the broader shift from generally positive to generally negative social mood in Finland between these periods. Our research makes several significant contributions at the methodological, theoretical, and practical levels. Our musical mood measurement scale enables researchers to quantitatively measure the mood of music. Our findings support Prechter's socionomic theory (1985, 1999, 2003, 2016), and our research has substantial implications for the ability of researchers to gauge the social psychology and mood of a nation through the study of the mood of its popular music.

Acknowledgements

We are grateful to Sara Sintonen for proctoring the testing procedure at the University of Helsinki and for her contribution to the design of the study, Eero Laakkonen at the University of Turku for help with statistics, Alyssa Hayden of the Socionomics Institute for a thorough proofreading of the manuscript, and Robert Prechter of Elliott Wave International for numerous helpful suggestions and comments. We would also like to thank the Foundation for Economic Education, Helsinki, for financial support for this study.

References

BBC News, 'Microsoft Sells Nokia Feature Phone Business', *BBC News*, 2016. www.bbc.com/news/technology-36320329 [retrieved 8 December 2016].

Bloomberg, 'OMX Helsinki 25 Index Profile', *Bloomberg Business*, 2015. www.bloomberg.com/quote/HEX25:IND [retrieved 27 September 2015].

Casti, John L., *Mood Matters: From Rising Skirt Lengths to the Collapse of World Powers* (New York: Copernicus Books, 2010).

Crouch, David, 'Rightwing Rant Exposes Tensions in Finnish Ruling Coalition', *Financial Times*, 2015. www.ft.com/content/cd775e86-3460-11e5-b05b-b01debd57852 [retrieved 7 December 2016].

Euronews, 'Finland Mourns the Loss of Iconic Phone Firm Nokia', *Euronews*, 2013. www.euronews.com/2013/09/04/finland-mourns-the-loss-of-iconic-phone-firm-nokia [retrieved 7 December 2016].

Eurostat, 'Economic Sentiment Indicator', 2015. http://ec.europa.eu/eurostat/en/web/products-datasets/-/TEIBS010 [retrieved 1 January 2015].

Fama, Eugene F., 'Efficient Capital Markets: A Review of Theory and Empirical Work', *Journal of Finance*, 25 (1970), 383–417.

Gorodnichenko, Yuriy, Enrique G. Mendoza, and Linda L. Tesar, 'The Finnish Great Depression: From Russia With Love', *American Economic Review*, 102 (2012), 1619–44.

Hall, Alan M., Matt Lampert, and Alyssa Hayden, 'Exploring Socionomic Causality in Social Health and Epidemics', *Working paper*, 2016. https://papers.ssrn.com/sol3/Papers.cfm?abstract_id=2234003 [retrieved 17 June 2016].

Hjelm, Titus, 'Metal Music Representing Finnishness', *Finnish Music Quarterly* *1/2013*, 2013. www.fmq.fi/2013/04/metal-music-representing-finnishness/ [retrieved 20 November 2016].

Kelly, Gordon, 'Finland and Nokia: An Affair to Remember', *Wired*, 2013. www.wired.co.uk/article/finland-and-nokia [retrieved 7 December 2016].

Ketovuori, Heikki, and Pekka Juhani Pöntinen, 'A Pain Vocabulary in Finnish – The Finnish Pain Questionnaire', *Pain*, 11 (1981), 247–53.

Kydland, Finn E., and Edward C. Prescott, 'Time to Build and Aggregate Fluctuations', *Econometrica*, 50 (1982), 1345–70.

Lampert, Matt, and Euan Wilson, 'Melody and Mood: An Update on the Socionomics of Popular Music', *The Socionomist*, (October 2009), 1–5.

Lorenz, Jan, Heiko Rauhut, Frank Schweitzer, and Dirk Helbing, 'How Social Influence can Undermine the Wisdom of Crowd Effect', *Proceedings of the National Academy of Sciences*, 108 (2011), 9020–25.

Mäkelä, Janne, 'Alternations. The Case of International Success in Finnish Popular Music', *European Journal of Cultural Studies*, 12 (2009), 367–82.

Makkonen, Teemu, 'Tales from the Thousand Lakes: Placing the Creative Network of Metal Music in Finland', *Environment and Planning A*, 46 (2014), 1586–600.

Melzack, Ronald and Warren S. Torgerson, 'On the Language of Pain', *Anesthesiology*, 34 (1971), 50–9.

Moisi, Dominique, *The Geopolitics of Emotion: How Cultures of Fear, Humiliation, and Hope Are Reshaping the World* (New York: Anchor Books, 2009).

Moore, David E., *History's Hidden Engine* (Gainesville, GA: New Classics Library, 2006).

Pepper, Stephen C., *World Hypotheses: A Study of Evidence* (Berkeley: University of California Press, 1942).

Prechter, Robert, 'Popular Culture and the Stock Market', *The Elliott Wave Theorist*, (August 1985), 1–20.

———, *The Wave Principle of Human Social Behavior and the New Science of Socionomics* (Gainesville, GA: New Classics Library, 1999).

———, *Pioneering Studies in Socionomics* (Gainesville, GA: New Classics Library, 2003).

———, 'Sociometrics: Applying Socionomic Causality to Social Forecasting', *The Elliott Wave Theorist*, (September 2004), 1–10.

———, 'Social Mood Regulates the Popularity of Stars – Cases in Point: The Beatles', *The Elliott Wave Theorist*, (July 2010), 1–40.

———, *The Socionomic Theory of Finance* (Gainesville, GA: Socionomics Institute Press, 2016).

Prechter, Robert R., Deepak Goel, Wayne D. Parker, and Matthew Lampert, 'Social Mood, Stock Market Performance and U.S. Presidential Elections: A Socionomic Perspective on Voting Results', *SAGE Open* (2012). DOI: 10.1177/2158244012459194.

Rea, Christopher, Pamelyn McDonald, and Gwen Carnes, 'Listening to Classical, Pop, and Metal Music: An Investigation of Mood', *Emporia State Research Studies*, 46 (2010), 1–3.

Rentfrow, Peter J., and Samuel D. Gosling, 'The Do Re Mi's of Everyday Life: The Structure and Personality Correlates of Music Preferences', *Journal of Personality and Social Psychology*, 84 (2003), 1236–56.

Scheel, Karen R., and John S. Westefeld, 'Heavy Metal Music and Adolescent Suicidality: An Empirical Investigation', *Adolescence*, 34 (1999), 253–73.

Sundberg, Jan, 'Who are the Nationalist Finns Party?', *BBC News*, 2015. www.bbc.com/news/world-europe-32627013 [retrieved 18 August 2016].

Swaminathan, Swathi, and E. Glenn Schellenberg, 'Current Emotion Research in Music Psychology', *Emotion Review*, 7 (2015), 189–97.

Whitmer, Brian, 'Re-opening the Tinderbox: Negatively Trending Mood and the European Union', *The Socionomist*, (April 2015), 1–7.

Ziegler, Chris, 'Nokia CEO Stephen Elop Rallies Troops in Brutally Honest 'Burning Platform' Memo? (Update: It's Real!)', 2011. www.engadget.com/2011/02/08/nokia-ceo-stephen-elop-rallies-troops-in-brutally-honest-burnin/ [retrieved 22 November 2016].

Nokia

http://company.nokia.com/sites/default/files/download/05-nokia-in-2006-pdf.pdf
http://company.nokia.com/sites/default/files/download/05-nokia-in-2007-pdf.pdf
http://company.nokia.com/sites/default/files/download/05-nokia-in-2008-pdf.pdf
http://company.nokia.com/sites/default/files/download/04-nokia-in-2009-pdf.pdf

IFPI Statistics (in Finnish)

http://www.ifpi.fi/tilastot/

This chapter was originally published as Mikko Ketovuori and Matt Lampert, 'From "Hard Rock Hallelujah" to "Ukonhauta" in Nokialand: A Socionomic Perspective on the Mood Shift in Finland's Popular Music from 2006 to 2009', *Popular Music*, Vol. 37, No. 2, pp. 237–52, reproduced with permission.

7   Translating Moods

Proust's 'Awkwardness'

Yasmine Richardson

Marcel Proust was an awkward man. Even those who have not read *A la recherche du temps perdu* are aware of his reputation as a member of the Parisian elite who spent most of the time in bed. When Proust's neighbours undertook refurbishments in their apartments, he beseeched his friends to arrange for the work to be postponed, or at least undertaken at hours more amenable to his nocturnal habits. When Proust wanted to go on holiday, he would ask them to investigate and report back on potential hotels, on the thickness of the curtains, and the amiability of the staff. When Proust agreed, rarely, to see these obliging friends, they were permitted to come only late at night, and were warned that he was likely to greet them in his bedclothes, for he could rarely tolerate clothes that were fitted. Proust was difficult to see, difficult to accommodate, and difficult to please: he was 'an awkward customer,' a description given to one of the characters in the novel, despite his extraordinary warmth and charm. While Proust's personal awkwardness has been the object of scrutiny and mirth, the importance of awkwardness in his writing has been neglected, most probably because the word itself does not exist in French. Both a feeling and a mood, awkwardness is a crucial phenomenon in the *Recherche*, linking its thematic, tonal, and structural elements. This article falls into two parts: the first provides context, outlining certain key questions at the intersection of Translation Studies and Affect Studies, and the second mounts an argument, namely that translation challenges can in fact help us to scrutinise the mood of a literary text, with the awkwardness in Proust's *Recherche* used as a case study.

Before exploring recent work on translation and affect, it is useful to briefly touch on the central debate of literary translation itself, namely whether a translation can ever be 'the same as,' 'as good as,' or 'equivalent to' the original, and whether this is more likely to be achieved through stricter (word for word) or freer (sense for sense) renderings. The title of Proust's chef d'oeuvre has provoked exactly this debate, and is known, to some confusion, by two titles in English. In its first translation by C.K. Scott Moncrieff (1922), the novel was titled *Remembrance of Things Past*, and it wasn't until a second revision of this translation by D.J. Enright in 1992 that the title became *In Search of Lost Time*.

At first glance, even for those who are not fluent French speakers, the newer title is a more accurate rendering of the original *A la recherche du temps perdu*: there is the action of searching (*In Search of*/*A la recherche du*) and the object of this search (*lost time*/*temps perdu*). In Moncrieff's version, by contrast, the act of searching becomes that of *Remembrance*, and the object of the search becomes *things past*. While it is evident that Moncrieff's 'freer' translation moves away from the meaning of the French title, one must also interrogate whether the newer, more 'direct' translation itself fully sustains the original meaning. In French, the word *recherche* has a technical aspect (academics talk about their *recherche*) which is absent in the English *search*, and likewise the double meaning of *temps perdu* (time lost or time wasted) is not carried over by the translation.

Yet Moncrieff's title is not even a sense for sense translation, as we have noted; indeed, 'remembrance of things past' contradicts the very claim the novel makes about time, namely that true memories are those which arise involuntarily, rather than through an act of remembrance. But Moncrieff, it seems, was less concerned with capturing the claims contained in the novel as he was with espousing its mood, or force of mood. His 'translation'—borrowed from the opening of Shakespeare's Sonnet 30—is allusive and evocative like the original title, in a way that the more perfunctory *In Search of Lost Time* is not. While Proust railed to Gallimard when he realised the English translation had been titled this way, and even wrote a letter to Moncrieff himself, his own experience as a translator of Ruskin had instructed him in the challenges of translating 'faithfully.' Indeed, although he did not take the same liberties as Moncrieff, Proust's methodology involved having his mother, whose comprehension of English was significantly better, translate Ruskin's phrases word for word, before he himself 'polished' them. However, when a friend suggested that the forthcoming translation of Ruskin was, considering Proust's imperfect English (and by extension, his method), bound to be flawed, the writer responded vehemently: 'I do not claim to know English. I do claim to know Ruskin.'[1] His linguistic shortcomings in English were more than compensated for, he argued, both by the sheer amount of time he had spent studying Ruskin's texts, and the meticulousness with which he reworked the translations in a three-step process; 'le sens de chaque mot, la portée de chaque expression, le lien de toutes les idées' ['the meaning of each word, the significance of each expression, the connection of all the ideas'].[2]

Proust's reminder that translation starts with a careful consideration of a single word raises the point that there are many categories of vocabulary which pose particular challenges to the literary translator,[3] and here it is the affective lexicon which shall be singled out. Each language contains, in its expression of moods, emotions, and feelings, certain terms which elude a word-for-word translation. This is not to say that they are untranslatable: as stated by David Bellos, a translator and translation theorist, 'One of the truths of translation—one of the truths that translation teaches—is that everything is effable.'[4] As a simple example, while the English language has no single word equivalent for the German term *Schadenfreude*, it is nonetheless possible to state its meaning: a feeling of delight arising from the perception of another's misfortune. Even terms which contain a more complex combination of feelings can be articulated, and thus 'translated.' The Russian term *toska*, for example:

> At its deepest and most painful, it is a sensation of great spiritual anguish, often without any specific cause. At less morbid levels it is a dull ache of the soul, a longing with nothing to long for, a sick pining, a vague restlessness, mental throes, yearning. In particular cases it may be the desire for somebody of something specific, nostalgia, love-sickness. At the lowest level it grades into ennui, boredom.[5]

While the meaning of *toska* can be translated into a foreign language, rendering it in the context of a literary translation poses a different challenge, as the text requires a substitute word as opposed to an extended definition. Hence when Nabokov was translating *Eugene Onegin* and came to a passage featuring the word *toska*, he put the full elaboration (cited above) in the book's notes, and in the text itself substituted *toska* with 'ache.'

The question as to why each language has its own 'untranslatable' feeling vocabulary is one which has produced many theories by and debates between scientists, psychologists, anthropologists, and linguists.[6] Studies of affective lexicons, facial expressions, and the dimensions implicit in comparative judgements of emotion, have revealed countless nuances in terms of how emotion and mood operate across different languages and cultures. With new technologies and approaches emerging, and with the vast amount of collected data increasingly shared by the various disciplines, providing a definitive account of the biological and social functions of emotions is progressively complex. When philosophical accounts of mood, as the background to emotion, are added to the mix, the possibilities for interdisciplinary exploration of affect are expanded almost infinitely: it is not difficult, then, to see why Affect Studies necessarily emerged to house a spectrum of theoretical positions and critical projects, united by a concern with the study of feeling.[7]

Although Affect Studies crystallised relatively recently, a number of intersections have already been established between this field and that of Translation Studies, which has experienced a similar surge in popularity since the turn of the century. A 2011 publication edited by Kathleen Shields and Michael Clarke, titled *Translating Emotion: Studies in*

Transformation and Renewal between Languages, brought together a collection of essays examining translation strategies for producing texts whose purpose is primarily to excite, in the receivers, the same emotions experienced by the translator-reader. While the essays use very different case studies, the majority of them have a dual-focus: the high degree of subjectivity of emotion and the difficulty of translating the figurative language writers employ for it. In light of these aspects, importance is placed not only on the role of translators generally, to determine suitable strategies to convey the message of the source text and the system of beliefs, but also specifically on their capacity to empathise with the original writer. This new emphasis on the importance of the translator's own emotions is developed further, and through a psychological analysis, in Severine Hubscher-Davidson's forthcoming monograph, *Translation and Emotion: A Psychological Perspective,* in which the author identifies three distinctive areas where emotions influence translators: emotional material contained in source texts, their own emotions, and the emotions of source and target readers.

While these writers, and others, are starting to explore the complex relations between emotion and translation, the question of mood and translation remains largely untouched, perhaps because it is all the more complex. This complexity derives, in the first, from the difficulty of circumscribing mood in the literary text. Whereas the emotions of the characters may be identified (both through the affective vocabulary employed and the behaviour they engage in), albeit ambiguously in certain cases, the mood of the text (both overall and within a particular section) is less easy to pinpoint and more likely to vary in terms of reader interpretation. Indeed, this is why *Stimmung,* a very difficult word to translate, is such a productive starting point for analysis of mood, because whereas in English the private feeling of 'mood' is separated from the public experience of 'climate,' the German *stimmen* collapses, through its connection with music and the hearing of sounds, the separation between what happens to our body and what surrounds it. For this reason *stimmen* is an apposite tool for literary analysis, because, as Hans Ulrich Gumbrecht argues, 'texts affect the "inner feelings" of readers in the way that weather and music do.'[8] The point here is not to attempt to conceptualise how mood functions in literature,[9] but to suggest that some of the debates between translators, debates which appeared to turn on technical questions of syntax and vocabulary, may in fact have been occasioned by the translators' differing modes of attunement to the mood of the text.

When Penguin published a new translation of *A la recherche du temps perdu* in 2002, the text was met with concern by a number of readers and academics. Edited by Christopher Prendergast, with a different translator for each of the volumes, the edition 'makes Proust less stuffy', mused Robert Douglas-Fairhurst shortly after its publication, 'but has something been lost in translation?'[10] André Aciman was less equivocal in his 2005 article 'Far from Proust's Way,' stating that

> this punctilious and ultimately priggish commitment to word-for-word accuracy turns out not only to be a cunning way of attracting attention and of publicizing a radically new translation out to make sweeping changes, but it is, all said and done, thoroughly deceptive. Accuracy, particularly in this volume, is proclaimed, not practiced, promised, not delivered.[11]

Prendergast and Lydia Davis, who translated the first volume, responded to the criticism leveled by Aciman (and others) insisting that in fact what was lost had finally been found, namely the clarity of Proust's style. The original translation by Scott Moncrieff (1922–30) was, they demonstrated in their letters, littered with his interpretive embellishments, and this despite the revisions made by Kilmartin in 1981 and Enright in 1993. Despite Davis's brilliant survey of the problems with Moncrieff's changes and additions, acknowledged by Aciman with the (not very Proustian) metaphor that trying to spot errors in Moncrieff's translation is like trying to spot rats in the New York subway, Aciman insisted that Moncrieff's was nonetheless the better translation. Why? Because, he said, translators 'have to depart from the text in order to capture not just its meaning, but its cadence, its luster, its stunning magic.'[12] Aciman's choice of words here is striking: 'cadence' has its musical connotation and 'luster' its visual connotation, but 'stunning magic' gestures towards something other than what is heard and seen in the reading of the text, instead emphasising the importance of what is ineffably *felt*. Aciman suggests, in other words, that Moncrieff just 'gets the feel' of Proust, as it were, in a way the contemporary translators have failed to. Of course he is more precise than this, and the published debate with Prendergast and Davis involves close scrutiny of the labyrinthine phrase which opens the second volume of the novel, and the translation solutions for it. But although Aciman does point to specific instances where he feels that, for example, the cadence created by a grammatical construction in French is lost in the new translation, it seems his greater concern is an overall 'magic,' which by another name might be called mood.

As already noted, identifying and agreeing on the mood of any literary text can be problematic, and this is all the more true with the *Recherche*, for a number of reasons. First, on a practical level, the lengthiness of the text, both in terms of the time Proust spent writing it (16 years, from 1908 to 1922) and the body of the text itself (almost one and a half million words), not to mention the time period the novel spans (1870s–1925s), means that it is likely to have not just one mood or skein of moods, but a number of moods which shift from volume to volume.

Indeed, one of the debates among Proust scholars is whether to understand the novel through the euphoric mood of the final volume, which concludes with the narrator's ecstatic discovery of the truth about time, or to be guided by the melancholy, pessimism, and skepticism which dominate the middle volumes of the work. This question is further complicated when one takes into account the non-linear fashion in which the volumes were written and edited. Put simply, the novel was originally intended as a short work, and its beginning and ending were part of Proust's first drafts: as time went on, it was the middle of the novel that he expanded, reflecting significant events in both his personal life (the death of family members and of a lover), and French society (the First World War). Indeed, it was thanks to the moratorium on publishing during the war that Proust had the time to reassess his plan for a three-part work and instead grow the *Recherche* from three to seven volumes. The fact that Proust died before he had finished revising the fifth volume of the novel, with volumes five, six, and seven then appearing posthumously, raises questions about whether, if Proust had lived long enough to edit the final volume, he might have modified the joyful ending which he had first drafted so many years ago.

The second factor behind the complexity of mood in the *Recherche* pertains to major social and aesthetic shifts at the time Proust was writing. As Antoine Compagnon emphasises in the title of his book, *Proust entre deux siècles* (1992[1989]), we are dealing with a writer of an indeterminate era. In his landmark work, which focuses on the medial volume of the *Recherche,* Compagnon demonstrates how Proust's idiosyncratic style both draws on the aesthetics of nineteenth-century giants such as Baudelaire, Wagner, and Ruskin, yet also reaches forcefully towards twentieth-century modernity. Added to these two contexts—the established moods of nineteenth-century society and literature on the one hand, and modernity's potential for new atmospheres and writing styles on the other—is a third, that of Decadence. This fin-de-siècle movement in literature emerged in France at the end of the nineteenth century through the writings of figures such as Joris-Karl Huysmans, Octave Mirbeau, and Jean Lorrain. Though by no means uniform in style or achievement, broadly speaking Decadent writing embraced and even celebrated the debasement and degradation of contemporary society, through a number of literary strategies, including radicalised subjectivity and an emphasis on sensations and fantasies to escape the banality of everyday life. And as Marion Schmid demonstrates in her work on the *Recherche,*

> Many of the novel's great themes—the struggles for social hegemony and the end of an era, the critique of aestheticism and idolatry, the subversion of gender and sexual roles, hereditary degeneracy and the collapse of the old social order—are indebted to Decadence.[13]

The significance of Decadence vis-à-vis mood and translation is revealed in a comment by Michael Wood, who suggests that the more recent English translations of the *Recherche* dismantle the image of 'the decadent Proust who emerges in Scott Moncrieff's flowery unrevised version.'[14] In other words, Moncrieff's stylistic flourishes promote the picture of Proust the Dandy, and, for those who are attached to this image, Moncrieff is evidently the most befitting translator. This (precarious) reasoning seems to underline Douglas-Fairhurst's argument when he says that 'Moncrieff, for all his occasional carelessness and prissiness, was probably temperamentally better suited than many later translators to making sense of a style which Robert de Montesquiou once described memorably as "a mixture of litanies and sperm."'[15] Rather than developing here the counterarguments to such a position (in sum, the mature Proust himself unravelled the dandy character of his youth[16]), it may be more fruitful to conclude this part of the discussion by reiterating that when it comes to translating a literary text, the temperament of the translator, their tendency to certain moods, is an important part of the process: for, even if it were possible for the translator to set aside their own affective disposition and read the text 'neutrally,' readers may approach and even judge the quality of a translated text through what they know of the translator's personality.

Clearly there is no easy answer to the question of which English translation is most faithful to the style and moods of the *Recherche*, and which the reader should be directed towards, but both versions share this advantage: the involvement of not one, but several translators. For Vintage this is so across the work as a whole (Moncrieff revised by Kilmartin revised by Enright), while for Penguin it is section by section (one translator per volume), but in both cases the plurality of translators with their variety of temperaments is, arguably, better suited than a single translator to confront the richness and multiplicity of mood in Proust's work.

Thus far, several issues at the intersection of Translation Studies and Affect Studies have been touched upon, and the specific difficulty of translating Proust has been highlighted. Not only does an 'untranslatable' affect lexicon pose a challenge to literary translators, but the temperament of the translators themselves is at stake when it comes to tuning into the mood of the source text. But the foreign translator also has an advantage over the native reader, namely their possession of a separate language, with its own nuances for describing ambience and feeling. While it may seem counterintuitive at first suggestion, the forthcoming paragraphs will demonstrate that by approaching a text in one language with the affective vocabulary from another, its mood may be brought to light in a new way.

The word 'awkward' does not translate directly into French. Henry James's novel *The Awkward Age* (1899) is known, for example, as *L'Age*

Difficile. This difficulty is not exclusive to the French tongue, but to all the major European languages: 'awkward,' ironically, is an awkward concept to pin down. Even in English, the phenomenon is easier to experience than to define. This difficulty is inscribed in the elasticity of the word itself, which is increasingly employed to denote a vast range of phenomena, from aesthetic style to material objects.[17] And this elasticity is all the more evident when we consider the word's etymological origins, as an adverb related to physical movement: somewhere between *forward* and *backward*, awkward is curiously performative of its own meaning, the word itself containing the clash of being 'turned the wrong way' (awk) despite 'having a specified direction' (-ward). Today, awkward most often indicates a feeling and/or mood, and as an adjective it is applicable to atmosphere ('it felt awkward'), interaction ('we had an awkward conversation'), and personhood ('an awkward person'). What makes 'awkward' more complex than the average adjective is the way it can describe both the thing ('he is awkward') and its effect ('he makes me feel awkward'), whereas feelings are often grammatically divided in terms of cause and effect ('it was embarrassing, I felt embarrassed'). One argument that may immediately raise itself in response to the idea of bringing the concept of 'awkward' to bear on a foreign text is the risk of projecting the peculiarities of the English temperament onto other cultures. But successful challenges to this kind of argument have already been made, for example by Michael Tilby in his work on the theme of embarrassment (a cousin to awkwardness) in André Gide's *Les Faux-Monnayeurs*.[18] Tilby disagrees with the idea that embarrassment is a 'narrowly English' sentiment, and in a similar way it is important to consider the way awkwardness operates beyond Anglo-Saxon cultures.

While the term embarrassment can be translated directly into French (*la gêne*), awkwardness lacks a singular equivalent. As a physical phenomenon, clumsy can be translated as *maladroit* or *gauche*, with both terms containing the idea of wrong direction. There are also fitting translations for the symbolic extension of awkwardness as a problem of movement or placement. An environment may cause an individual to feel uncomfortably out of place or *mal à l'aise*; an action or utterance may be ill-fitting or *déplacé*; an individual may be put in an awkward position or *être en porte-à-faux*. What is immediately clear is that while the French language lacks a single adjective that can be used to describe the awkwardness of composure, interaction, and personality, there is a plethora of vocabulary which suggest different aspects of the phenomenon; a situation or interaction can be *délicat* or *difficile*, a person can be *étrange* or *peu commode*, and most of us are at risk of making the occasional blunder, that is *des gaffes* or *des maladresses*. Thus while the French language lacks an overarching term for awkwardness, a work of French literature may depict the phenomenon through a multitude of terms. Indeed, Proust's *Recherche* is teeming with the French lexicon mentioned above, but this is more likely to become apparent to an English reader who has 'awkward,' as an umbrella term, at hand. The concept of awkwardness provides a means of bringing the French terms together and of perceiving its contribution to the mood of the text. While the lexicon of embarrassment and uneasiness which describes the characters' feelings and interactions alerts us to certain themes, this in turn directs our attention to the way a broader mood of awkwardness functions as a backdrop to the novel, against which such themes can stand out. Before looking at two of these themes in detail, it is worth noting that the context in which Proust was writing, as discussed earlier in this essay, necessitates the presence of awkwardness. The unprecedented rapidity of social change meant that the rules of engagement—between the classes, between the sexes—no longer functioned smoothly, and consequently individuals were unsure of which direction to take in everything from casual conversations to intimate relationships. As Adam Kotsko puts it, far more potent than 'everyday awkwardness,' when social rules are broken, is 'radical awkwardness,' when the rules themselves are in flux.[19]

One of the most commented aspects of the *Recherche* is its depiction of romantic love, and the social upheavals mentioned above are portrayed with particular acuity in the unhappy love affairs when the novel's male characters become besotted with women of a lower social class. Scholars dealing with this theme have, naturally, written about the feelings associated with romance and mésalliance in the novel, including obsessive, destructive jealousy, a suffering that is as physical as it is psychological, and the fear and sense of loss inevitably wrought. The narrator himself makes extensive analysis of his own emotions and thought patterns, and such sustained excavations of consciousness are what make the novel such an achievement. The novel both shows and discourses on a bleak vision of love, which is almost always unreciprocal, based on one's own imagination rather than the attributes of the loved one, or based on their unexpected unavailability: hence, love gives rise to anxiety, disappointment, and despair. Such are the feelings of the characters unhappily 'in love,' but what of the atmosphere in which these characters exist? From the earliest pages of the novel, which is to say from the dawn of the narrator's consciousness, romantic love is inseparable from social awkwardness. In the first volume alone, he bumps into a family friend embarrassed to be caught with a lover, and pays a surprise visit to his uncle, who is embarrassed to be caught with a courtesan. Furthermore, the young protagonist learns from his family's behaviour that marriage is not enough to sanctify a romance—his parents refuse to acknowledge the wife and child of one of their dearest friends, Swann—and that even the depiction of romantic love in literature is off limits, with his mother censoring those parts of the novel she reads aloud to him at bedtime. When the adolescent protagonist, from the second volume of the novel, begins to engage in conversations about love, he discovers that the conversation inevitably turns sour, and this even happens without him saying anything at all. In one scene, for example, Swann is theorising aloud that it is wiser for men to love women of a lower class, but by the end of his phrase he realises that the protagonist may be applying this truth to him. The protagonist knows this because he feels the atmosphere change dramatically: 'he was seized by a violent ill-will towards me. But this was made manifest only in the uneasiness of his glance. He said nothing more to me at the time.'[20] Such awkward conversations proliferate throughout the novel, establishing a mood of awkwardness within which particular stories can then stand out.

The love affairs of nearly all the couples in the *Recherche* are stories involving social embarrassment and psychological torture, yet the tone surrounding these characters and their exploits is not limited to the melancholic or the tragic. Instead, while the characters are ascribed feelings such as jealousy and despair, their behaviour is depicted in such a way as to establish a certain 'comedy of awkwardness.' Often, this is through the paralleling of physical awkwardness with psychological unease or unbalance. Swann, for example, is tormented by the idea that Odette is cheating on him with another man. Having become mentally disturbed to the point of physical illness, he decides to catch her *in flagrante delicto*. Stationed outside of her house that night, he reflects on what is about to ensue, aware that 'what he was going to do would be extremely awkward, and she would detest him for ever after [...] But his desire to know the truth was stronger.'[21] At this point, the reader may feel both empathetic towards Swann, sharing in his pre-awkwardness at the thought of catching Odette in the act, and embarrassed for him, which is to say embarrassed to see an intelligent man reduced to this.[22] The conclusion to Swann's espionage allows him to feel embarrassed about himself, and in this way shifts the tone from emotional desperation to comedic awkwardness. Having finally garnered the courage to knock on the window, Swann is not met by the faces of Odette and her lover, but by two elderly gentlemen: in the darkness, in his confusion, he has the wrong house. While being positioned outside of the wrong house is not exactly slipping on a banana, there is something akin to slapstick here, a phenomenon which Mary Cappello describes as 'choreographed awkwardness.' As Cappello observes, 'Awkwardness so regularly threatens us that we've invented the situation comedy to help us cope.'[23] Proust, though, uses the comedy of awkwardness to help the reader cope with the overwhelming despair of his lovesick characters: in the same way the narrator both participates in events and observes them as a writer, the reader is able to both identify with the characters' emotions and, through the contrast in tone, take a step back.

While awkwardness is used to bring comic relief to the theme of love and its agonies, it is also used in the form of dark humour to intensify the theme of death. Throughout the novel, where there is death there is also awkwardness, in such a way as to amuse and pain the reader in equal measure. One of the most striking examples is when Swann reveals to Oriane, his closest and oldest friend, that he has just three or four months to live. The timing of this revelation is, for Oriane, most importune: about to drive off in her carriage to a glamorous party, she is 'placed for the first time in her life between two duties as incompatible as getting into her carriage to go out to dinner and showing compassion for a man who was about to die.'[24] Swann's news places Oriane in both a physically and psychologically awkward position, caught as she is between stepping into her carriage and remaining with her dying friend, between social ambition and compassion. The dark humour is introduced to the scene not only through the narrator's sardonic commentary, cited above, but also Oriane's own clumsy attempt to transform the tone, by telling Swann that he must be joking. Later in the novel, the dark humour linked to Swann's devastating love life and consequent early death are continued through socially awkward scenes featuring his daughter, Gilberte. When Oriane finally meets Gilberte, having refused to acknowledge her when Swann was alive, their conversation inevitably veers towards him, but both women choose to avoid the subject. On the one hand, this is extremely sad, with Swann's memory being deliberately suppressed by both his daughter and best friend. On the other, the ridiculous solutions proposed by Oriane's husband may make the reader laugh bitterly at the lengths these people will go to in order to place anything uncomfortable under the carpet. Hence after Gilberte remarks on some drawings and Oriane almost makes a slip—'in fact it was your fa ... some friends of ours who made us buy them'[25]—Oriane's husband tells her to simply remove them from the walls, 'since they make you think about Swann. If you don't think about Swann, you won't speak about him.'[26] These are just a few examples of how awkwardness functions as the atmospheric backdrop to the themes of love and death in the novel, with a lighter, more entertaining form of the phenomenon marking some incidents, and its more intense, sometimes excruciating manifestation used for others.

Awkwardness not only underlies and unites thematic concerns in the *Recherche*, fostering tonal modulations between the humorous and the tragic, but also helps us to understand the structure of the novel. The link between mood and music was touched upon earlier in the chapter, and with a work of the length and complexity of the *Recherche*, the comparison to a symphony is inevitable: Edith Wharton, for example, lauded it for being one of those novels which 'beginning very quietly—carelessly, almost—yet convey on the opening page the same feeling of impending fatality as the first bars of the Fifth Symphony.'[27] When it comes to the beginnings and endings of the subsequent six volumes (and sections within them), seemingly quite disparate in their concerns and tone, awkwardness provides a useful way of bringing these strains, chords, and cadences together. Often, a volume begins or concludes on a surprising revelation or incident which induces awkward feelings for the protagonist, the reader, or both. Swann's maddening obsession with Odette in Volume One concludes with his painful understanding, thanks to a dream, that he does not even find her attractive: the reader presumes that this is the end of their courtship, only to discover in the next section that the couple are now married and have a child. The aforementioned conversation between Swann and Oriane, in which Swann's impending death is revealed, concludes Volume Three, while the opening of Volume Four involves sexual awkwardness for two male characters as they seduce one another, for the protagonist who accidentally finds himself watching them have sex, and for the reader who understands, before the protagonist himself does, what is happening. But it is in the concluding section to the final volume of the novel where the full versatility of awkwardness is shown, in its link to elation and even redemption. The wary, aged protagonist is making his way to a social event when he stumbles on a paving stone, and the strange felicity his physical clumsiness produces—in summoning a memory, just like the madeleine at the beginning of the novel—strengthens his resolve to understand the meaning of this joy. What he comes to realise is that he has the writing subject he has been searching for: all the embarrassing memories of his youth, all the evenings spent at salons watching the gaffes and humiliation of snobs and social climbers, all the years awkwardly hiding the woman he loved from his friends, these were not wasted moments, but material gathered for his art.

This exposition has allowed us to observe the rich potentiality of bringing an affective term from the English language to bear on a literary work written in French. This opens up a host of possibilities: how many texts, we may wonder, might be illuminated through idiosyncratic concepts such as the German *Fernweh* (homesickness for a place one has never been to, literally 'far-sickness') or Japanese *aware* (the melancholy appreciation of the transiency of existence, literally 'the pathos of things')? How might studies in comparative literature, moreover, benefit from such an approach? Proust, after all, was not the only novelist writing at a moment of social upheaval, when rules of etiquette, not to mention, ways of seeing the world, were coming undone. Work on mood across authors of different languages within the same period, like the fin-de-siècle, may allow us to see things which thematic or stylistic analyses do not, or at the very least it can enhance existing research. Of course there are dangers to be avoided, chiefly the projection of a mood onto a text, but this danger exists in any act of literary criticism and not only in cross-lingual readings. Furthermore, there are realities to be acknowledged, namely that every translator, just like every reader, experiences the text through their personal situation and temperament. The moods of great literary texts, like Proust's *Recherche*, necessarily elude definitive description, partly because they will be felt to differing degrees by the reader, partly because mood is by nature ineffable: as the narrator of the *Recherche* says, 'what we feel about life not being felt in the form of ideas, its literary, that is to say intellectual expression describes it, explains it, analyses it, but does not recompose it.'[28] But by bringing together theories of affect with practices of translation and criticism, as this essay has done, a new space for grappling with mood opens up.

Notes

1 'Je ne prétends pas savoir l'anglais. Je prétends savoir Ruskin,' in *Correspondance de Marcel Proust*, ed. by Philip Kolb, 21 vols. (Paris: Plon, 1970–1993), vol. III, p. 221. All translations are my own.

2 *Correspondance de Marcel Proust*, pp. 220–1.

3 Words with significant phonaesthetic effects, for example, or concept words with different emphases in different communities ('liberalism,' 'bureaucracy'). This is not to mention cultural metaphors, idioms, proverbs, puns, neologisms, nor the peculiar syntactic structures unique to certain languages.

4 David Bellos, *Is That a Fish In Your Ear?: Translation and the Meaning of Everything* (New York: Farrar, Strauss & Giroux, 2011), p. 153.

5 Aleksandr S. Pushkin, *Eugene Onegin: A Novel in Verse* (Princeton, NJ: Princeton University Press, 1990), trans. by Vladimir Nabokov, vol. II, *Commentary and Index*, p. 141.

6 In contemporary linguistics, Anna Wierzbicka's *Emotions across Languages and Cultures* (Cambridge: Cambridge University Press, 1999) is a seminal text, and Wierzbicka also co-edited, with Jean Harkins, *Emotions in Cross-linguistic Perspective* (Berlin and New York: Mouton de Gruyter, 2001), which offers a variety of fascinating perspectives. More recently, an important contribution has been made by Hans-Jürgen Diller's *Words for Feelings: Studies in the History of the English Emotion Lexicon* (Heidelberg: Universitätsverlag Winter, 2014).

7 While the field of Affect Theory is difficult to circumscribe, Melissa Gregg and Gregory J. Seigworth, editors of *The Affect Theory Reader* (Durham, NC: Duke University Press, 2011), set out 'as a set of necessarily brief and blurry snapshots, eight of the main orientations' in their 'Introduction,' pp. 6–8.

8 Hans Ulrich Gumbrecht, *Atmosphere, Mood, Stimmung: On a Hidden Potential of Literature*, trans. by Erik Butler (Stanford, CA: Stanford University Press, 2012), p. 5.

9 I share Gumbrecht's skepticism 'about the power of "theories" to explain atmospheres and moods' and his doubt 'about the viability of "methods" to identify them.' *Atmosphere, Mood, Stimmung*, p. 17.

10 Robert Douglas-Fairhurst, 'In Search of Marcel Proust,' *Guardian*, 17 November 2002. www.theguardian.com/books/2002/nov/17/classics.higher education [accessed 1 October 2017].

11 André Aciman, 'Far from Proust's Way,' *The New York Review of Books*, 15 December 2005. www.nybooks.com/articles/2005/12/15/far-from-prousts-way/ [accessed 1 October 2017].

12 André Aciman, 'Proust's Way: An Exchange,' *The New York Review of Books*, 6 April 2006. www.nybooks.com/articles/2006/04/06/prousts-way-an-exchange/ [accessed 1 October 2017].

13 Marion Schmid, 'Decadence and the fin de siècle,' in *Marcel Proust in Context*, ed. by Adam Watt (Cambridge: Cambridge University Press, 2013), pp. 51–8 (p. 54).

14 Michael Wood, 'Translations,' in *Marcel Proust in Context*, ed. by Adam Watt (Cambridge: Cambridge University Press, 2013), pp. 230–40 (p. 233). Here, he is speaking about both Kilmartin (in his revisions of Moncrieff) and Prendergast.

15 www.theguardian.com/books/2002/nov/17/classics.highereducation [accessed 1 October 2017].

16 As Wood points out, 'Proust himself invented the old Proust, and was his first acolyte so to speak; the beauty of the critical situation is that he also invented, and had done from the very beginning, the new, sceptical Proust, the ironic doubter who allows us to give the other one a hard time,' *Marcel Proust in Context*, p. 233.

17 When 'the word awkward' is typed into Google, one of the first suggestions generated is that 'the word awkward is overused.'

18 Michael Tilby, 'Les Faux-Monnayeurs: A Novel about Embarrassment,' *French Studies*, 35(1), 1981, pp. 45–59.

19 Adam Kotsko, *Awkwardness: An Essay* (Hants: O Books, 2010), p. 16.

20 Marcel Proust, *In Search Of Lost Time, Vol 2: Within a Budding Grove*, trans. by C. K. Scott Moncrieff, Terence Kilmartin, and Dennis J. Enright (London: Vintage, 1996), p. 688. All references to the English text will be to the Vintage edition, translated by Moncrieff, Kilmartin, and Enright.

21 Proust, Marcel, *In Search Of Lost Time, Vol 1: Swann's Way*, trans. by C. K. Scott Moncrieff, Terence Kilmartin, and Dennis J. Enright (London: Vintage, 1996), p. 330.

22 We can note that some languages have vocabulary for this feeling of embarrassment by proxy, for example the Mexican Spanish term *Pena ajena* which denotes the embarrassment felt when watching someone else's humiliation.

23 Mary Cappello, *Awkward: A Detour* (New York: Bellevue Literary Press, 2007), p. 25.

24 Proust, Marcel, *In Search Of Lost Time, Vol 3: The Guermantes Way*, p. 688.

25 Proust, Marcel, *In Search Of Lost Time, Vol 5–6: The Captive, The Fugitive*, p. 667.

26 Ibid., p. 675.

27 Wharton, Edith, 'Edith Wharton, *The Writing of Fiction*,' entry 110 in *Marcel Proust: The Critical Heritage*, ed. by Leighton Hodson (New York: Taylor & Francis, 2005[1989]), pp. 319–22 (p. 320).

28 *In Search Of Lost Time, Vol 5–6: The Captive, The Fugitive*, p. 427.

Works cited

Aciman, André, 'Far from Proust's Way', *The New York Review of Books*, 15 December 2005. www.nybooks.com/articles/2005/12/15/far-from-prousts-way/ [accessed 1 October 2017].

——, 'Proust's Way: An Exchange', *The New York Review of Books*, 6 April 2006. www.nybooks.com/articles/2006/04/06/prousts-way-an-exchange/ [accessed 1 October 2017].

Bellos, David, *Is That a Fish In Your Ear?: Translation and the Meaning of Everything* (New York: Farrar, Strauss & Giroux, 2011).

Cappello, Mary, *Awkward: A Detour* (New York: Bellevue Literary Press, 2007).

Compagnon, Antoine, *Proust entre deux siècles* (Paris: Seuil, 1989).

Diller, Hans-Jürgen, *Words for Feelings: Studies in the History of the English Emotion Lexicon* (Heidelberg: Universitätsverlag Winter, 2014).

Douglas-Fairhurst, Robert, 'In Search of Marcel Proust', *Guardian*, 17 November 2002. www.theguardian.com/books/2002/nov/17/classics.highereducation [accessed 1 October 2017].

Gregg, Melissa, and Gregory J. Seigworth, eds., *The Affect Theory Reader* (Durham, NC: Duke University Press, 2011).

Gumbrecht, Hans Ulrich, *Atmosphere, Mood, Stimmung: On a Hidden Potential of Literature*, trans. by Erik Butler (Stanford, CA: Stanford University Press, 2012).

Hubscher-Davidson, Severine, *Translation and Emotion: A Psychological Perspective* (New York and London: Routledge, forthcoming 2017).

James, Henry, *The Awkward Age*, ed. by Vivien Jones (Oxford: Oxford University Press, 2009[1899]).

Kotsko, Adam, *Awkwardness: An Essay* (Hants: O Books, 2010).

Massumi, Brian, 'The Autonomy of Affect', *Cultural Critique*, 31, 2 (1995), 83–109.

Proust, Marcel, *Correspondance de Marcel Proust*, ed. by Philip Kolb, 21 vols (Paris: Plon, 1970–1993).

———, *In Search Of Lost Time, Vol I: Swann's Way*, trans. by C. K. Scott Moncrieff, Terence Kilmartin, and Dennis J. Enright (London: Vintage, 1996).

———, *In Search Of Lost Time, Vol II: Within a Budding Grove*, trans. by C. K. Scott Moncrieff, Terence Kilmartin, and Dennis J. Enright (London: Vintage, 1996).

———, *In Search Of Lost Time, Vol III: The Guermantes Way*, trans. by C. K. Scott Moncrieff, Terence Kilmartin, and Dennis J. Enright (London: Vintage, 1996).

———, *In Search Of Lost Time, Vol V-VI: The Captive, The Fugitive*, trans. by C. K. Scott Moncrieff, Terence Kilmartin, and Dennis J. Enright (London: Vintage, 1996).

Pushkin, Aleksandr S., *Eugene Onegin: A Novel in Verse*, trans. by Vladimir Nabokov (Princeton, NJ: Princeton University Press, 1990).

Schmid, Marion, 'Decadence and the fin de siècle', in *Marcel Proust in Context*, ed. by Adam Watt (Cambridge: Cambridge University Press, 2013), pp. 51–8.

Sedgwick, Eve Kosofsky, and Adam Frank, 'Shame in the Cybernetic Fold: Reading Silvan Tomkins', *Critical Inquiry*, 21, 2 (1995), 496–522.

Shields, Kathleen, and Michael Clarke, eds., *Translating Emotion: Studies in Transformation and Renewal between Languages* (Bern: Peter Lang, 2011).

Tilby, Michael, 'Les Faux-Monnayeurs: A Novel about Embarrassment', *French Studies*, 35, 1 (1981), 45–59.

Wharton, Edith, 'Edith Wharton, *The Writing of Fiction*', entry 110 in *Marcel Proust: The Critical Heritage*, ed. by Leighton Hodson (New York: Taylor & Francis, 2005[1989]), pp. 319–22.

Wierzbicka, Anna, *Emotions Across Languages and Cultures* (Cambridge: Cambridge University Press, 1999).

Wierzbicka, Anna, and Jean Harkins, eds., *Emotions in Crosslinguistic Perspective* (Berlin and New York: Mouton de Gruyter, 2001).

Wood, Michael, 'Translations', in *Marcel Proust in Context*, ed. by Adam Watt (Cambridge: Cambridge University Press, 2013), pp. 230–40.

8 'He wept for a way home'
The *Stimmung* of Odysseus's *Nostos*

Madeleine Scherer

In popular imagination, classical epics have long been conceptualised as larger-than-life stories of warfare, male friendship, and fickle gods; stories driven by their incredible plots and captivating characters. But the Homeric epics that detail the fall of Troy, the travels of Odysseus, and the slaughter of Penelope's suitors feature equally pivotal scenes that detail the calmer moments of the heroes' journeys, scenes that, at times, serve as one of our first introductions to the heroic characters. After his dramatic confrontation with Menelaus, for instance, one of the first moments in which we re-encounter Achilles is in his tent, when the great hero gently plays the lyre, melancholically recalling the *klea andron*, the fame of (other) men. Likewise, our very first introduction to the hero of the *Odyssey* does not detail Odysseus's great deeds or cunning intelligence, but instead we see him bitterly weep by the seashore:

> [Kalypso] set out searching after great-hearted Odysseus,/ and found him sitting on the seashore, and his eyes were never/ wiped dry of tears, and the sweet lifetime was draining out of him,/ as he wept for a way home, since the nymph was no longer pleasing/ to him. By nights he would lie beside her, of necessity,/ in the hollow caverns, against his will, by one who was willing,/ but all the days he would sit upon the rocks, at the seaside,/ breaking his heart in tears and lamentation and sorrow/ as weeping tears he looked out over the barren water.[1]

This scene, like others across the two Homeric epics, focuses largely on setting out not only the themes, but also the larger atmosphere that will shape the rest of the poem, an entanglement of leitmotifs, emotions, and mood this chapter sets out to explore.

The mood of ancient Greek epic has received little attention in scholarship to date. Major issues arise when trying to assess the inner lives of characters whose thoughts and feelings are almost entirely kept obscure by the poets, within a society whose understanding of emotions is fundamentally different to our own. Some of the most significant works on mood in epic poetry include Donald Lateiner's discussion of affect displays, which reads nonverbal signs in the poems as expressions of the heroes' thoughts, feelings, and disposition towards their social environments.[2] Samuel Eliot Bassett's 1928 *The Poetry of Homer* is also still fundamental to the study of mood in epic thanks to the connections it draws between the musical nature of the epic genre and the emotions it creates within its listeners—although Bassett uses the concepts of 'mood' and 'atmosphere' without much qualification.[3] There have been some works which have picked up on the prominence of references to the past in the *Odyssey*, the most substantial of which may be François Hartog's *Memories of Odysseus*, which has substantially influenced my own reading of the *Odyssey* in this chapter. Hartog writes:

> As soon as the poem begins, we move into the time of memory. Forgetfulness, now feared, now longed for, lurks. The memory of the dead haunts the living [...] In his wanderings over the sterile sea, Odysseus is in danger of losing everything, his possessions, his reputation, even his name, and in the end returns home all alone, obliged to pass himself off as someone else, after losing all his ever-forgetful companions.[4]

Many other scholarly works have argued that the *Odysseys*'s preoccupation with the past creates, what they term, the epic's 'nostalgic' mood.[5] These works include, for instance, 'Philosophy's Nostalgia' by Jeff Malpas, 'Homeric Nostalgia' by Norman Austin, and *The Past Is a Foreign Country* by David Lowenthal. And indeed, there can be no doubt that the Greek word *nostos* has been absolutely key to the formulation of the modern term 'nostalgia': etymologically speaking, nostalgia derives from the Greek *nostos*, meaning home or homecoming, and *algos*, denoting pain or suffering.[6] At least in antiquity, as is most clearly showcased by Odysseus's own *nostos*, the return journey is inherently interwoven with experiences of longing as well as pain. However, one of the questions I want to pose through this chapter is whether the term nostalgia is still appropriate for reading a poem which, from our modern standpoint, is so far removed from our own cultural contexts; particularly as nostalgia is often, as critics such as Malpas himself outline, seen as a product specifically of modernity, 'and, more specifically, of modernity understood as a mode of historical experience that is essentially given over to a process of unceasing change and renewal.'[7] The term nostalgia was originally coined in 1688 by Swiss medical student Johannes Hofer to describe the feeling of homesickness, but it came to be severed from this background over time and now describes 'a structure of internal feeling, typically understood in terms of temporality, memory, and desire'[8]—whereby especially the internal quality of the term's contemporary meaning will be shown to stand at odds with its origin in the *Odyssey*.[9]

Despite possible conceptual problems of applying a 'modern' term to a poem composed in the Early Iron Age, in most pieces of scholarship which discuss the poem's mood, nostalgia is referenced with little quali-fication: Lowenthal talks about how in the *Odyssey* 'nostalgia combined physical pain and mental grief with the prospect of redemptive recov-ery,'[10] while Austin enthusiastically writes:

> Nostalgia! Now there's a theme that calls for high poetry. Homer, Virgil, Dante, Milton – remove nostalgia from their palette and what would we have? Some noble sentences no doubt, but dry as a biscuit when what we crave is cake, Proust's madeleine, dipped in Madame's tisane.[11]

While Austin recognises that '[n]ostalgia is not an ancient word,' he claims that 'if the word is modern, the idea is as ancient as poetry it-self,' and that '*nostos* and nostalgia become almost synonymous.'[12] A primary issue with these readings lies in the fact that ancient Greek emotions and moods are, in many ways, fundamentally different from our own and that such etymological connections may thus no longer be relevant. As David Konstan explains in his seminal monograph on *The Emotions of the Ancient Greeks*, in antiquity the word *pathos*, which is now rendered as 'emotion,' referred more generally to the things which happened *to* a person, relating the emotional state of a character or qual-ity of a situation more to outside contingencies than an inner state of be-ing.[13] I wish to take note of the influence that the epic's outer world and the characters' social context have on the mood created within the poem to propose that the complex web of connotations around *nostos* in the *Odyssey* are not sufficiently embodied by the modern term nostalgia. In-stead, they prescribe a different, at times even contradictory, mood both of longing and being haunted; a mood which comes into being through outside influences as much as the characters' innermost feelings.[14]

This chapter then attempts to approach the nature of the *Odyssey*'s mood and its poetic invocations, albeit carefully, in view of Hans Ulrich Gumbrecht's all-too-true warning that

> [r]eading for *Stimmung* [moods] cannot mean 'deciphering' atmo-spheres and moods, for they have no fixed signification. [...] Instead, it means discovering sources of energy in artifacts and giving oneself over to them affectively and boldly – yielding to them and gesturing towards them.[15]

Conceptualising a literary mood has long been a contentious topic, with difficulties arising not only in how to define 'mood' as a concept but also in how it is produced. The feelings and atmospheres invoked within a piece of literature are not necessarily synonymous with the text's overall mood, but David E. Wellbery, quoting Schmitz's *Der Leib, der Raum und die Gefühle*, has convincingly argued for an inherent connection between feelings, emotions, atmospheres, and mood, which this chapter relies on.[16] As I explore the differences between our ideas of emotions and nostalgia, and those of the ancient Greeks and the *Odyssey*, I want to focus in particular on the dynamic between inner feelings and the influence of the outside world, which Konstan has written of with regards to archaic and classical Greek literature. In our own scholarly understanding of moods, for a long time they have been conceptualised as purely inward-looking, subjective experiences based on one's individual personality and feelings; something that is echoed within our modern understanding of nostalgia. Recently, however, there have been a number of scholars who aim to divide mood from this idea, including Rita Felski and Susan Fraiman who, in their introduction to *New Literary History*, argue that 'mood circumvents the clunky categories often imposed on experience: subjective versus objective, feeling versus thinking, latent versus manifest.'[17] This increasing academic distance from a focus purely on subjectivity and inwardness was perhaps most famously introduced by Martin Heidegger's essential work *Being and Time*, which argues for the existence of a mutual dynamic relationship between self and world, between being and Being. In the wake of the prevailing importance of his philosophy, I attempt a reading of the *Odyssey*'s mood in parts inspired by Heideggerian approaches, which acknowledges the importance the ancient Greeks saw in the state of the world in addition to one's own subjective experiences.[18] My aim in this chapter is thus twofold: first to show how the mood of the *Odyssey* comes into being, and therein how the dynamic between self and world, individual and community, is negotiated. The interactions between the larger world, the community and the individual will be foregrounded in particular, interactions which produce something we can conceptualise through what Heidegger refers to as *Dasein*, a sense of Being-in-the-world. Second, although I think there is no word in English that can directly encapsulate the complex dynamics around Odysseus's *nostos*, through my readings of the interactions between subjects and their surroundings, I want to offer a more in-depth analysis of the *Stimmung* of the *Odyssey*, which continues to shape the mood of its hero, and even, at times, guides his journey back on course.

I. 'as when a man': *Stimmung* and the Dynamic between Individual and Community

Heidegger's understanding of *Stimmung* necessitated a radical reconception of what the academic community had understood as mood; no longer merely reflective of inwardly and purely subjective feelings, Heidegger instead proposed that our emotions are always inherently influenced by a sense of *Dasein*, Being-in-the-world, a state of the world related to and yet separate from oneself.[19] He famously used the example of the *Katheder*, the lectern he was speaking from at a university, as an example of what *Dasein* is, namely our surrounding world which we rarely become conscious of; until, that is, the *Katheder* is suddenly too low for us to speak from, and we are forced to acknowledge its presence in order to readjust its position.[20] *Dasein* becomes closest and most familiar to us in what Heidegger terms *Welt,* the world, but also *Umwelt*, the world around us; wherein the relationship of *Dasein* to this world influences how we engage with our surroundings, our *'going about* the world' and our 'looking around, [our] *circumspection.*'[21] Therein Being—in the Heideggerian sense with a capital 'B'—is a state of existence, not of a mind or a body but something that is 'always already outside itself.'[22]

In *Being and Time*, Heidegger conceived of moods as central to *Dasein*, to our very existence in and experience of the world.[23] In writing about specifically nostalgia as a mood, Heidegger has emphasised the importance of time for our experience of *Dasein*, whereby he seems particularly fascinated by the influence of the past and our memories on our identity in the present.[24] Remembering our past self or state of existence is thus fundamental to our sense of Being itself, the past shaping the ways in which human beings frame both their current and future existence. Recent sociological studies conducted on the relationship between memory and mood tend to support such a thesis, wherein memories take on the function of 'mood-regulation' strategies.[25] A mood such as that of the *Odyssey*, which is so inextricably linked to the pain of but also longing for memory, is illuminating to read through a philosophy that acknowledges the processes of remembering as constitutive for *Dasein* itself, and thereby for its moods. As I will show, the lasting effects of the past become part of the very fabric of Being in the *Odyssey*, of its *Welt*, and has a profound impact on the moods of the epic's main characters. Through reading their actions and expressed emotions, we can draw conclusions about the *Stimmung* of the *Odyssey*: one, I argue, encapsulates a haunting and yet alluring draw of the past which simultaneously leads characters towards and away from their *nostos*.[26]

Scholars have agreed that the *Odyssey* is characterised by the repetition of consistent themes such as 'the unquenchable desire of the long-absent warrior and wanderer to return'[27]; themes that are underlined by frequent similes complementing the poem's main narrative and modal dimension.[28] I likewise suggest that the poem's themes and narratives bring forth a certain mood not only for the characters immersed in it but also for the audience—it creates a certain sense of *Dasein* and, as Heidegger writes, *Dasein* always has a certain mood.[29] Thanks to Milman Parry's groundbreaking work on oral composition, many features of the epic's structure and language are now better understood within the context of communal performance and memory.[30] The epic's language, for instance, is formulaic, made up of type-scenes and words which are 'most fundamentally units of utterance, logical chunks of expression,'[31] whereby John Foley in particular argues that Homeric poetry often uses particular signs, *sêma*, which in the manner of *pars pro toto* express an 'ambient tradition,' 'a larger, immanent whole.'[32] Particularly similes have been shown to adapt and underline what is often described as an overall 'tone of the whole passage,' a mood which certain poetic phrases and images try to complement or convey.[33] The oral nature of the Homeric poems thereby favours general and universally applicable themes, which both reflect a sense of community in the poem as well as immediately resonate with their audiences: as Joseph Russo and Bennett Simon convincingly propose, 'poetry of a traditional oral character will naturally favor traditional language and thought, and discourage ideas or phrases that are too novel or idiosyncratic,' and as such oral poetry naturally 'emphasises the communal and the collective, rather than the personal and the idiosyncratic; the influences one person has on another, rather than the autonomy of each person.'[34] It is this universality of the Homeric language, the resonance of the poem's similes, terms, and themes with the concerns of the poet's audience which forecloses the *Odyssey*'s mood. Gumbrecht has already argued that it is often poetic form which allows for a coherent tone to establish itself,[35] and an oral epic that uses a language that reflects the concerns, ideas, and hopes of its own contemporary audience can perhaps serve as a unique example for a reciprocal dynamic between poetry and mood.

Russo and Simon's reading underlines a sense of collectivity in the Homeric epics, as the personal dimension of experiences is de-emphasised in order to link a single narrative to a communal mnemonoic hemisphere. As the Homeric bard(s) work(s) hard to establish a collective dimension through his (their) poem's form and language, experiences are not purely subjective but also shaped by the world which the characters are created and immersed in. Bruno Snell and E.R. Dodds have likewise distanced their analysis from a focus on the private and subjective and have, in turn, identified a tendency in the epics to represent the 'common and publicly observable, as contrasted with that which is idiosyncratic and private.'[36] In a partial parallel to Heidegger whose *Being and Time* moved away from a purely subject-based system of moods to one which acknowledges the influence of one's surroundings, in Homeric epic poetry there is no traditional sense of self: as Charles Segal writes, 'Homer has no concept of, indeed no word for, the unconscious, let alone the "self."'[37] Rather than explicitly describing inner mental processes, conflicts, or thoughts, feelings are, if at all, expressed through the characters' actions and conversations, through which the audience can identify the general themes and atmosphere of a scene rather than a unique emotional experience. Jan Söffner even goes so far as to argue that Homer moves away entirely from the subjective, proposing that feelings in the epics are completely determined by the situation that characters find themselves in,[38] a statement that, perhaps, reads deliberately polemic but is useful for underlining the lack of subject-based psychology in Homeric poetry. While Heidegger does not, of course, discount the subjective or completely remove his analytic focus from the self, his work is singularly important in emphasising the influence of the *Umwelt* on individual experiences. In the later analysis, I will rely on a comparable approach to Heidegger's to show how being conscious of the social *Umwelt* the epic protagonists find themselves immersed in allows for more informed analyses of the Homeric epics and ancient Greek emotions more generally, which are, on the whole, significantly more concerned with outside influences than a subjective state of being.

Damian Stocking has extensively written about the Homeric sense of self, arguing that it is defined through the *biê* and the *is*, that is, the power and capability to change the state of the world,[39] whereby he draws on a comparable connection between self and *Umwelt* as the one on which Heidegger bases his ideas around mood. Being or existing in Homeric poetry is dependent on a relationship to the world, a dynamic which echoes the notion that the moods of individuals interact with an overall *Dasein*. Interestingly enough, Stocking subtitles part four of his essay on the Homeric self 'On Being, and Not Being, in the World,'[40] whereby he likewise draws a connection between the Homeric self and Heidegger's ideas about *Dasein*, although this is not a connection he elaborates on in the essay itself. Stocking does, however, explicitly suggest that there exists a general mood in each Homeric poem when he writes: 'Against the sorrows of the *Iliad*, the sorrows that belong to the failure to be, the *Odyssey* sets joy [...], which is not the joy of being, but the joy of "not-being"—of *becoming*—in the world.'[41] As he uses what seems reminiscent of Heideggerian terminology here, he implies that it is through the interaction with the world, through a sense of 'becoming,' that the protagonists experience and/or produce the poem's mood. This dynamic interaction between self and outside, between the individual and the world, is what Heidegger also envisions in his conception of moods; for Heidegger a mood 'comes neither from "outside" nor from "inside," but arises out of Being-in-the-world, as a way of such Being.'[42] In a similar vein, Homeric moods are inherently determined by both the individual protagonist and his social *Umwelt*, both of them caught in an interaction of mutual influence without which there can be no true Being for the heroes, no *biê* and no *is*.

The importance of the interactions between an individual and his surroundings can be taken further still. In David Konstan's monograph on the emotions of the ancient Greeks, he explains how through Aristotle's treatises on *pathos*, we can reach certain conclusions on the cultural tendencies in classical and archaic Greece to see emotions as 'a reaction rather than an inner state to be disclosed.'[43] An example he uses is

Aristotle's writing on Achilles's resentment against Agamemnon in the *Iliad*, claiming that the ancient hero's anger is a reflex to the pain and harm caused to him by his king, and more specifically, to the public humiliation he undergoes as his war prize Briseis is taken away from him.[44] Quoting Jon Elster, Konstan notes how Aristotle's descriptions of anger use such readings to claim that emotions are 'intensely confrontational, intensely competitive, and intensely public; in fact, much of it involves confrontations and competitions *before* a public.'[45] In the world of archaic and classical Greece, emotions were never merely internal states, but always inherently dependent on the situation and actions of the surrounding community. And it is, as I will propose now, communal moods which shape and describe the mood of individual scenes, and even of the poem itself.

How such communal moods are formed is best shown within the relationship between the Homeric hero or king on the one side,[46] and the people on the other: the *basileus* and the *laos*. Although the *laoi* (pl. *laos*) are seldom individualised or given much space in the Homeric poems, they are a vital part of epic, as Chester Starr notes, since a leader is inherently dependent on his followers.[47] The role of the *laoi* has received little critical attention until Johannes Haubold's pivotal study *Homer's people* analysed the relationship between the hero as an individual and the people as his community, and many of my readings of Homer's 'communal mood' rely on his foundational work.[48] Haubold argues that certain members of the *laoi* like, for instance, a shepherd are always already social composites, 'combining as he does the one (ποιμήν in the singular) with the many (λαοί in the plural) in a close functional relationship.'[49] It is the companions in particular who usually function as a coherent group,[50] whereby their fate serves as an extension or expression of Odysseus's own story. Haubold writes how:

> Their fate is seen not as one aspect of their leader's suffering but as its most salient feature. Without their death, there can be no return, no *Odyssey*. [...] The misfortunes of the collective come to stand for those of its leader; they make his fame, as reported by the odyssean Muse and by himself.[51]

Hereby, the companions serve as reflections of Odysseus's own experiences, emotions and, arguably, the very mood of his *nostos*. They share his longing for home as well as the temptation to simply forget about the past, although those feelings occur at different times in the epic. Odysseus's companions are tempted to give up on their *nostos* most memorably in the episode with the Lotus-Eaters where they consume a flower which induces forgetfulness in their minds and hearts, until Odysseus has to force them to leave the island with him. The situation later reverses when Odysseus stays with the sorceress Circe for a year, seemingly happy to forget about his *nostos* himself, and has to be convinced by his companions to return to his journey.[52] As Haubold describes, in the *Odyssey* any emotion experienced in the group at large, such as 'anger' and 'grief', is caused by the feelings of the leader, describing a reciprocal relationship between individual and community.[53] I suggest further that as much as Odysseus shapes the mood of his followers, the emotional state of his followers further impacts his own emotions and concerns. Odysseus's companions reciprocate his longing for *nostos* as well as his wish to simply forget about the past, and although his wit and wisdom surpass theirs, allowing him to ultimately be the only survivor to reach Ithaca, in some parts of the epic, it is the surrounding mood of companions or otherwise surrounding people which causes Odysseus to adapt his own emotional state and to take action. Both in the examples from Odysseus's wanderings as well as more generally speaking, I propose that the mood of the *laoi* or other social groups is hereby reflective of a more general sense of Being, reflective, one may say, of the poem's sense of *Dasein*. This 'public' mood then influences both Odysseus's—and other heroes'—own feelings of longing for home as well as suppressing their wishful forgetfulness or sorrow in order to allow for the poem to reach its successful conclusion.

II. 'forget the way home': Haunting Memory and Tempting Forgetfulness

I now wish to examine the mood of the poem in more detail, to approach the question of how the dynamic between community and individual influences the *Stimmung* of the poem as it follows the twists and turns of Odysseus's *nostos*. I have already implied that it is both a longing for home as well as a wish for forgetfulness which I see reflected in the companions' narrative arc, which is a reading I now extend to the rest of the poem. One of scenes most clearly mirroring this interweaving of longing and pain, of *nostos* and *algos*, with thoughts of the past, occurs early on in book I when Penelope asks her court-singer Phemius to change his tune, as his songs about Odysseus cause her emotional pain.[54] Although overtly it seems like she is indulging her wish to forget about the past rather than wanting to remember her husband, the language of the scene makes it clear that she is, in fact, longing for the past but also that this longing always involves suffering, as she is reminded of Odysseus's long absence. For instance, the verb ποθέω is used to describe Penelope's longing for her husband, a word which has implications of missing what one once had and has now lost.[55] Her strong reaction to the singer's tale merely emphasises her yearning for the past, for her husband's presence at court, which cannot be replaced by a mere invocation of memories. Keeping the stories about Odysseus alive in a communal setting is nonetheless shown as important, however, and Telemachus's intervention assures that his father's presence is not entirely lost at the Ithacan court.[56] Penelope's temptation to no longer listen to tales of the past complements other scenes of threatened forgetfulness in the epic, most of which occur during Odysseus's wanderings. The scenes in the *Odyssey* which tempt its characters with the sweet oblivion of forgetfulness reference the pain of remembering a past that is, either temporally or spatially, removed. Although even in a modern sense, nostalgia may be said to encapsulate a sense of loss and grieving for a past one wishes to return to, as I continue to analyse the mood of the poem, I want to return to the question of whether all the instances in which characters wish to escape their past either through silencing songs, through drugs, or other means can be said to truly reflect what is nowadays understood by nostalgia; the longing for an absent past and the bittersweet joy of remembering. The function of songs such as Phemius's is a complicated one in the *Odyssey*: at times, song is a source of pain, *penthos*, but elsewhere in the epic as well as overall in Greek hexameter poetry, it is what allows people to forget their pain through recalling eternal glory, *kleos*,[57] which Gregory Nagy names the antidote to *penthos*.[58] Segal suggests that a 'pleasurable forgetting of sorrows' is the expected response to the evocation of memories from the past—and such a reaction does, at least in parts, fit within the parameters of our modern understanding of nostalgia. According to Segal, it is Penelope's rejection of song and Odysseus's tears at recalling Ithaca which are inappropriate responses, the latter of which will be discussed shortly.[59] What I want to suggest here, then, is twofold: first, I echo the suggestion that the *Odyssey* sets a precedent in ancient Greek hexameter poetry for a new set of reactions to songs of the past, and second, I propose that *penthos*, the pain many of the characters experience in response to memories, is not to be equated with nostalgia.

Certainly, reactions to songs are given a lot of space in the poem—as DeJong notes in her commentary, long narratives in the *Odyssey* are usually introduced by an emotional preamble wherein the speaker describes the specific emotions which he aims to evoke by reciting his story.[60] It would thus appear that there are important differences between the effects which individual stories have both on their speaker and the audience. However, as I discussed throughout the last section, a communal mood is also invoked in certain moments of the poem, which then influences the individuals who are immersed in it; and, as I will propose now, such a communal mood is particularly prevalent and has the greatest influence during those scenes featuring songs or other means of recollection. Perhaps the most famous example for the grieving process invited by stories of the past is the song of the bard Demodocus in book VIII. Early on in the book, the Trojan War is called a πῆμα, 'an evil,' using the emotive language which is typical of recollection scenes in the *Odyssey*.[61] Odysseus in particular typically refers to the Trojan War through words with negative connotations: he uses οἶτος to speak of the doom of the Achaeans, whereby in 7 out of 11 cases he further qualifies the word with κακός, 'evil,' although οἶτος already has an inherently negative tone in Homeric epic.[62] The intended effect of Demodocus's storytelling is laid out just before he starts singing; despite speaking about an evil such as the Trojan War, the purpose of the story is to cause delight, and even to 'enchant.'[63] This intended dynamic comes close to describing actual nostalgia in the *Odyssey*, as it acknowledges the delight the process of remembering can bring. The actual effect of the storytelling, however, is defined by Odysseus's own memories, which do not cause nostalgic longing for the hero but instead cause him to weep with sorrow upon his recollections. It is the evocation of the living memory of the Trojan War, an evil of the past, which causes Odysseus pain upon remembering.

There exists an important communal dimension to this scene: Hartog convincingly suggests that Odysseus weeps because the bard speaks of him in the third person, as though he were already dead—and, indeed, to the other listeners in the court it is exceedingly likely that Odysseus has died in the ten years since the events that are described, since no one knows where he is and he is unable to reveal himself to them.[64] Odysseus is thus removed not only from his past self, but also from his past glory, the *kleos* he accrued through his vital role in conquering Troy. As Hartog describes, the space Odysseus has travelled through on his wanderings is *aklees*, devoid of glory, where no songs are sung about his deeds, so he has been unable to collect any more fame through his travels by the time he reaches Scheria.[65] Realising that due to his absence he is no longer directly linked to the hero from the tales—and that, thus, he may no longer be able to return home as the rightful king of Ithaca— triggers memories that cause Odysseus pain through his disassociation from them. As Zachary Biles argues,

> [f]or the living at least immortalising *kleos* carries with it a certain measure of loss. In the process of securing his own homecoming, Odysseus must confront the old songs of Troy and establish a theme that will bring him closer to the fulfilment of his journey.[66]

He has to confound his new identity as a survivor, as the wandering traveller, with his old role of the hero at Troy if he wants to recover his *kleos*, as well as complete his return to his home in Ithaca where his status of king is still associated with this glory. It is thereby the perspective of the community on his current persona which causes his emotional shift to grief; as his role and position in the public sphere has descended from that of an epic hero to that of a nameless traveller. Like Achilles in the *Iliad*, his mood shifts upon being confronted with an open indignity— even if, in the *Odyssey*, this is entirely unintended by those surrounding the hero. Overall, there is a kind of mixture between nostalgic longing and fear of the past interwoven into book VIII. On the one hand, Odysseus longs for the status of his past, which is inherently connected to the possibility of his *nostos*, but on the other hand, the memories of the past are emotively designated 'evil,' memories Odysseus is inherently tempted to avoid. As previously suggested, then, I uphold that while there are elements of nostalgia in the *Odyssey*, the layers of connotations in the poem are more complex than could be described merely by this term. Menelaus is amongst the veterans who suffer most from remembering the Trojan War; although he is described as often dwelling on the past, this reminiscence only brings him sadness.[67]

Both the Spartan king and the *laoi* at his court, the veterans of the Trojan War, then speak of Troy only with reluctance.[68] Menelaus's suffering and Telemachus's simultaneous insistence on information about his father's past lay the groundwork for one of the most interesting scenes in the poem, which breaks with the seemingly established dynamic of seeing forgetfulness as inherently threatening and remembrance as positive—an assumption which builds the foundation for seeing the *Odyssey* as purely nostalgic. When Telemachus visits the court of the Greek king, the audience realises that despite his wealth and accrued fame, Menelaus is unable to forget either the comrades that fell on his behalf, or the betrayal of his own wife, Helen, although he does not mention the latter explicitly. Still, Mihoko Suzuki suggests that, in fact, the most important event in his past was Helen's treason, since now his identity is reduced to that of the betrayed husband: 'Menelaus cannot be content, since he is unable to refrain from looking backward to the traumatic disruption of his domestic peace and to the war that came in its wake.'[69] Such an obsession with the past, however, is not portrayed as healthy or sustainable in the epic, and thus requires intervention. It is, in fact, Helen herself who drugs Menelaus and the men at his court with a memory drug imported from Egypt which makes them forget the pain associated with their past and allows them to talk openly about the events Telemachus is interested in. As Justine McConnell notes, this drug is close in effect to the lotus flower which threatens to make Odysseus and his companions fully forget about their journey home.[70] Its effects are described as a 'madness [...] bestowed' on the Greeks, invoking connotations of external forces which leave the men powerless.[71] Nevertheless, a significant difference between this drug and the lotus flower lies in its link to Egypt: Egyptian culture and medicine are throughout this scene held up as superior and more advanced than the Greeks', implying that the drug's effects are not necessarily negative but may actually be helpful.[72] DeJong likewise argues that

> [f]or once in the *Odyssey* forgetfulness is seen in a positive light [...] all those crying in 183–6 need this drug [...] but it seems that Helen and Menelaus, who are still in the grip of their past, need them most.[73]

Likewise, it is worth remembering that the effects of this drug are only temporary, providing transient relief rather than the all-consuming oblivion that was promised by the lotus flower.[74]

Despite the dangers the drug may yield, it does seem that the partial forgetting allowed by the scene ultimately yields positive consequences: Telemachus finally gains more knowledge of his father, which is the reason he visited the court of Menelaus in the first place.[75] The successful *Telemacheia*[76] ultimately facilitates Odysseus's own *nostos*, whereby the temporary forgetting allowed to Menelaus directly prefigures the success of Telemachus's—and Odysseus's—journey. The Greek warriors, still haunted by the painful memories of the Trojan War, also finally gain an outlet for their past grievances through recounting and listening to stories that soothe their pain and trauma.[77] It is significant that this shift in Menelaus's and the veterans' perspective on the past occurs, once more, in a communal setting, in which the king's mood comes to reflect that of his former war companions and vice versa—and where even Telemachus is influenced by the shift in this dynamic, so that he is able to painlessly recall memories of his father, a moment which possibly foreshadows their later reunion in book XVI. It is then the mood of their social surrounding, of the *laoi*, which comes to stand in a reciprocal relationship with the scene's main characters, Menelaus and Telemachus, and thus allows for the success of the *Telemacheia*, which in itself is necessary for the success of Odysseus's *nostos*. Social remembrance creating an atmosphere which affects the characters' emotions in a given scene, I argue, shapes what critics have identified as the poem's overall mood, the sense of *Dasein* in its imaginative *Welt*.

In the *Odyssey*, forgetting can both create pleasure as well as produce danger. The characters of the poem are constantly at risk both of oblivion as well as of losing themselves in their memories and being overcome by longing or regret for the past. As in Homer—and in Heidegger—the past is essential to one's sense of being, memory as well as forgetting are processes which need to influence the hero to accommodate his growth and achievements. Due to these positive effects of forgetfulness particularly outlined in book IV, I must disagree with Austin, who writes that '[f]orgetfulness is not magic in the *Odyssey*. It is the greatest calamity short of death; in fact, it is death.'[78] I concede on the large importance Austin places on memory, as well as the initially threatening nature of forgetfulness, which is most likely pronounced even further through the context of the *Odyssey* describing and recounted in an oral society. Still, the *Odyssey*'s relationship to the past and the various ways characters engage with it is more complex than the absolute veneration of remembrance and the presentation of forgetfulness as purely threatening.[79]

Nostalgia has come to be understood as a mood which relies on such reverence of the one's memories, and which rejects oblivion as an inherent threat to its existence. As noted in the introduction, however, nostalgia has yet another dimension, that of a 'structure of internal feeling,' one largely shaped by personal and subjective emotions. In contrast to this, my analysis has emphasised the communal element of the mood which permeates Homer's *Odyssey*, whereby its role has to be understood as implicitly connected to the sociopolitical *Umwelt* the poem sets up. Therein, the memories recounted by many of the heroes and bards in social settings not only influence the mood of the scene—while the heroes are, in turn, influenced by those voices around them—but this reciprocal process also serves to forge a kind of communal memory. As mentioned previously, emotions, mood, and affect have often been examined as individual-level phenomena, ones that originate purely from a subjective state of mind. Research on communal moods originated largely in Émile Durkheim's 1912 study *The Elementary Forms of the Religious Life*, which has prompted investigations of the influence of group affect on collective emotions and atmospheres. Prompted also by Heidegger's foundational work on mood, subsequent studies in philosophy, sociology, psychology, and even neuroscience have proceeded to give more attention to the interpersonal roles which emotions can play, and the ways in which affect is related to social interactions.[80] A recent study conducted by Sigal Bararde and Donald E. Gibson, for instance, shows 'clear evidence that group affect has significant consequences on groups as a whole and on the individuals within them.'[81] In the *Odyssey* a group's affective state, that is the emotions and general atmosphere which the poet conveys through the poem's language and descriptions, shapes the mood of certain scenes, and therein also the individuals' emotions who come into contact with it. This dynamic Bararde and Gibson describe echoes how the Greeks perceived emotions as not only external but also as influenced by one's surroundings and social context. Particularly scenes of recollection, songs performed by bards or Odysseus himself, have a strong impact on the collective mood, a dynamic interesting to observe through recent approaches such as Louis van den Hengel's which view '[r]eenactment [...] as an embodied mode of collective or social memory,' as performative modes profoundly shaped by affect.[82] Performative recollection thereby becomes a social activity which stands in a reciprocal relationship with the communal mood of its setting.[83] As the listeners become attuned to the singer's tale, certain attitudes to what is being recollected become homogeneous across their group, as is, for instance, the case when Penelope and Odysseus's sorrow transforms expected pleasant recollections into a pervasive mood shaped by sadness and grief. This attunement process helps to formulate an overall mood not only within individual scenes but within the *Odyssey* as a whole, with the poem largely made up of recollection scenes and journeys into the past, and thereby fundamentally tied to the question of how to approach one's memories. This is not to suggest that modern research on collective emotions can be neatly applied to a poem from a fundamentally different time and cultural context. At the same time, however, recent approaches to the social aspects of mood, both from philosophy and the social sciences, seem to confirm that the Greeks' conception of emotions as constituted by both individual and social influences was grounded in an important understanding of affect, and this dyamic between individual and community deserves more attention when analysing their artistic expressions.

III. 'I should not have sorrowed so over him dying': 'Belated' Attunement in the *Odyssey*

It is a certain past-oriented mood which infuses the *Odyssey*, creating a *Stimmung* which both its hero and its people are attuned to, but this mood is not sufficiently encapsulated by 'nostalgia' alone. It is a mood which can cause both joy and sorrow upon invoking memories of the past, a mood often dependent on the listener, emphasising the subjective component Heidegger names as partially constitutive of mood in relation to the world. At the same time, this *Stimmung* takes on a particularly strong and important role in communal settings, whereby the hero's emotions stand in a reciprocal relationship with those of the people around him. In situations when the hero's pain threatens to drive him off course or into despair, this communal dynamic can even allow for the continuation of Odysseus's *nostos*, the ultimate destination of the poetic narrative. It is possible that with an epic which is both so far removed from our own cultural context and which, furthermore, features so many different characters, some of which have had very different experiences and motives, a single term cannot possibly encapsulate the complexities of the epic's mood. Perhaps, like Heidegger, we need to continually search for new terminology in order to gather a sense of the shifting realities of the *Odyssey*'s *Dasein*.[84] What this chapter has shown, however, is that a lasting focus on the past continues to impact the characters' emotions, both on an individual level and through scenes of the poem which invoke a communal mood. Thus, perhaps a good starting point to approach the epic's mood is to retrace our steps to the sense of 'becoming' in the *Odyssey*, the constant journey from past to present—encapsulated, perhaps best, by the term 'belated,' used prominently by Jonathan Burgess. For Burgess, the hero's journey is constantly delayed as Odysseus continues to be informed of travels which precede his own, whether it be by Circe, the shade of Herakles in the Underworld, or the songs of bards singing of already completed *nostoi*.[85] The scene with Demodocus is perhaps the most evident of this pattern as therein Odysseus not only discovers new information which has already been long known to those around him, but the poem's language also implies a more general sense of belatedness. DeJong notes how the narrator's use of τότε in an absolute sense, 'at that time (in the past)' permits not only for the present to be contrasted with the past of the Trojan War but more generally for the *Odyssey* to meta-poetically portray itself as the last in a long line of song.[86] It is this overall sense of being continuously influenced by and drawn to the past that is interwoven into the characters' Being-in-the-world, and therefore, into the mood of Homer's second epic. Whether this sense of belatedness causes a longing nostalgia or feelings of sorrow and haunting is, as I have shown, dependent on both the individual characters and the communal mood within a certain scene; a dynamic which is, in itself, dependent on the (belated) *Dasein* all characters are and become attuned to. Of course, such parallels between Homer and Heideggerian philosophy are by no means exact, but they have helped to emphasise the importance of both the individual and the communal component of the poem's mood, and to develop the somewhat reductive notion of nostalgia into an approach which has the potential to more deeply and comprehensively encapsulate the *Stimmung* of the *Odyssey*.

Notes

1 Homer, *The Odyssey*, trans. Richmond Lattimore, 2nd edition (New York et al.: Harper Perennial Classics, 2007), *V.150–.158*.
2 Donald Lateiner, 'Affect Displays in the Epic Poetry of Homer, Vergil, and Ovid,' in *Advances in Nonverbal Communication: Sociocultural, Clinical, Aesthetic and Literary Perspectives*, ed. by Fernando Poyatos (Amsterdam; Philadelphia, PA: John Benjamins Publishing Company, 1992), pp. 255–69 (p. 265). An expanded study of non-verbal behaviour in both Homeric epics can be found in his monograph *Sardonic Smile: Nonverbal Behavior in Homeric Epic* (Ann Arbor: The University of Michigan Press, 1998).
3 Samuel Eliot Bassett, *The Poetry of Homer*, New Edition (Lanham, MD; Boulder, CO; New York; Oxford: Lexington Books, [1928]2003), comp. especially pp. 27, 149ff. Other works to touch on the mood of epic include: Thomas Munro's, 'The Failure Story: A Study of Contemporary Pessimism,' *The Journal of Aesthetics and Art Criticism*, 17(2), 1958, pp. 143–68 which specifically discusses failure as a kind of mood in epic poetry (145ff.); Beata Agrell, 'Consolation of Literature as Rhetorical Tradition: Issues and Examples,' *LIR*, 4, 2015, pp. 10–35, which touches on suffering and consolation as emotional evoked in the participants of rituals; George Kurman, 'Ecphrasis in Epic Poetry,' *Comparative Literature*, 26(1), 1974, pp. 1–13, which discusses ecphrasis as a way to create resonances with the epic poem's mood.
4 François Hartog, *Memories of Odysseus: Frontier Tales from Ancient Greece* (Edinburgh: Edinburgh University Press, 2001), pp. 18, 21.
5 Although it is mostly the *Odyssey* that has been associated with nostalgia, there exists some research on nostalgia in other works of Greek literature, theatre, and epic. An example of this is Gary S. Melzer's *Euripides and the Poetics of Nostalgia* (Cambridge: Cambridge University Press, 2006).
6 Comp. Erica Hepper, Timothy S. Ritchie, Constantine Sedikides, and Tim Wildschut, 'Odyssey's End: Lay Conceptions of Nostalgia Reflect Its Original Homeric Meaning,' *Emotion*, 12, 2012, pp. 102–19 (p. 103); Jeff Malpas, 'Philosophy's Nostalgia,' in *Philosophy's Moods: The Affective Grounds of Thinking*, ed. by Hagi Kenaan and Ilit Ferber (Heidelberg; London; New York: Springer, 2011), pp. 87–105 (pp. 87–8). The concept of nostalgia truly

entered the *Sprachgebrauch* in the seventeenth century in the form of a med-
ical ailment which affected the 'fibers of the middle brain' (Johannes Hofer,
'Medical Dissertation on Nostalgia' (1688), *Bulletin of the Institute of the
History of Medicine* (1934), pp. 376–91 (p. 384); qtd. in David Lowenthal,
The Past is a Foreign Country – Revisited (Cambridge: Cambridge University
Press, 2015), p. 46). Meanwhile, with reference to the aforementioned 2008
study by Sedikides, Wildschut, Arndt, and Routledge, critics Hepper, Ritchie,
Sedikides, and Wildschut suggest that while 'nostalgia serves vital psychologi-
cal functions' (p. 3), today its use has transcended purely medical applications.

7 Malpas, 'Philosophy's Nostalgia', p. 90. Malpas also quotes the historian
Peter Fritzsche on the subject:

> nostalgia is a fundamentally modern phenomenon because it depended
> on the notion of historical process as the continual production of the
> new [...] it was in the middle of the nineteenth century that nostalgia
> found a secure place in household vocabularies, its general usage made
> tenable by the massive displacing operations of industrialization and ur-
> banization, which also standardized its meaning as a vague, collective
> longing for a bygone time rather than an individual desire to return to a
> particular place. Nostalgia retains this general and temporal meaning; it
> distils the "dispirit of the age".
>
> (Qtd. in Ibid., p. 90)

8 Tammy Clewell, 'Past "Perfect" and Present "Tense,"' in *Modernism and
Nostalgia: Bodies, Locations, Aesthetics* (New York; Basingstoke: Palgrave
Macmillan, 2013), pp. 1–25 (p. 5).

9 This is not to suggest, of course, that the social component of nostalgia has
never been studied, or that nostalgia is inherently a subjective and private
emotion, only that the development of the term in modernity has tended
to privilege a focus on the internal instead of foregrounding a communal
dimension. As I will elaborate later on in the chapter, this is one of the reasons I deem the term unhelpful to describe the mood of the *Odyssey*, as the
communal aspect of the emotions which are developed in the poem is one
which, I argue, needs to be foregrounded more.

10 Lowenthal, *The Past is a Foreign Country – Revisited*, p. 43.

11 Austin, 'Homeric Nostalgia,' *Yale Review*, 98, 2010, pp. 37–64 (p. 37).

12 Ibid., p. 37.

13 David Konstan, *The Emotions of the Ancient Greeks: Studies in Aristotle and Classical Literature* (London; Toronto: University of Toronto Press,
2006), pp. 3–5.

14 At this point, I would like to draw a distinction between a mood and a
mode, as I believe Homer sets up a certain mood in the *Odyssey* through
his a 'commodified style or commodified set of practices' (Michael Pickering
and Emily Keightley, 'The Modalities of Nostalgia,' *Current Sociology*, 54,
2006, pp. 919–41 (p. 932)), a mood constituted through a mode, which is
the use of events and objects that continuously recall the past to the characters as well as the audience. I thus believe that through using certain modes,
Homer sets up this mood of simultaneous fear of, and longing for, the past,
rather than through elaborations on the characters' inner lives. It is through
the characters' actions and reactions to events that the audience learns about
their preoccupation with the past rather than through introspective scenes.

15 Hans Ulrich Gumbrecht, *Atmosphere, Mood, Stimmung* (Stanford, CA:
Stanford University Press, 2012), p. 14. Gumbrecht also warns against 're-
constructing or analyzing [the] historical or cultural genesis [of *Stimmungen*]'

(p. 14). In the middle part of this chapter, I will draw on some research on the structures of emotions in archaic Greece, but as they were formulated within Aristotle's writings on the *Iliad*, the first Homeric epic, they are too significant for a reading of the *Odyssey* to not be included.

16 'Alle Gefühle bezeichne ich, sofern sie weit sind, und weil sie als Atmosphären sämtlich weit sind, als Stimmungen, als reine Stimmungen aber insofern, als sie nichts als weit (d.h. frei von Richtungen) sind. Gefühle als Atmosphären, die von Richtungen oder Vektoren durchzogen sind, nenne ich Erregungen, mit einem Fremdwort könnte man auch von >Emotionen< sprechen' (Hermann Schmitz, *Der Leib, der Raum und die Gefühle* (Ostfildern 1998), pp. 63f.; qtd. in David E. Wellbery *Ästhetische Grundbegriffe* (Stuttgart; Weimar: J.B. Metzler, 2003), p. 730). Mikkel Bille, Peter Bjerregaard, and Tim Flohr Sørensen provide a comprehensive summary of various approaches to atmospheres in their article 'Staging Atmospheres: Materiality, Culture, and the Texture of the In-between,' *Emotion, Space and Society*, 15 (2015), pp. 31–38 (comp. particularly pp. 34ff.). Therein, they emphasise that in its conceptual properties, mood is not entirely synonymous with atmosphere or affect (p. 35), but since this chapter largely discusses the mood of the *Odyssey* through its atmosphere, I here rely on the connection Wellbery draws between the two.

17 Rita Felski and Susan Fraiman, 'Introduction,' *New Literary History*, 43(3), 2012, pp. v–xii (p. vi).

18 I need to disclaim here that I am not arguing for a straightforward application of a twentieth-century philosophy to the Greek poem. Heidegger himself believed that philosophy can only work in its own time; he writes 'Die Philosophie setzt am heute an,' roughly translatable as 'philosophy addresses the present.' Rather, through this reading I want to identify certain commonalities between Heidegger's and the *Odyssey's* conceptions of mood to underline certain elements I deem essential to Homer's conception of his epic's tone and themes, and, in part, to suggest that Heidegger's *Stimmung* may provide a gateway for modern readers to better understand how the *Odyssey's* mood is constructed.

19 Andreas Elpidorou and Lauren Freeman, 'Affectivity in Heidegger I: Moods and Emotions in Being and Time,' *Philosophy Compass*, 10(10), 2015, pp. 661–71 (pp. 661–4).

20 Heidegger used the example of the *Katheder* in his early lectures in Freiburg. The example is discussed, for instance, in Georg Imdahl, *Das Leben Verstehen: Heideggers formal anzeigende Hermeneutik in den frühen Freiburger Vorlesungen (1919–1923)* (Würzburg: Königshausen & Neumann, 1997), p. 54.

21 Magda King, *A Guide to Heidegger's 'Being and Time'* ed. by John Llewelyn (Albany: State University of New York Press, 2001), pp. 69–70; emphasis in original.

22 Stephen Mulhall, 'Can There Be an Epistemology of Moods?' *Royal Institute of Philosophy Supplement*, 41, 1996, pp. 191–210 (p. 193).

23 Ibid., p. 289. Heidegger also gives his *Stimmungen* a temporal dimension, arguing that moods are closely linked to an experience of the past (Wayne J. Froman, 'Attentiveness: A Phenomenological Study of the Relation of Memory to Mood,' in *Philosophy's Moods: The Affective Grounds of Thinking*, ed. by Hagi Kenaan and Ilit Ferber (Heidelberg; London; New York: Springer, 2011), pp. 27–39 (p. 31). He claims that every mood implicitly involves an engagement with the past, present and future, arguing that because one is always looking back to the past from the perspective of

the future, one is always 'in the process of having-been' (Ibid., p. 31). This link Heidegger draws up between moods and one's relationship to the past could be used to read Odysseus's and the other characters' obsession with the past and the lasting importance of the Trojan war for the events of the poem.

24 Comp. 'Philosophy's Nostalgia,' pp. 93, 95.

25 Seth J. Gillihan, Jennifer Kessler, and Martha J. Farah, 'Memories Affect Mood: Evidence from Covert Experimental Assignment to Positive, Neutral, and Negative Memory Recall,' *Acta Psychologica*, 125 (2007), pp. 144–54 (p. 145).

26 It is interesting to note that Jonas Grethlein links the exchange of objects and gifts between heroes to a temporal dimension set up in the Homeric epics, focussed on remembering certain events of the past. He notes that these instances are notably more frequent in the *Odyssey* than the *Iliad*, something I argue may imply that there is a larger focus on the past in Homer's latter epic ('Memory and Material Objects in the *Iliad* and the *Odyssey*,' *The Journal of Hellenic Studies*, 128, 2008, pp. 27–51 (p. 37)).

27 Charles Segal, *Singers, Heroes, and Gods* (Ithaca, NY; London: Cornell University Press, 1994), p. 12.

28 Richard Buxton, 'Similes and Other Likenesses,' in *The Cambridge Companion to Homer*, ed. by Robert Louis Fowler (Cambridge: Cambridge University Press, 2004), pp. 139–56 (p. 149).

29 Mulhall, 'Can There Be an Epistemology of Moods?', p. 194.

30 The Homeric bard is thereby set apart from the later, more individualised and independent poetics of archaic lyric, exemplified by Simonides and Pindar (Segal, *'Singers, Heroes, and Gods'* p. 141).

31 John Miles Foley, '"Reading" Homer through Oral Tradition,' *College Literature*, 34(2), 2007, pp. 1–28 (p. 27). Also comp.: Matthew Clark, 'Formulas, Metre and Type-Scenes,' *The Cambridge Companion to Homer*, ed. by Robert Fowler (Cambridge: Cambridge University Press, 2004), pp. 117–38 (p. 117); Johannes Haubold, *Homer's People* (Cambridge: Cambridge University Press, 2000), p. 72; Chester G. Starr, *Individual and Community: The Rise of the Polis, 800-500 B.C.* (Oxford: Oxford University Press, 1986), p. 17.

32 John Miles Foley, *Homer's Traditional Art* (University Park: Pennsylvania State University Press, 1999), p. 13.

33 William Scott, *The Oral Nature of the Homeric Simile* (Leiden: Brill, 1974), p. 164. Joseph Russo and Bennett Simon also discuss the Homeric use of similes as part of a replacement of explicit descriptions of mental processes, using the example of the simile which compares Penelope to a lion as a way to portray general themes of threat, encroaching helplessness, and defensive hostility ('Homeric Psychology and the Oral Epic Tradition,' *Journal of the History of Ideas*, 29, 1968, pp. 483–98 (pp. 487–8)).

34 Ibid., pp. 491–92, 97.

35 Gumbrecht, *Atmosphere, Mood, Stimmung*, p. 7.

36 Russo and Simon, 'Homeric Psychology and the Oral Epic Tradition,' p. 487.

37 Segal, *Singers, Heroes, and Gods*, pp. 62–3.

38 Jan Söffner, 'On Nostalgia (and Homer),' in *Habitus in Habitat I: Emotion and Motion*, ed. by Sabine Flach, Daniel Margulies, and Jan Söffner (Bern: Peter Lang AG, 2010), pp. 81–94 (p. 85).

39 '"Res Agens": Towards an Ontology of the Homeric Self,' *College Literature*, 34(2), 2007, pp. 56–84 (p. 61). Stocking gives as an example the case of Achilles who, he argues, needs to engage with the world in order to exist

as himself, while at the same time his interaction with the world limits his prowess as a hero and thus his sense of self (p. 63).

40 Ibid., p. 62.

41 Ibid., p. 64. By 'not-being' he refers to Odysseus's unstable identity which he keeps having to change according to which situation he finds himself in.

42 *Being and Time*, p. 176, transl. by John Macquarrie and Edward Robinson (Oxford: Basil Blackwell, 1962). Matthew Ratcliffe elaborates on this statement further, describing how for Heidegger moods are 'not experienced as states of mind possessed by psychological subjects, and [...] we do not experience moods as "out there" in the world either. Moods constitute a sense of being part of a world that is pre-subjective and pre-objective' (Matthew Ratcliffe, 'Why Mood Matters,' in *The Cambridge Companion to Heidegger's Being and Time*, ed. by Mark A. Wrathall (Cambridge University Press, 2013), pp. 157–76 (p. 157)).

43 David Konstan, *The Emotions of the Ancient Greeks: Studies in Aristotle and Greek Literature* (Toronto et al.: Toronto University Press, 2006), p. 31. It is worth noting that most of the examples Konstan uses are not from Aristotle's writings on the Homeric epics, but they are still used and discussed at several points.

44 Ibid., p. 75.

45 Jon Elster, *Alchemies of the Mind: Rationality and the Emotions* (Cambridge: Cambridge University Press, 1999), p. 75, my emphasis; qtd. in Konstan, p. 75.

46 The ancient Greek term for hero is ἥρως. In the *Odyssey*, the figure of the king and the hero are one and the same, embodied in Odysseus as the poem's primary protagonist.

47 Starr, *Individual and Community*, p. 23. Starr argues that this is a reflection of Greek society before 700 BCE; the communities of Greece must 'be seen as possessing a fundamental unity' if one is to explain the emergence of the *polis* (p. 32).

48 In his book, Haubold draws important distinctions between the role of the *laoi* in the *Iliad* and the *Odyssey* which are worth taking note of but are not relevant for the point I make in this chapter. For instance, a dynamic which exists much stronger in the *Iliad* than it does in the second Homeric poem is the tension between 'singing the fame of some (κλέα ἀνδρῶν) and deploring the fate of others (ὤλεσε λαόν)' which is epitomised by Achilles allowing his fellow Greeks to die for the sake of his own fame (*Homer's People*, p. 98).

49 Ibid., p. 10.

50 This is despite the fact that while the Greek for 'people' always refers to a group, Haubold notes how the term for companions always draws attention to the individual (Ibid., p. 129).

51 Ibid., pp. 134–5. In his monograph, Haubold does draw a distinction between the companions and the *laoi*, which is important to acknowledge but ultimately not relevant for the more general argument on communal mood I am drawing out here. For Haubold's explanation on this distinction, comp. Ibid., pp. 134–5ff.

52 Of course his companions are not reflective of Odysseus's feelings for the entirety of the epic as his superior self-control and intellect allow him to survive where they could not. Haubold elaborates at large how unlike in the *Iliad*, Odysseus does not pay for the collective disaster around him but instead the perishing of his companions ultimately constitutes his fame (Ibid., p. 133).

53 Ibid., p. 130. The words Haubald translates as anger and grief are χόλος and ἄχος, respectively.

54 *Odyssey*, pp. 1.336–.344.

55 *Odyssey*, I.115–.117; Irene DeJong, *A Narratological Commentary on the 'Odyssey'* (Cambridge; New York: Cambridge University Press, 2001), p. 37.

56 Parallels to the story of Agamemnon's death throughout the *Odyssey* further underline the importance of Phemius's song, since by comparison at Clytemnestra's court there were no singers reminding her about her husband, which is an absence that could be related to her ensuing adultery.

57 *kleos* encapsulates a sense of eternal glory, of being forever remembered in song.

58 Hilary Mackie, 'Song and Storytelling: An Odyssean Perspective,' *Transactions of the American Philological Association*, 127, 1997, pp. 77–95 (p. 82). Mackie takes Hesiod's *Theogony* as an example for this when she writes:

> Among the programmatic statements about song in the proem to Hesiod's *Theogony*, we find the statement that the Muses' song makes the person afflicted with 'grief in a newly-troubled heart' (p. 98) ... 'forget (ἐπιλήθεται, p. 102) and give no thought to his cares.' The poetry of the Muses brings 'forgetfulness' (λησμοσύνην, p. 55) of pain.

59 Segal, *Singers, Heroes, and Gods*, p. 134.

60 DeJong, *A Narratological Commentary on the 'Odyssey'*, p. 75. In fact, De-Jong argues that there is only one case in the *Odyssey* in which the speaker is caused joy by repeating stories about the past (Ibid., p. 75).

61 Ibid., p. 197.

62 Ibid., p. 251.

63 Ibid., p. 197. DeJong uses 'delight' to translate τέρπειν/ εσθαι and 'enchant' for θέλγειν and κηληθμός.

64 Hartog, *Memories of Odysseus*, p. 18. Zachary Biles adds: 'In Odysseus's case, Demodocus' ability to retell the events of his life with such accuracy effectively drives a wedge between the hero and his past. As a subject of song Odysseus loses some control over his own person' ('Perils of Song in Homer's "Odyssey,"' *Phoenix*, 57, 2003, pp. 191–208 (p. 203)).

65 Ibid., p. 28.

66 Ibid., pp. 199–200.

67 Comp. 3.103–.117; DeJong, *A Narratological Commentary on the 'Odyssey'*, p. 94.

68 Comp. Menelaus in 4.76–.112.; Odysseus in 8.83–.92, 489–90, 521–31nn.; Achilles in 11.482–.491 and 24.27; and Agamemnon in 24.95–.97 (DeJong, *A Narratological Commentary on the 'Odyssey'*, p. 75–6.).

69 Mihoko Suzuki, *Metamorphoses of Helen: Authority, Difference, and the Epic* (Ithaca, NY; London: Cornell University Press, 1989), p. 64; qtd. in Andrea Doyle, '"Unhappily Ever After?": The Problem of Helen in *Odyssey* 4', *Akroterion*, 55, 2010, pp. 1–18 (p. 4).

70 Justine McConnell, *Black Odysseys: The Homeric 'Odyssey' in the African Diaspora since 1939* (Oxford: Oxford University Press, 2013), p. 33.

71 *Odyssey*, IV.261–.262.

72 McConnell, *Black Odysseys*, p. 33.

73 DeJong, *A Narratological Commentary on the 'Odyssey'*, pp. 100–1. Helen's own presentation in this scene is as notably ambiguous. Through her inducement of a form of forgetfulness she is directly contrasted to her relative Penelope, Odysseus's wife, who serves as a beacon of memory as she swears to keep her husband's memory alive even if she is forced to remarry (*Odyssey*, XXI.75–.79). Using Egyptian magic, Helen transgresses the boundaries of mortals as she takes on the role of a sorceress, linking her to other characters like Circe and Calypso, who tempt Odysseus to forget his *nostos* and to stay with them. The temptations of their sorcery deliberately oppose

the strong association inherent to the Homeric epics between women and memory, as female characters are usually considered to be responsible for keeping the memories of heroic warriors alive. This can be seen in particular with Briseis's lament for Patroklos, with Andromache, Hekabe and Helen's lamentations for Hektor in the *Iliad*, and, of course, Penelope throughout the *Odyssey* (For more information on the link between female lamentation and memory, compare Casey Dué, *The Captive Woman's Lament in Greek Tragedy* (Austin: University of Texas Press, 2006)). Here, however, Helen seems to take on a role which allows her to achieve the opposite effect, forgetfulness, by which she undermines her supposed function of remembering the deeds of the veterans around her, and acquires a sense of agency unique to mortal women in the Homeric epics.

74 As Doyle points out, there exists a certain amount of ambiguity around the question of whether the stories Helen wants the warriors to recount in their moment of emotional forgetfulness are entirely truthful: Helen employs the term μύθοις, which although can be applied to any kind of speech, is primarily associated with legends and myths, 'and thus sits diametrically opposed to λόγος (verbal account or word) which implies truth or historical veracity' ('Unhappily Ever After?', pp. 10–1.). We can also not be entirely sure about Helen's motivation in this scene; while it could be an act of kindness to the warriors to still their painful memories, it could also be her attempt to shape their perception of her own questionable role in the *Iliad*, a theory that gains more credibility through the fact that the tale she recounts is one in which she was trying to help the Greek invaders, an account whose veracity is questioned by Menelaus himself (*Odyssey*, IV.271–.279). Menelaus here contrasts her account of trying to help the Greeks, specifically Odysseus, with his own tale of how she tried to lure the Greek soldiers out of the Trojan horse by imitating the voices of their wives.

75 Austin argues that Helen's memory drug 'induces not forgetfulness but "forgetfulness of evils." Like a strong sedative, it removes the pain but keeps the memory intact' ('Homeric Nostalgia,' p. 52.). I believe that he is assuming too much when he suggests that the memories that are recounted afterwards are 'intact': first, as I mentioned above, the Greek word Helen uses for these stories is ambiguous in regards to the truth value of these tales. Second, the stories recounted in this section were not included in the *Iliad*, leaving it ambiguous to the audience whether they would have been correct, something I believe may have been a deliberate move of the composer(s) to leave the question open of whether or not the stories are entirely truthful. Likewise, we must question whether memories without the emotions associated with them can still be considered to be 'accurate' or, at least, the same memories they were before the removal of an arguably key part or recollection itself.

76 *Telemacheia*: The journey of Telemachus's adolescence and later development into adulthood.

77 While here the process of remembering the past comes to lose its negative connotations and becomes helpful for the veterans in overcoming their war trauma, their remembrance should not be equated with a nostalgic longing to return to their time in the war.

78 Austin, 'Homeric Nostalgia,' p. 52.

79 In fact, there is one more scene which complicates this dichotomy between memory and forgetfulness further, and this is the encounter which the Sirens, a scene which introduces the possibility of threatening knowledge from both the past and the future. The Sirens' song both functionally and linguistically recalls the heroic songs of bards like Phemius and Demodocus; it enchants (θέλγουσιν: 40, 44) and provides delight (τερπόμενος/ τερψάμενος: 52, 188) (DeJong, *A Narratological Commentary on the 'Odyssey'*, p. 298).

The Sirens promise Odysseus to sing about his past and thereby about his heroic status in the Trojan War as well as the future, offering a kind of limitless knowledge otherwise only accessible through invocations of the Muse. Nugent describes how especially for Odysseus, a man of natural curiosity, the Sirens' offer would be irresistibly tempting, and indeed, his heart is described as wanting to listen (12.191–.193; Pauline Nugent, 'The Sound of Sirens; *Odyssey*, 12.184–.192,' *College Literature*, 35(4), 2008, pp. 45–54 (p. 49)). The knowledge and pleasure they offer, however, necessitate a complete detachment from the human community as well as the realm of the living, as Odysseus would have to jump into the *aklees* sea in order to listen to their song permanently, separated from his companions and unable to fulfill his *nostos*. It is a transcendent knowledge of both future and past they offer but, as Segal notes, it necessitates the obliteration of his very self (p. 134). Although it is here both knowledge about the future and the past that is offered, it is still overtly portrayed as a danger which Odysseus needs to avoid in order to finish his quest.

80 Gavin Brent Sullivan, 'Collective Emotions,' *Social and Personality Psychology Compass*, 9(8), 2015, pp. 383–93 (p. 383 ff.).

81 Sigal Bararde and Donald E. Gibson, 'Group Affect,' *Current Directions in Psychological Science*, 21(2), 2012, pp. 119–23 (p. 121).

82 Louis van den Hengel, 'Archives of Affect' in *Materializing Memory in Art and Popular Culture*, ed. by László Munteán, Liedeke Plate, and Anneke Smelik (New York; Abingdon: Routledge, 2017), pp. 125–243 (p. 135).

83 Comp. Stephen D. Brown and Paula Reavey, *Vital Memory and Affect: Living with a Difficult Past* (New York: Routledge, 2015), esp. pp. 32, 41–2, 137ff.

84 In line with Modern philosophical thought, Heidegger realises the inseparability of his philosophy from language but nonetheless mistrusts its ability to convey true meaning. He thus wishes to create the possibility of an authentic language through language criticism. See Pelagia Goulimari, *Literary Criticism and Theory: From Plato to Postcolonialism* (London; New York: Routledge, 2015), p. 257.

85 Jonathan S. Burgess, 'Belatedness in the Travels of Odysseus,' *Homeric Contexts*, ed. by Franco Montanari, Antonios Rengakos, and Christos Tsagalis (Berlin; Boston, MA: De Gruyter, 2012), pp. 269–91. Particularly Menelaus's *nostos* thereby parallels Odysseus's very closely; as DeJong notes,

> he too wandered around for many years, was driven off course by a storm, detained on an island (cf. Calypso), suffered from starvation (cf. Thrincacia), was advised by a supernatural woman (cf. Circe) to consult a clairvoyant person, who tells him about the fate of his comrades, his journey home, and the end of his life (cf. Tiresias).
>
> *A Narratological Commentary on the 'Odyssey'*, p. 106.

86 DeJong, *A Narratological Commentary on the 'Odyssey'*, p. 197.

9 Altering the Mood

Boredom and Anaesthesia in Itchy Park

Joshua Burraway

Itchy Park

Aside from the wind tearing its way into London's financial quarters like a commuter on the wrong side of their morning alarm, the defining sound of the park benches on which I find myself sitting is the hissing of recently opened beer cans, their sibilant pressures escaping into the air like the sighs of invisible serpents. It is mid-afternoon in *Itchy Park*, an interstitial slither of grass and concrete on the border of Tower Hamlets and the City of London. Sandwiched between the world's financial capital and one of London's most impoverished boroughs, *Itchy Park* is the stamping ground for the area's collection of homeless addicts, a place where company was sought, drinks drunk, drugs scored, and stories shared. The story of the day, like the one before it, is of boredom.

At the beginning of the day there is not a lot of talking. Instead people hang their heads in calloused and weather-beaten hands. They stare up at the skies, at the trees. Or else they stumble off to the station to try their luck panhandling. Pockets are sought through and mined for loose change as people try to work out how much bang they can expect for their buck. Someone is sent to the shop for booze, always super-strength. Some scavenge for tobacco along the pavement, urban foragers looking to forge cigarettes from leftover butts; *Roadside Virginia*. They give a whole new meaning to secondhand smoke. I turn to John and ask him how he slept. Terrible, he tells me. But that's not the worst part, he says. For sure, finding a place to bed down for the night is a drag, he tells me. The rain. The cold. The concrete bleeding its way through his cardboard mattress past his sleeping bag and into his marrow. The constant fear of assault. But at the very least you're occupied, he reminds me. Sleep allows the world, allows time, to move on behind his back, allows his consciousness to ignore its own demands while also withdrawing from a world that brutalises and alienates him. It's the daylight hours, John tells me, that are the worst part. All that time that needs to be filled. Finding stuff to do. Why do I think he's such a raging alcoholic? It's because there's quite frankly nothing else to do. Do I think he wants to be out here every day, getting pissed out his head? He just doesn't have anything else. No job. No money. No family. 'You just end up so fucking bored the whole time,' he tells me. Homelessness is *so fucking boring*. Alcohol is John's only way of getting through the day, his only means of killing time. And boy, is there an awful lot of it, time. Time everywhere. Overflowing. Endless.

Every single one of my homeless friends lamented this feeling of end-lessness that permeated their waking hours, of experience reduced to the deep ache of chronic boredom, of time and being dislocated out-of-joint. Every day they drank, smoked, and injected themselves into variant forms of memoryless abyss, anaesthetic oblivions that took them out of time, and by extension, out of boredom. The problem was that every morning the (anaesthetised) clock would reset, the hands at once moving and not moving, trapping them within the cyclical architecture of homeless addiction. In short, to understand the social, political, and existential nuances of addiction amongst the homeless, it is paramount that we pay proper ethnographic and analytical attention to boredom, not as a fleeting emotion, but as a distinct ontological mood, inseparable from being itself.

Moody Anthropologists

It is fair to say that anthropology is the kind of discipline that likes to have its fingers firmly in the pies of others, liberally borrowing terminology, concepts, and ideas and appropriating them into its own theoretical frameworks. Historical pies, philosophical pies, psychological pies to name but a few; all digitally probed and mined for fillings. Hence all the 'turning' that seems to be constantly going on within anthropology—the ethical turn, the ontological turn, the historic turn, the feminist turn. The list goes on. At times we just don't know which pie to turn our eager little fingers towards. As such it feels all the stranger that anthropology has devoted so little to the study of mood,[1] especially when so much has been written about the power of emotion to shape the social world.

But then what is the difference, exactly, between mood and emotion? Where does one end and the other begin? Are they not simply synonyms of each other? Is the emotion of anxiety distinct from an anxious mood? According to psychologist Richard Davidson (1994), emotion drives be-haviour, whereas mood shapes cognition (see Frijda 1994; Parkinson et al. 1996; Ekman 1999). From this perspective, emotions are triggered by a specific stimulus—someone cutting you up in rush hour traffic—whereas moods are shaped by broader existential and social circumstances—the experience of finding yourself stuck in rush hour traffic, day in day out. The car cutting you up might spark a sudden and ultimately tempo-rary flare of violent road rage, whereas the daily experience of embedding yourself in traffic for a job you despise might inspire a far more encom-passing and chronic sense of existential and personal dread, the kind that might linger deep into the day, long after you disembark the car and collapse into your cubicle. As with any two words that share a large degree of semantic overlap (take morals and ethics, for example), how you distinguish them from one another will invariably have a fair amount to do with the researcher's particular area of interest and intellectual background (Beedie, Terry, and Lane 2005). So, as an anthropologist, fingers covered in pie or not, it is about time I set out my own position on the emotion/mood debate, for the conjoined sakes of brevity and clarity.

For the purposes of this chapter, I'm going to adopt the conventional view outlined above that emotions are responses, often extremely powerful and with potentially far-reaching consequences (consider the case of murder, for example), directed at specific objects, in specific times and places. Furthermore, an emotional reaction to an object does not mean that the object in question is the cause of that reaction (think of when, in the midst of a blazing telephone row, your antagonist on the other end of the line decides to callously hang up; and you, feeling jilted by the sheer inhumanity of it all, hurl the phone to the ground in a blinding roar of simian rage. What did the phone ever do to you?).

Moods, on the other hand, are, I intend to argue, far less specific in their origin. We can float (or struggle) through an entire day, experience all manners of diverse experience and interaction, and still remain anchored in a particular mood. If emotions can be described as reactions to particular external contexts, we might say that mood is the internal context through which our reactions to the world are filtered. In this sense, I take my lead from a small handful of anthropologists (Lee 1998; Daniel 2000; Throop 2014, 2017; Zigon 2014; Ram 2015) who have written about mood, drawn in particular to Jason Throop's idea that 'moods are temporally complex phenomena that that transform through time and yet often entail a durativity that extends beyond the confines of particular morally salient events, narratives, and interactions' (2014:68). From this perspective, mood is not something we are able to take on and off like some kind of psychic sweater based on how hot or cold we feel; rather it is irremovably stitched into the most intimate contours of what Heidegger called *Dasein*, Being-in-the-world. In this way, we might say that really there are no moods, only *'changing moods'*: (see Ch. 1 by Hagi Kenaan in this volume). Viewed from this angle, moods—determined by perpetual flux—are inexorably tied to the intersubjectivity and temporality of being, forever shape-shifting into new configurations that are at once incontestably tangible and indeterminately ethereal.

Though scholars such as Throop and Zigon are explicitly concerned with how the temporality of moods intersect with our moral concerns, I will be leaving questions of morality to one side, choosing instead to focus on how the temporality of one particular mood, boredom, has permeated the addictive pursuits of *Itchy Park's* homeless. In the ethnographically informed analysis that follows, I will argue that boredom, more than any other mood, holds together the context for the field of experience that defines their homelessness and their addictions.

Locating Boredom

It is easy to use boredom as a broad category that contains any experience that is somehow empty. As such, it has been tempting to assume that boredom enjoys something of a universal quality, a transhistorical condition of humanity. However, a number of scholars have disputed this idea, rejecting the notion that boredom (as it is understood today) is 'inherent' and instead tracing out its specific historical genealogy (Spacks 1995). As it turns out, the study of boredom arose historically from the study of melancholy, the deepest roots of which can be traced to early Christianity and a group of ascetic monks known as the 'Desert Farmers' who, owing to their extreme isolation, were often beleaguered by experiences of *acedia*, best understood as a deep feeling of listlessness which impeded them from fulfilling their religious obligations. This state of torpor was intrinsically linked to the presence of 'the noontide demon'—a demonic apparition with the power to induce in them 'a dangerous form of spiritual alienation' (*ibid*:11). Though the historical connections with the acedia demon are salient, it is important to recognise that boredom as we understand it now is a distinct phenomenon in its own right. Boredom, in other words, is very much a modern problem (Musharbash 2007; Pezze and Salzani 2009; Clare 2012).[2]

Martin Heidegger (1995) made a similar claim, arguing that it is above all else boredom—understood as a kind of ontological mood—that constitutes our attunement to the world, what he described as the 'concealed destination' of modernity. Heidegger describes this kind of ontological boredom as 'profound,' in the process drawing a theoretical distinction between boredom as a reaction to some identifiable object/event and *being* bored as deep existential predicament. Informed by Heidegger among others, Svendsen (2005) makes a similar distinction, dividing boredom into two types, 'situative' and 'existential.' Situative boredom is closer to the feeling of indifference. It has a particular object as its focus, something which is unstimulating or tedious in and of itself, such as waiting for a bus, or watching paint dry. In this sense, Svendsen's situative boredom is closer to what the psychologists from the previous section would described as an emotion.

Existential boredom, on the other hand, is constituted by the disembowelment of world and self, the consequence of which is a sense of emptiness that can feel impossible to shed. Under these conditions, boredom shapes reality by transforming the normative flow of temporality, elastically stretching the present to an almost endless degree, and in the process divorcing existence from the mutual bracketing of past and future. It is this notion of getting bogged down in the tarpits of a boundless and meaningless present—what I will explore more specifically as 'getting stuck'—that I will bring into my discussion of homelessness. So, borrowing from Heidegger and Svendsen, this essay will pay explicit concern to the existential over the situative, the idea being to recast boredom as a mood that simultaneously discloses and encompasses the homeless' ongoing experience of the world, in the process shaping access to different modes-of-being.

Breaking Down: Same Shit Different Day

Recall John's assertion that alcohol was the only means he had of driving himself through the waking hours of the day. The reason that any of John's numbered days are more than just the cyclical rising and setting of the sun is that he, like all human beings, is inextricably temporal in his makeup. Indeed, as Henri Bergson (1991) argued, the temporal flow of consciousness means that being is not just a state, but a state-in-motion. For the homeless, their ejection from the normal social order—in particular the relational, material, economic, and temporal security this order entails—means that the motile flow of being is experienced as a kind of relentless breakdown.

Consider Jimmy, a 50-year-old man who has been rough sleeping for almost two years. With his gravelly stubble and bag heavy eyes, Jimmy often looks like the definition of sleep debt. For the majority of his adult life he had worked as a tree surgeon. He spoke to me with eloquence about the thrill of working outdoors, of breathing fresh air, about the meaning he took from working with his hands, about the detailed technical knowledge required to carry out this kind of work. He spoke with great seriousness about what tools were required to handle what tree, keen to assert that it was not simply a case of strapping on a harness and thoughtlessly wielding an axe. Beaming with nostalgic pride he emphasised that the skills required to do the job properly and safely were not easy to come by, that they required time and dedication, and no small amount of bravery. He regularly regaled me with stories of epic climbs up ancient trees, having to scale acrophobia-inducing heights whilst keeping a sufficiently cool head to carry out the required surgery. He spoke of panoramic views and warming sunlight, of the simple pleasures of sweat and hard work: in short, the pleasures of purpose. However, following an accident involving a faulty harness, Jimmy was forced to cease work for a prolonged period, the damage to his back serious enough to warrant a long course of prescription painkillers. The complexity of the injury in conjunction with the physical intensity of the work meant that Jimmy found it increasingly difficult to return to arboricultural work, and was forced in the end to stop altogether. With his job, nay, his purpose taken from him, Jimmy lapsed into a double vacuum of depression and unemployment, a void that became increasingly filled with prescription opioids. Eventually Jimmy's marriage also suffered a terminal injury, his wife unable to cope with his depression and increasingly acute addiction. With his intimate and professional life in tatters, Jimmy fell into rent arrears and quickly found himself on the streets, thrown into a purposeless existence defined on one hand by its scarcity of human relationships, and on the other by its overabundance of time. And nothing takes the edge off of time like the anaesthetic abyss of an opioid binge. As Jimmy himself puts it,

> Everything in my life is just falling apart at the moment. I can't catch a break, like the rug is being taken out from under me. The longer I go without contact [with his family], the harder it is to make it back. I just feel like my life is slipping through my fingers.

Notice the usage of the present participle: fall*ing*, slipp*ing*. It is commonplace to describe the homeless as those who have fallen through society's cracks. This expression is misleading in the sense that it takes as axiomatic that the worst is somehow over; in saying that they have fallen through, that the experience is or *was* one of dislocation is to suggest, to some extent, that the experience is already in the past. Locking someone's predicament in the past tense often has the effect of creating a moral distance that can seriously dilute the empathic potential of a person's reaction to another's misfortune: *"What's done is done," "it's in the past now," "it's history now," "they've made their choices."* Using the past tense in this manner is part of a wider repertoire of objectification and marginalisation that ultimately serves to neglect the realities of the homeless condition as it unfolds sequentially in the present. Jimmy's use of the present participle, the -ing, reminds us that the lived feeling of breakdown is continuous, exponential, and perceptibly unending. It also reminds us that time does not stop for them, that each recurring day has to be faced and occupied in some way, shape or form.

In Jimmy's case, his unemployment and homelessness meant that he was no longer able to contribute value to the liberal market economy. Instead he became just another skiver, another socioeconomic failure unable to 'invest' in the spirit of an entrepreneurial future.[3] In this sense Jimmy, like so many of the addicted homeless, is shut out from the capitalist project. He becomes an aberration of a market society that has effectively found him surplus to requirements, just another soul in the riptide of human ruin—*lumpenized*, in Bourgois' (2009) sense of the word. Important to recognise here is that the neoliberal project of deregulated capitalism is equally fixated on the ordering of time as it is with the ordering of money. The division of time into commoditised units of exchange—such as the hourly wage—is part of a distinctly modern disciplinary regime, constitutive of capitalism's very ethic of productivity (Papadopoulos, Stephenson, and Tsianos 2008). The subjectivity of the modern citizen is defined not just by how they spend their money, but also by how they spend their time. In this way, how much time one has (be it too much or not enough) becomes an explicitly political statement; one that speaks to the deep tension between the embodied experience of time and the representation of time as a space for work. When Jimmy fell out of that tree and out of work, through the branches of his marriage and into the bowels of addiction and homelessness, he also fell through the trapdoor of good citizenship and into its penumbral obverse, what Saris (2013) calls 'anti-citizenship.' On this, the dark side of the moon, the homeless are forced to live within the conventional brackets[4] laid down to them by the dominant temporal and moral order—viz. work and consumerism—despite having none of the structural support and material resources required to live in such a way. As a result, their daily life becomes reduced to begging, waiting, self-intoxicating, and aimless wandering. Take Lenny, for example, made homeless when he was unable to make up the shortfall in his rent following the sudden death of his long-term partner. With nothing to do, nowhere to go and no one to see,[5] Lenny spends his waking hours walking through London's streets, devoid of direction or destination:

> They say I've got to get off my feet, stop walking so much. Or else my feet are gonna get even worse, like I'm gonna need surgery and all that. They say I need new boots, that these ones aren't designed for all the walking I'm doing. I mean yea, fair enough. My feet are fuckin' killing me. But where the fuck am I gonna get the money for new shoes? I've got barely enough to make it through the day as it is. What do they expect me to do? I walk to the day centre in the mornings, eat as much as I can, you know, trying to pack on the calories. I tell you, I've lost so much weight, down to almost twelve stone. I used to be sixteen! I just can't seem to get enough calories down me, to keep my weight up, y'know? I should be at least three four heavier, at least! But I don't have a choice, I've got to keep walking. When this place closes at lunchtime what else do I have to do? Can't go to sleep yet, wouldn't be able to anyway, too many people around. Plus, I've got to keep my bag with me, or else someone'll just fucking nick it. Only thing I can do is keep moving, keep out of people's way, out of trouble, keep my eye out for a new place to skip. Thing is I'm fuckin' wasting away at the moment, y'know? At this rate I'll be dead by the end of the month, just another number.

Getting to know Jimmy, John, and Lenny was like watching structural violence in motion, a front-row-seat to the way in which life on the streets mutates from condemnation into a tragic home unto itself. In Lenny's case, his relentless steps were as much about eating up time as they were about moving through space. In this sense we can see his wanderings as homologous with John's imperative to kill time through alcohol, to use whatever resources are available to help him to get through the day. The problem is that any such solution, be it walking or drinking, is a bit like using your pinkie to plug a bursting dam. Suspended in a kind of material and temporal purgatory, the homeless find themselves ensnared in a situation where their means of existence no longer square up with the values of wider society, a tension that gives rise to what Musharbash, in her ethnography of an aboriginal settlement, describes as 'meaningless fits' (2007:315). Using insights borrowed from Edmund Leach (1968), Musharbash argues that boredom at Yuendumu emerges in the absence of meaning, a chronic situation borne of a motionless present devoid of the novel events necessary to generate meaningful breaks in everyday life.

The homeless of *Itchy Park* suffer from a comparatively similar existential malaise, summed up by the commonplace saying: *same shit different day*. This expression crops up time and time again on the benches, as much a statement of existential fact as it is a cultural idiom. For Larry, another of the park's frequent fliers, the experience of homeless time is defined by the same chronic meaninglessness that pervades the Yuendumu settlement. Originally from Glasgow but drawn to London as a young adult by the lure of greener pastures, Larry was never able to achieve the economic security he craved, becoming part of London's precarious day-labour force for his first few years in London, eventually subsidising his income through dealing drugs, predominantly heroin. Though his slippage into the informal economy provided a roof over his head, it wasn't long before Larry started getting high off his own supply, the long stretches of empty time between construction jobs providing fertile ground of anaesthetic experimentation. In the end Larry's double life closed violently in on itself, reaching a critical point when he was accused by another user of being a police informant. Not taking these charges lightly, Larry seriously assaulted his would-be accuser, the ensuing damage severe enough to warrant a police inquiry. Not only did the ensuing investigation find Larry guilty of ABH (actual bodily harm), it also happened upon his heroin portfolio, compounding his custodial sentencing, the afterlife of which continues to haunt him to this day.

Indeed, Larry fell into homelessness after being released from prison, a situation that affects a large proportion of ex-offenders, the causes of which are complex and multilayered, though they can be partially explained by lack of advice during prison itself, the lack of appropriate accommodation, lack of income and savings, poor job prospects, the stigma of incarceration, and the absence of stable relationships on the outside (Clancy et al. 2006; Lewis et al. 2003; Maguire and Nolan 2007). As Larry puts it,

You get out of prison, it's just you and twenty other junkies waiting to be kicked out onto the streets. You've got forty-six quid in your pocket, or whatever it is they give you when you leave, and you can't get money from signing on for six weeks, is that gonna last you? Fuck off it is. You've got nowhere to go, so you get together and score some drugs to sell. You end up drifting between other people's houses and the streets. Nowhere to go and nothing to do but stick gear up your veins and try and block it all out.

Larry's account reveals that incarceration does not end when the cell door is eventually unlocked; rather, it possesses its own kind of stubborn temporality, one that weighs down the future with the gravity of the past, a temporality folded into the social label of the 'ex' offender. The 'ex' is a prefix Larry must carry around like a millstone around his neck, one that will constitute the suffix of his remaining life, whether he likes it or not. Like any other X worth its salt, it marks the spot where the structural violence and criminal trajectories of his illicit past become inexorably folded into the cyclical architecture of homelessness. Larry knows the dangers of this cycle intimately well, his most recent brush with the law for heroin possession coinciding with the death of his parents:

I lost both parents when I was on remand. Had to attend their funerals in shackles. I was found not guilty a week after my father's death. I should have been able to bury my parents. I'm an atheist, my parents were my Gods.

Larry's long-standing entanglement with drugs, both economically and experientially, have built for him a prison that goes beyond the spatial and temporal dimensions of his original penal term, encompassing not just his past but also his future. Tainted by all that surrounds the untimely death of his parents, he now finds himself locked within an addicted state-of-being that is defined by a limitless and stagnant present, where mourning and existential boredom have bled into one another to form a filter that is deeply nihilistic—*same shit different day*:

I wish I could grieve properly. Instead I just sit here and drink, shoot up. Sometimes I wish I could just scream. I go to sleep hoping I don't wake up. I'm fed up. Sick of it.

Larry's thinly veiled suicidal impulses are reflected in the sorry state of his flesh, his arms and legs acned with post-injection abscesses that evoke deep lunar craters. According to Tony, one of his closest confidants in the park, Larry is on a one-man frog march towards the abyss, telling me in no uncertain terms that '*he's gonna kill himself. He'll die with a needle sticking out of him. He plays roulette every time he shoots up.*' Larry is under no illusions about the game he's playing with his life. He knows the stakes. Indeed, he often frames himself in almost zombie-like terms, regularly describing himself to me as a dead man walking, a ghostly figure trapped in a warped and meaningless reality. The death of his parents haunts his everyday life, his unresolved grief made manifest in each heroin-steeped descent into anaesthesia, a practice that is destined to ensnare him deeper and deeper into the cycles of social alienation that have come to define his world. His, like so many others who have suffered the double-blow of intimate loss and structural violence, is a Beckettian existence where '*everything stays the same. You just get stuck, it's fucking hard to get out of. Impossible maybe, for me anyway.*' With his body collapsing in on itself under the needled weight of his escapist impulses, and the weight of his criminal past weighing down on his neck like an invisible pillory, Larry understands himself as 'stuck' in a social and temporal vacuum, an (un)dead man excluded from the flow of meaningful life, trapped in a situation where there is little else to punctuate the day other than seek oblivion. Each day Larry, he of already deadness, finds himself waking up alive, the asphyxiating nothingness of the present drowning him beneath swollen waves of time.

This vignette reveals that boredom in *Itchy Park*—what Larry configures as 'stuckness'—is not in a person's head, as it were. Rather than buying into the psychological assumption that boredom represents but one emotional state of mind among many, I have taken boredom to be a prime existential condition of homeless-addicted being—within the local parameters of *Itchy Park* at least. In this sense, Larry's sense of stuckness should not be understood as an internal or cognitive process, but rather as a mood that discloses his attunement to his situated place in the world—what Heidegger calls 'disposedness' (*Befindlichkeit*). Our disposedness is intrinsically related to the contingency of our place in the world, how disposed and attuned we are to the situation in which we find ourselves always already embedded. The notion of disposedness means that we intrinsically possess attachments to the world as it unfolds, attachments that cannot be severed, for they are constitutive of Dasein itself. These are not experiences that occur at the sunken and opaque level of the spirit or soul, but rather they are part of an ongoing and embodied reflection of how we are, there, *in the moment*. Moods then (understood here in terms of disposedness and attunement) are not categorisable as either subjective or objective; rather, they are the embodiment of the continuous moment of inbetweenness—that is to say that we constantly find ourselves in specific situations that contingently determine the very possibilities for living. Borrowing the language of Throop (2014), moods are responsive to how we 'come along' in the world.

Crucially though, for the homeless person tragically ensnared in the bear-trap of existential boredom, the 'coming-along' that conditions their 'disposedness' can be viewed as somewhat kinked, sparking a narrowing of possibilities to the extent that what may once have felt like embedded continuity is now experienced as discontinuity or blockage, a 'stuckness,' in Larry's terms. Indeed, if we are prepared to entertain the Heideggerian position that a person's ontological attunement, that is to say their situated 'being,' is always already coterminous with the world as it unfolds, we can understand how the abject 'nothingness' of Larry's everyday puts a knot in the flow of existence, forcing him to live within the knot, so to speak. It is worth noting in this that this predicament is not an intrapsychic one, rather it denotes the way in which Dasein senses itself within the assembled complexity of particular situations; an understanding of self, surrounding, and time that is fundamentally implicit. So, if we take 'disposedness' as something implicit, world-relating and thus ultimately 'non-cognitive,' we can perhaps approach the mood of boredom experienced in *Itchy Park* as something that stalls a person's temporal and ontological motor. Boredom can therefore be said to pose a radical threat to the possibility of being, creating an ever-narrowing future in which certain options for living no longer exist. In this sense, the relational tragedy and temporal precarity that constitute existential boredom as an embodied mood can be said to have pervaded, suffused, and coloured the very conditions of their reality.

Narcotic anaesthesia constitutes a temporary exit from this condition of stuckness. Consider the temporal absenteeism of the drug-induced blackout—an alternative bodily state experienced disproportionately by homeless drinkers and drug-takers, and one that was all too familiar to the residents of *Itchy Park*. For those unfamiliar with this state-of-being, a blackout (not to be confused with passing-out) can be said to have occurred when a person continues to act in the world but has no memory of their actions when they eventually sober up—kind of like a post-binge amnesia. In these moments, where the past becomes a non-reflexive void and a person's agency effectively goes on behind their back, my interlocutors continuously told me the same thing: that under these conditions, they were categorically *not themselves*, that they had *become somebody else*. Whilst the complexity intrinsic to this state-of-being deserves an entire article to itself, what we are dealing with in such situations is not, I claim, a mere figure of speech, but rather the inducement of a highly dissociative trance-like state, in which, through the narcotic temporality of blacking-out, a person *really does become somebody else*. Or, put another way, a self is temporarily interrupted and reinvented as an Other— an Other that emerges, phantom-like, beyond the dual jurisdiction of extreme boredom and disciplinary time.

Faced with the tyranny of existential boredom, the transcendental promise of anaesthetic intoxicants can thus be conceptualised as a kind of jump lead, as a means of untying the knot in which they are forced to exist. Ultimately, I am proposing that drugs are often the primary tool through which the homeless attempt to loosen this existential entanglement, of finding meaning in a world otherwise constituted by nothingness. I will now return to *Itchy Park* as a means of ethnographically enriching this idea of 'nothingness,' of teasing out the complex ways in which the temporality of boredom works to fan the flames of sociopolitical abjection, to explore in greater depth what it is like to live within the knot.

Doing Nothing, Being Nothing

In his revealing cross-cultural study of psychiatric hospitals in Romania and America, Jack Friedman (2012) explores the ways in which studying the experience of inactivity can provide a distinct methodological challenge to the project of ethnography. Whilst acknowledging the myriad ways that the anthropological lens has enabled us to go beyond the experience of inactivity itself, in the process opening up the various social, political, and existential forms that emerge from this particular condition, Friedman is simultaneously wary of the hermeneutic impulse hardwired into anthropology's mainframe. He claims that the anthropological imperative to tease deeper meaning and connection from the puzzle of human experience makes it tricky to take, at face value, situations where people claim to be 'doing nothing'—particularly when, at the surface level, this may well appear to be the case. As he puts it: 'this is the great challenge, for, to write an ethnography of inactivity is, in the end, both the challenge of writing of the experience of nothing while, simultaneously, being an exercise in challenging the nature of ethnography itself' (2012:8). The nature of my fieldwork ensured that this was a challenge I had no choice but to accept. Accordingly, in a bid to surmount Friedman's challenge—at least partially—I will now offer some thoughts on the difference between nothing and vacuity, the aim being to ethnographically illuminate the ways in which people endure 'nothingness,' with particular focus on how these endurance trials relate to the (narcotic) transcendental jump lead mentioned just above.

The thing about getting wasted on park benches is that it *takes time*. On waking, the first few hours in the park are a solemn, funereal affair. There are few exchanges between the park's protagonists, many of whom say nothing at all. At the beginning of the day, many of the bodies are folded over themselves like rows of deflated queries. With the day set upon them the cold and interrupted nature of the last night's sleeping arrangements produce a collective lethargy that stains the space with a sensation of piercing insomnia. Above all there is quiet, punctuated mainly by weary exhalations of breath, as it dawns on park's residents that they have to go through it all again, just like the day before, and the day before that. This is precisely the challenge laid down by Friedman: how do you provide descriptive thickness to situations where, overtly at least, nothing seems to be happening?

On this particular day, a waiter from the new pizza restaurant across the road walks through the park, looking to give free samples out to passers-by. He walks right past our group, offering not so much as a glance in our direction. As Larry remarks right after, '*he walked right past us like we were a bunch of fucking lepers.*' Max, another heroin addict, mumbles something under his breath, I make out the words '*invisible*' and '*untouchable*.' Later I ask Max to elaborate on what I overheard:

> These people man, they think there's something wrong with us. Like we're dangerous, or diseased. They just look right through us, like we don't even exist, just because we got a drink in our hands. Like we're nobody. People look at us and think we're the plague, makes us feel like shit. All it takes is for someone to just say hello. It's part of being human. You're the first person in time to actually approach us and have a conversation. Do you understand how nice that feels for someone to actually stop and talk to us? We ain't bad people man, we're just doing it differently. We're the undesirables, we know that.

Walking past a bunch of homeless people, huddled together on benches, beer in one hand, head in the other, it is easy to say that nothing is happening. In such situations, it is so much easier to look through the space than directly at it. Furthermore, if your worldview happens to be shaped by the capitalist ethos of synchronicity and productivity, happening upon this inert gathering of down-and-outers, it seems self-evident to suggest that no-one is 'doing' anything. From this perspective, if you 'do' nothing, *you are nothing*. However, as Max and Larry demonstrate, they are very much aware of their marking as an undesirable Other. They are acutely aware of the conditions of their own invisibility, perceiving themselves as transparent ghosts, or else 'untouchable' lepers. They understand themselves as under a very specific gaze, the gaze of exile, of abandonment.

Indeed, the longer I spent on the benches, the more obvious it became that each person was acutely aware of this disgusted gaze, of their own repulsive alterity. Even when they were bent-double under the pressure of their own solitude, each and every one went through moments of acute self-awareness that was marked by a highly amplified sensitivity to self and surroundings. Indeed, the more one zooms in on intervals of 'empty' time, the less empty they seem to be. Indeed, when examined through the right kind of lens, they turn out to be rather swollen—not of deducible complex events or exertions in an objective sense, but of emotions, thoughts, fantasies, illusions and, perhaps most significantly, *moods*—what Goffman (1961) would describe as 'engrossment.' So when a routine passer-by tells herself that these people are 'doing' nothing, she is conceptualising the 'nothing' as an absence, a vacuum, empty. She forgets that nothing is an ongoing experience, an integral component of the break(ing)down of 'normal life' that I analysed in the previous section above here. Julie, a woman in her late-fifties, has been homeless on-and-off for over 30 years, during which time she has intermittently kept a diary. Julie kindly permitted me to read some of her entries, and transcribe parts that I felt might be analytically pertinent:

> I have never been so lonely. I've been trying to figure out how my life has gotten this bad. I have thought I should end my life. The biggest mistake of my life was not going to Denver with Jamie; but I got cold feet. I have been trying to figure out how my life got so bad. I looked out from my bench this morning and just thought what's the point of all this. It felt like nothing.

The more time I spent with Julie, the more it became apparent that Jamie wasn't 'real' in the biological sense of things. Indeed, whilst at first Julie made only passing references to her mystery partner, as we began to spend more time together, the more elaborate, convoluted, and downright contradictory the stories became. Ultimately the more attuned I became to the divergent flow of these 'street stories,' the more I came to see them as a window into the reality from which the homeless had been frozen out, and their ongoing attempts to either re-enter or circumnavigate it. In a sense, these performative fragments of truth made concrete the social rejection that had since been embodied in the viscera of their everyday experience. Moreover, for the homeless themselves, these narratives were spaces in which the 'nothingness' of their daily lives was rethought and re-evaluated.

Significantly, the 'nothingness' of Julie's existence is brought about not by the claustrophobic inertia of the three-by-three cell as in solitary confinement, but rather the sheer vast facelessness of the cityscape. Julie's words are a reminder that 'nothing' is something that a person gets stuck in, something that *happens* to that person, day in, day out. Nothingness is *not* synonymous with vacuity. The person may feel 'empty' (that is to say isolated, fragile, alone) but that does not mean that they do not feel in their bones the unravelling of the day, even if this unfolding does not take the form of manifest, external stimuli. Rather, that which is so readily misjudged as time devoid of overt complexity or intricate praxis is in fact loaded with the moody syntax of existential boredom on the part of those who are privately, actively, and self-reflexively engrossed by their immediate circumstances, irrespective of the surface appearance of uneventfulness.

The intention of these ethnographic examples is to flush out the particular connection between boredom and the experience of time. As John expressed to me one morning, *'these days just seem to go on forever, like they're never going to end.'* This sense of time lengthening, what in more technical terms can be described as 'protracted duration,' is a common feature of homeless temporality, one that all my informants attested to at one point or another. The relentless monotony of the everyday holds a particular kind of tedium for the homeless individual. As I have already shown, the 'dragging on' of the day inflicts a special kind of violence on a homeless person's existential foundations. As such, it demands a special kind of violence in return, the *killing* of time. As Tony puts it, *'that's the thing, you've got to find a way to kill the time somehow, otherwise it'll just fuckin' eat you up.'*

For the residents of *Itchy Park*, their endurance of existential boredom really does give them what Joseph Brodsky (1997) would call a 'full look at the worst'—insofar as their sense of self and world becomes swallowed up by the tar pit of 'pure, undiluted time in all its repetitive, redundant monotonous splendour' (*ibid*:109). As part of his reflections on boredom, Brodsky suggests that one should 'let boredom squeeze you,' the idea being that 'the sooner you hit bottom, the faster you surface' (*ibid*). Heidegger sings a similar tune, arguing that the experience of *Hingehaltenheit* (one of boredoms key 'structural moments')—translated literally as being-held-out-into-the-nothing—sparks a moment of profound reflective distance in which Dasein becomes entranced by this 'pure' time; a distance through which the possibilities-of-being that sustain Dasein in its authenticity are suddenly made manifest, whilst also remaining just out of reach. Paradoxically then, it is through this very entrancement that Dasein can make sense of its potentiality-for-being. For Heidegger and Brodsky, boredom is the means through which Dasein achieves 'self-disclosure' and learns to speak the language of time. In other words, the means by which human beings navigate the realities of their existential situation become pronounced in profound boredom precisely through their disappearance, their 'telling refusal' in Heidegger's terms. So, by pulling things out of their usual context and hanging Dasein out to dry in limbo, deep boredom supposedly cleaves open new configurations of existential meaning.

How then might the homeless addicts of *Itchy Park*, conspicuously stripped of their possibilities for living meaningfully, react to this call to actively retrieve these features of existence? As it turns out, for those people who are forced to endure the alienating political and material conditions of urban homelessness, Heidegger and Brodsky's advice is all but impossible to follow. Instead of propelling them into the kind of resolute action that might 'free' them from their situation, their ongoing sense of nothingness is so pervasive that Heidegger's 'message' simply cannot get through. Consequently, Larry and those around him find themselves severed from any meaningful temporal context—at once divorced from history and from any meaningful projection towards the future. Stuck in a limbo where nothing happens and nothing matters, their entire existence transforms them into a 'nobody.' Max is especially pronounced in his sense of limbo, telling me that *'we're nothing to society, just ants to be stepped on. You know, like we don't matter. Just a bunch of nobodies.'* As someone who is consciously able to consider his life situation in relation to the societal and temporal whole, Max shows himself to be fundamentally attuned to the realities of his existential predicament, aware that, in his current state, being a valued member of society—'a somebody'—is simply beyond the realm of possibility. This pervasive sense of insignificance is continually ossified and made gut-wrenchingly real through the temporal, relational, and material conditions of existential boredom.

Conclusion

Already on the verge of bursting, and forced to live in a world that already offers almost nothing of significance, the homeless simply cannot afford to let boredom 'squeeze' them anymore than it already does. Rather than operating as anything revelatory, the existential boredom experienced by *Itchy Park's* homeless addicts serves instead to affirm their nothingness. For Heidegger, this incapacity to find one's way through to the other side of boredom and 'reignite' existence constitutes a form of failure, an 'inauthentic' means of being-in-the-world. From an anthropological perspective, this conclusion is simply not acceptable insofar as it fundamentally neglects the myriad ways in which human beings are able to find moments of significance in the wilderness of an otherwise meaningless world. As Max puts it,

> When you become homeless, you become invisible. Life ain't no longer ahead of you, so you have to create a new time for yourself. This life, it's like a cancer. On the streets you have to drink, smoke, shoot up, whatever; it's the only way to get through the situation. If you start to intelligently reflect on the whole thing, it will become too much.

For Max as with the other addicts I worked with, drugs and alcohol are often the only means of dwelling within the meaningless abyss of existential boredom. Max's imperative to craft a 'new time' in the face of nothingness through anaesthetic intoxicants is a reminder that selfhood, temporality, and existential meaning can fit together in any number of ways, the configurations of which are intimately contingent on a person's social, political, and material conditions. Indeed, this becomes immediately clear when we consider the often overwhelming tendency for homeless people to heavily intoxicate themselves as a means of 'getting through their day.' That psychoactive substances are often described as mood-altering, is not, I suggest, a coincidence.

Indeed, this case study shows that boredom and intoxication, explored in terms of the temporality of mooded experience, are deeply interrelated. In the homeless context, boredom is the primary filter through which the homeless experience and make sense of time, and by extension the truncated nature of their social reality. As time swells into a meaningless abyss, the homeless use anaesthetic intoxicants to alter the prevailing mood of their existence, changing the filter of their world: kill (time) or be killed (by time). The ethnographic account of existential boredom provided in this work has gone some way to illuminating the state of world that the homeless find themselves thrown into, a world constituted above all by an excess of time and scarcity of intimate relations. Stuck in a seemingly endless cycle of the same, the homeless addicts of Itchy Park actively seek anaesthesia, the radical temporality of which is able to temporarily neutralise the compound paralysis of deep boredom, structural alienation, and tragic loss, in the process negating the exhausting regime of time so intimately woven into the late-liberal sales pitch.

Notes

1 There are, of course, notable exceptions. All of which will receive proper mention in due course.

2 For further anthropological studies that take boredom as their ethnographic focus, see Frederiksen (2013); Jervis, Spicer, and Manson (2003); Mains, Hadley, and Fasil (2013); Masquelier (2013); and Wexler (2009).

3 See Casas-Cortés (2014), Moore and Robinson (2015), and Standing (2014) for a more detailed analysis on the precarity inherent to liberal capitalism's entrepreneurial spirit.

4 The concept of bracketing is inspired by Povinelli's (2011) provocative analysis of late-liberalism. She uses the image of bracketing to capture what she describes as the 'enforced suspension' of social difference. The homeless, refugees, ethnic minorities—any social group that does not fit easily into the political frameworks set out by free market dynamics become suspended in a kind of material, social, and temporal limbo. As part of their tragic abandonment, in which they are rendered 'neither something nor nothing,' they are unable to properly shake the bondage of their bracketing, being forced instead to continually resist this constriction through exhausting trials of daily endurance. As the indigestible remainder, and reduced to something resembling Agamben's (1998) 'bare life,' the homeless find themselves caught in a kind of purgatory, locatable neither on one side nor on the other of the temporal organisation of being—found instead in the messy space that lies somewhere just outside of these arrangements. Between the brackets, boredom is the order of the day, and it is served non-stop.

5 Lenny's predicament, like so many others, viscerally evokes the metaphysical anguish experienced by Vladimir and Estragon in *Waiting for Godot*, their waiting described by Beckett as an 'awful' place where 'nothing happens, nobody comes, nobody goes.'

Bibliography

Agamben, Giorgio, *Homo Sacer: Sovereign Power and Bare Life*, trans. Daniel Heller-Roazen (Stanford: Stanford University Press, 1998).

Beckett, Samuel, *Waiting for Godot* (New York: Grove Press, 1954).

Beedie, Christopher, Peter Terry, and Andrew Lane, 'Distinctions between Emotion and Mood', *Cognition and Emotion*, 19, 6 (2005), 847–78.

Bergson, Henri, *Matter and Memory* (New York: Macmillan, 1991). First published 1911.

Bourgois, Philippe, and Jeffrey Schonberg, *Righteous Dopefiend* (Berkeley et al.: University of California Press, 2009).

Brodsky, Joseph, *On Grief and Reason: Essays* (Harmondsworth: Penguin, 1997).

Casas-Cortés, Maribel, 'A Genealogy of Precarity: A Toolbox for Rearticulating Fragmented Social Realities In and Out of the Workplace', *Rethinking Marxism*, 26, 2 (2014), 206–26.

Clancy, Anna, Kirsty Hudson, Mike Maguire, Richard Peake, Peter Raynor, Maurice Vanstone, and Jocelyn Kynch, *Getting Out and Staying Out: Results of the Prisoner Resettlement Pathfinders* (Bristol: Policy Press, 2006).

Clare, Ralph, 'The Politics of Boredom and the Boredom of Politics in David Foster Wallace's "The Pale King"', *Studies in the Novel*, 44, 4 (2012), 428–46.

Daniel, E. Valentine, 'Mood, Moment, and Mind', in *Violence and Subjectivity*, ed. by Veena Das, Arthur Kleinman, Mamphela Ramphele, and Pamela Reynolds (Berkeley: University of California Press, 2000), pp. 333–66.

Davidson, Richard J., 'On Emotion, Mood and Related Affective Constructs', in *The Nature of Emotion*, ed. by Paul Ekman and Richard J. Davidson (Oxford: Oxford University Press, 1994), pp. 51±5.

Ekman, Paul, 'Basic Emotions', in *Handbook of Cognition and Emotion*, ed. by Tim Dalgleish and Mick J. Power (New York: Wiley, 1999), pp. 3–19.

Frederiksen, Martin D., *Young Men, Time, and Boredom in the Republic of Georgia* (Philadelphia: Temple University Press, 2013).

Friedman, Jack R., 'Thoughts on Inactivity and an Ethnography of "Nothing": Comparing Meanings of "Inactivity" in Romanian and American Mental Health Care', *Newsletter of the Society for the Anthropology of North America*, 15, 1 (April 2012), 1–9.

Frijda, Nico H., 'Varieties of Affect: Emotions and Episodes. Moods and Sentiments', in *The Nature of Emotion*, ed. by Paul Ekman and Richard J. Davidson (Oxford: Oxford University Press, 1994), pp. 59–67.

Goodstein, Elizabeth S., *Experience without Qualities: Boredom and Modernity* (Stanford, CA: Stanford University Press, 2005).

Goffman, Erving 'Fun in Games', in *Encounters: Two Studies in the Sociology of Interaction* (New York: Bobbs-Merrill, 1961), pp. 15–81.

Heidegger, Martin, *The Fundamental Concepts of Metaphysics: World, Finitude, Solitude*, trans. by William McNeill and Nicholas Walker (Bloomington: Indiana University Press, 1995). First published in 1929.

Jervis, Lori L., Paul Spicer, and Spero Manson, 'Boredom, "Trouble," and the Realities of Postcolonial Reservation Life', *Ethos*, 31, 1 (2003), 38–58.

Leach, Edmund, *Rethinking Anthropology* (London: Athlone Press, 1968).

Lee, Nam-In, 'Edmund Husserl's Phenomenology of Mood', in *Alterity and Facticity: New Perspectives on Husserl*, ed. by Natalie Depraz and Dan Zahavi (Dordrecht: Kluwer Academic, 1998), pp. 103–20.

Lewis, Sam, Mike Maguire, Peter Raynor, Maurice Vanstone, and Julie Vennard, *The Resettlement of Short-Term Prisoners: An Evaluation of Seven Pathfinder Programmes*. Research Findings 200 (London: Home Office, 2003).

Maguire, Mike, and Jane Nolan, 'Accommodation and Related Services for Ex-prisoners', in *Prisoner Resettlement: Policy and Practice*, ed. by Anthea Hucklesby and Lystra Hagley-Dickinson (Cullompton: Willan Publishing, 2007), pp. 144–73.

Mains, Daniel, Craig Hadley, and Tessema Fasil, 'Chewing Over the Future: Khat Consumption, Anxiety, Depression, and Time Among Young Men in Jimma, Ethiopia', *Culture, Medicine, and Psychiatry*, 37, 1 (2013), 111–30.

Masquelier, Adeline M., 'Teatime: Boredom and the Temporalities of Young Men in Niger', *The Journal of the International African Institute*, 83, 3 (2013), 385–402.

Moore, Phoebe, and Andrew Robinson, 'The Quantified Self: What Counts in the Neoliberal Workplace', *New Media and Society*, 18, 11 (2015), 2774–92.

Musharbash, Yasmine, 'Boredom, Time, and Modernity: An Example from Aboriginal Australia', *American Anthropologist*, 109, 2 (2007), 307–17.

Papadopoulos, Dimitris, Niamh Stephenson, and Vassilis Tsianos, *Escape Routes: Control and Subversion in the Twenty-First Century* (London: Ann Arbor, 2008).

Parkinson, Brian, Peter Totterdell, Rob B. Briner, and Shirley Reynolds, *Changing Moods: The Psychology of Mood and Mood Regulation* (Harlow: Addison Wesley Longman, 1996).

Pezze, Barbara D., and Carlo Salzani, *Essays on Boredom and Modernity* (New York: Rodopi, 2009).

Povinelli, Elizabeth A., *Economies of Abandonment: Social Belonging and Endurance in Late Liberalism* (Durham, NC and London: Duke University Press, 2011).

Ram, Kalpana, 'Moods and Method: Heidegger and Merleau-Ponty on Emotion and Understanding', in *Phenomenology in Anthropology: A Sense of Perspective*, ed. by Kalpana Ram and Christopher Houston (Bloomington: Indiana University Press, 2015), pp. 29–49.

Saris, A. Jamie, 'Committed to Will: What's at Stake for Anthropology in Addiction', in *Addiction Trajectories*, ed. by Eugene Raikhel and William Garriot (Durham, NC and London: Duke University Press, 2013), pp. 263–84.

Spacks, Patricia Meyer, *Boredom: The Literary History of a State of Mind* (Chicago, IL: Chicago University Press, 1995).

Standing, Guy, *The Precariat: The New Dangerous Class* (London: Bloomsbury, 2014).

Svendsen, Lars, *A Philosophy of Boredom* (London: Reaktion Books, 2005).

Throop, C. Jason, 'Moral Moods', *Ethos*, 42, 1 (2014), 65–83.

———, 'Despairing Moods: Worldly Attunements and Permeable Personhood in Yap', *Ethos*, 45, 2 (2017), 199–215.

Wexler, Lisa, 'Identifying Colonial Discourses in Inupiat Young People's Narratives as a Way to Understand the No Future of Inupiat Youth Suicide', *Indian and Alaska Native Mental Health Research: The Journal of the National Center*, 16, 1 (2009), 1–24.

Zigon, Jarrett, 'Attunement and Fidelity: Two Ontological Conditions for Morally Being-in-the-World', *Ethos*, 42, 1 (2014), 16–30.

10 Registering the Charge

Mood and Lawrence Durrell's *The Alexandria Quartet*

Rex Ferguson

Introduction

Why think about the mood of text? In what way can mood form a useful category in the analysis of literature? Where is the mood of text to be found? Answering these questions involves a certain insistence upon the exceptionality of literature: it means thinking about the relationship between mood and text as unique. This, in turn, requires seeing the questions posed as being part of a scholarly background which includes the range of recent work on literature and the emotions (and the history of emotions) and the now well-established field of scholarly work which has investigated the various embodied states that impinge upon and are reflected in text.[1] While this chapter will do this, it is also crucial to recognise (as this book does) that mood's import is not discipline or genre-specific. As such, the mood of text is perhaps best thought of as specific rather than singularly unique. Recent special issues of *New Literary History* and *New Formations* have emphasised a cultural studies approach to 'mood-work' which finds mood in an array of aesthetic forms.[2] Importantly, this work is typically centred on the philosophical (specifically ontological) significance of mood and is couched in terms which place it in the context of the body of work which has, since the early 2000s, appeared under the umbrella title of 'affect studies.' Thus, in Ben Highmore's estimation, 'in the ongoing attention that the humanities and the social sciences have been lavishing on emotion, sentiment, and affect, a space seems to be opening up for the study of mood.'[3] I would go further than this and claim that attending to mood—especially the Heideggerian form of mood, or *Stimmung*, which underpins the work of Highmore, Hans Ulrich Gumbrecht, and others—is the clearest way in which affect studies can shift emphasis and save itself from recent, valid, criticism.

The range of literary scholars who are doing 'mood-work' (even when they don't quite call it that) is significant but it is still in the process of establishing itself. What it currently lacks is enough material on specific texts and examples of what an examination of the moodiness of a text might look like. To this end, this chapter will take Lawrence Durrell's

The Alexandria Quartet and subject it to a mood-reading, explicating the philosophical significance of mood as it does so. Alexandria's mood is made manifest through an abundance of descriptive passages which activate complex lines of connection between the city's physical environment, social conditions, and tangled history. Crucially, such passages are also tied to the equally complex narrative content of the series—in other words, the quartet's plot is, in part, constitutive of its mood. That plot can be seen as forming a fundamental plank in the genesis of mood is significant because it reverses the dominant critical stance which tends to position the evocation of atmosphere and emotion as a feature of text that is primarily employed to produce meaning. Equally, it moves against affect studies' fixation upon identifying affect in precisely those regions of text which are not driven by meaning. By contrast, this essay is concerned, ultimately, with the moodiness of plot.

Affect, Mood, and Intentionality

What's wrong with affect studies? The first answer to this is nothing at all. As it has developed since the early 2000s, affect studies has offered an admirably rich means by which contemporary critical theory could move beyond the dominance of a linguistically conceived version of post-structuralism.[4] As it is most commonly articulated, affect studies is seen as coalescing around the writing of Eve Kosofsky Sedgwick and Brian Massumi who, in taking foundational cues from Baruch Spinoza, Gilles Deleuze and Felix Guattari, and Silvan Tomkins, have insisted that sense-making is not restricted to cognition and that the body is immanently affected and affecting.[5] This prospect has been taken up in order to account for the apparent irrationality of, amongst other things, political allegiance and gender construction while it has also given rise to studies focussed upon the peculiarity of aesthetic affect.[6] What affect studies has also given rise to is one of the most interesting scholarly debates in recent years, this taking place through a series of critiques and rebuttals in the pages of *Critical Inquiry* in 2011–2012. This began with Ruth Leys's now well-known essay 'The Turn to Affect: A Critique.' Leys takes aim, mainly, at the foundational work of Sedgwick and Massumi and in the conclusions they reach from contemporary research in psychology and neuroscience. For Leys,

> both the new affect theorists and the neuroscientists from whom they variously borrow—and transcending differences of philosophical background, approach, and orientation—affect is a matter of autonomic responses that are held to occur below the threshold of consciousness and cognition and to be rooted in the body. What the new affect theorists and the neuroscientists share is a commitment to the idea that there is a gap between the subject's affects and its

cognition or appraisal of the affective situation or object, such that cognition or thinking comes "too late" for reasons, beliefs, intentions, and meanings to play the role in action and behavior usually accorded to them. The result is that action and behavior are held to be determined by affective dispositions that are independent of consciousness and the mind's control.[7]

Leys concludes that, for affect-theorists, 'affect is the name for what eludes form, cognition, and meaning.'[8] Her objection to this position is not that it suggests there is a realm of behaviour and activity which takes place subliminally (who would argue against that, she claims) but, rather, the conclusion reached that such activity is completely divorced not just from cognition but, more crucially, from meaning and intention. Especially in the case of Massumi's work, Leys thus sees affect theory as reopening an ultimately regressive mind-body dualism. Since Leys's essay was published, there have been several attempts to rebut her claims and arguments made to suggest that she has misinterpreted the affect theory she seeks to critique.[9] It is beyond the scope of this chapter to attend to the details of all the arguments made in this context—this task also being made redundant by the admirable clarity with which Leys herself has countered most of them.[10] But there is one attempt at rebuttal which is particularly noteworthy, not because it is more successful in undermining Leys's interpretation of affect studies, but rather because, in one brief moment, it points towards a possible way in which affect studies could be reoriented. This comes from Charles Altieri, whose response was published in *Critical Inquiry* in 2012 and who writes that

in opposition to Leys, I will argue that there are diverse and valuable forms of nonconceptual emotions and that these are present in moods and in esthetic experiences [...] Consider first the question of mood. What kind of intentionality can one attribute to moods, given the fact that they alter our sense of agency? Moods typically are imperialistic; moods do not compete, but only one dominates at any given time because they are without boundaries. Moods are total because they set affective atmospheres and color all that the atmosphere contains. And moods seem a strange combination of passive and active. There is a thinning of the powers of agency because agents become the participants in this shaping totality and come to feel that powers of action seem distant and not particularly relevant. Moods also seem particularly resistant to concepts, especially if one recognizes that there are two possible states of the agent here. One can simply be aware of the world as filtered through the mood. Or one can be aware of oneself as being shaped by the mood. Only the second is at all conceptual. And even then the concept that one is in a mood covers very little of what is going on for an intending agent.

Even when one identifies the mood one need not take any practical orientation toward it.[11]

Intention is certainly the nub of the problem, but in writing about its complexity and reach, Altieri seems to argue more that Leys has not gone far enough in her critique than anything else. What is extremely significant about this passage, though, is that intention is nuanced by way of thinking about mood and that Altieri's version of mood is derived almost entirely from Heidegger. There are several important points here.

First, as Altieri points out, one of the most noticeable things about moods is their constancy. Affects are often described in terms which emphasise a vitality which is necessarily transitory.[12] To use an analogy, affects could be compared to the dynamic activity of an electronic device while mood is the continuous hum of an electrical current which is always 'on.' As Heidegger writes, 'in a state-of-mind Dasein is always brought before itself, and has always found itself, not in the sense of coming across itself by perceiving itself, but in the sense of finding itself in the mood that it has.'[13] I am always in a mood, no matter how banal or innocuous that might be—quiet contentment is as much of a mood as melancholy—and, in Heidegger's thought, a mood can only be removed by its replacement with another mood.

Altieri is also being Heideggerian when he talks about the liminal agency which moods entail. According to Heidegger, 'a mood assails us. It comes neither from "outside" nor from "inside," but arises out of Being-in-the-world, as a way of such Being.'[14] Moods are therefore important precisely because they are not within our ultimate control and yet are also not solely grounded in the external world.[15] To describe them in this manner thus builds on the very project of phenomenology which, in its Husserlian origin, was inspired by the aim of collapsing scientific (objective) and psychological (subjective) philosophies in favour of the description of pure 'phenomena.' This tradition informs Altieri's definition of mood but is more openly referenced in Hans Ulrich Gumbrecht's brilliant discussion of the German word *Stimmung*, which refers to both 'mood' and 'climate.' Gumbrecht writes:

> 'Mood' stands for an inner feeling so private it cannot be precisely circumscribed. 'Climate,' on the other hand, refers to something objective that surrounds people and exercises a physical influence. Only in German does the word connect with *Stimme* and *stimmen*. The first means "voice" and the second "to tune an instrument"; by extension, *stimmen* also means "to be correct."[16]

In paying close attention to the musical reference contained in these meanings, Gumbrecht writes of the complexity of haptic experience— the fact that hearing does not take place through the ears alone but involves the skin's response to the lightly vibrating touch of sound waves. Inspired by the form of phenomenological analysis, Highmore has argued that many sensory experiences are similarly 'synaesthetic.'[17] While this is significant, it is also important that, in Gumbrecht's account, music *touches* the body. He elaborates further on this by pointing out that 'another dimension of reality that happens to our bodies in a similar way and surrounds them is the weather.'[18] Intimately physical, mood is literally an atmosphere that lightly touches and surrounds the body: the 'climate' which is inhabited. At the same time, and perhaps precisely because of the very lightness of that touch, it is also encountered as interior: my mood is fundamentally related to my sense of inner being.

To return to the issue of intentionality, this formulation of mood seems to raise a problem: namely, how intentional can an encounter with weather conditions be? Certainly, one does not intend the rain in a strictly determinate sense. There are two key points to make here. First, *Stimmung* activates a sense of climate and atmosphere but is not a precise synonym for either. In fact, the overlap rather than mirroring of significance is what allows so many writers, including Durrell, to play in such complex ways with the evocation of mood through descriptions of the weather.[19] Second, and more importantly, to think in such terms is to miss the point of intentionality as it was conceived by the phenomenological project following the insight of Franz Brentano. By this logic, whatever comes into consciousness *must* be encountered as an intentional relation: as Steven Connor puts it, 'there can be no pure consciousness, only consciousness *of*.'[20] Thus while I don't intend the rain, I intend my consciousness *of* the rain and, to push the point, what the state of being in the rain is.

This is all very well but consciousness *of* is precisely what Sedgwick and Massumi (in Leys's account) think comes too late in matters of affect. In other words, affects unconsciously motivate behaviours which are then only cognised latterly by an intentional consciousness. This is when the peculiar intentionality of mood becomes so potent, for moods are not like other objects in the world. Nor, even, are they something that we have in relation to a particular object in the world—I am not depressed about the kitchen table for example. Rather, as Heidegger sees it, mood is what allows for consciousness to happen just as it does (and for the kitchen table to *be* just as it is). As Jonathan Flatley puts it, 'in a real sense, when one is experiencing shame, a different world is being perceived than when one is joyful or fearful.'[21] Altieri must surely be quite wrong, then, to say that we do not take any practical orientation in relation to our moods. Rather, we must by necessity experience the world in, through, and as the particular mood that we have because, in Heidegger's terminology, they 'attune' us to the world in very specific ways. The further implication of this point is summarised succinctly by Charles Guignon, in a passage favoured by Highmore:

> Our moods modulate and shape the totality of our Being-in-the-world, and they determine how things can count for us in our everyday concerns. Heidegger's point is that only when we have been 'tuned in' to the world in a certain way can we be 'turned on' to the things and people around us. Moods enable us to focus our attention and orient ourselves. Without this orientation, a human would be a bundle of raw capacities so diffuse and undifferentiated that it could never discover anything. What we do encounter in our attuned situatedness is not just worldhood, but rather a highly determinate cultural world.[22]

One of the key concepts here is 'care.' Heidegger writes that *'existentially, a state-of-mind implies a disclosive submission to the world, out of which we can encounter something that matters to us'* (italics in original).[23] Moods orient us towards a 'highly determinate cultural world' which we are concerned with and which is encountered as meaningful. In a brief reply to one of her critics, Leys writes that *'intentionality* carries with it the idea that thoughts and feelings are directed to conceptually and cognitively appraised and meaningful objects in the world.'[24] Affect theory might, at the very least, be hazy on this point but a phenomenologically inspired version of mood-work has this kind of intentionality and more. This is because rather than springing from an entirely physiological basis which then contributes to a delayed meaning-making, moods are characterised by an extended version of intentionality which is geared towards our particular situatedness. In other words, mood is not of a particular object but is of that 'highly determinate cultural world' which Guignon writes of. Moods are thus an entanglement of physical touch, state of mind, and cultural meaning.

Mood-Reading

Given this combination of character and significance, what would it be to read for a text's mood? Well, one of the first things to say is that mood's entanglement with meaning does not mean that mood-reading should be devoted to the task of explicating a particular interpretation which may not be apparent to the casual reader. Gumbrecht has spoken, by contrast, of moving towards a practice not of excavating meaning but of 'pointing' towards significance.[25] Highmore, likewise, has written of resisting the appeal to 'disentangle.' Rather, it is 'the sticky entanglements of substances and feelings, of matter and affect [which] are central to our contact with the world' and that 'what is required is a critically entangled contact with affective experience. This means getting in among the murky connections between fabrics and feelings, between the glutinous and the guffaw.'[26]

The sticky entanglements of 1930s and 1940s Alexandria is precisely what *The Alexandria Quartet* describes. Yet, on the face of it, Durrell's text might seem specifically designed to promote a different kind of readerly disentanglement. The four separate novels—*Justine* (1957), *Balthazar* (1958), *Mountolive* (1958), and *Clea* (1960)—cover a period which can roughly be dated from the late 1930s to the late 1940s. *Justine* tells the story of an affair between Darley, the novel's narrator, and the eponymous Justine, who is married to a prominent Alexandrian banker, Nessim. The novel charts the passion of this affair and Darley's increasing concern that Nessim knows about it, with this fear culminating in his paranoid belief that Nessim will stage an 'accident' in which Darley is shot during the annual duck hunt on Mareotis Lake which he hosts. As it happens, the novel does indeed conclude with an accident during the duck hunt but it is another prominent character, Capodistria—who sexually abused Justine as a child—that is killed.

As the succeeding volumes of the quartet proceed, they offer numerous corrections and supplements to Darley's (and the reader's) partial knowledge of events. The initial conceit of the second volume is that Darley's friend, Balthazar, having received Darley's manuscript of *Justine*, writes to him with a series of annotations. These are collectively referred to as the 'interlinear,' with these notes providing a very different account of the period Darley has described—most notably by asserting that Justine never loved Darley but was, in fact, all the time in love with another character, the flamboyant writer, Pursewarden. *Mountolive*, which focusses upon David Mountolive, the British Ambassador in Egypt, adds political intrigue to the mix with a narrative centred around Nessim's involvement in running guns to Palestine. What this ultimately leads to is Nessim instructing Justine to begin an affair with Darley in order to distract him from this activity—so, by this account and on Justine's side, the affair has been entirely instrumental, functional, and passionless. This volume also contains the revelation that Capodistria was not the body found at Mareotis Lake and that his death was faked—with this, again, being motivated by Nessim's dealing in arms. *Clea* concludes the quartet by moving forward in time and charting the realisation of Darley's love for the artist, Clea.

This mode of narrative is set out by Durrell in a brief Preface where he claims it is based on a rough analogy with the relativity proposition such that the first three novels are 'related in an intercalary fashion, being "siblings" of each other and not "sequels."'[27] This is intended to be a challenge to the 'serial form of the conventional novel.'[28] It is also hinted at in *Balthazar* when a novel is planned that would act 'like some medieval palimpsest where different sorts of truth are thrown down one upon the other, the one obliterating or perhaps supplementing the other.'[29]

Taken at face value, then, the quartet is an epistemological puzzle—a mysterious narrative in which the reader is motivated by the desire to move from partial to full knowledge. Yet what is most noticeable about the quartet is the way in which a full knowledge of events is never really attained, partly because a full disentanglement is impossible. On top of the basic outline summarised above, there are multiple other overlapping storylines including those in which Nessim fathers an illegitimate child with the prostitute Melissa (who is later cared for by Darley) and three important deaths in the shape of Nessim's fanatical brother Narouz (assassinated), the elderly cross-dressing policeman Scobie (beaten to death by sailors), and Pursewarden (suicide). These interconnected strands could be disentangled but what makes things more complicated is the way in which, despite Durrell's own words, the earlier 'truths' of the quartet are not 'obliterated' by the later ones: for example, it is impossible to believe, following a reading of *Justine*, that Justine was never actually in love with Darley. What I want to suggest is that this is because the mood of that earlier time, which is encountered as an immersion in an Alexandria of raw emotion, physical location, and fleshly being, is so palpably felt. Thus, from the very opening pages, there are descriptions such as the following:

> Notes for landscape-tones...Long sequences of tempera. Light filtered through the essence of lemons. An air full of brick-dust—sweet-smelling brick-dust and the odour of hot pavements slaked with water. Light damp clouds, earth-bound yet seldom bringing rain. Upon this squirt dust-red, dust-green, chalk-mauve and watered crimson-lake. In summer the sea-damp lightly varnished the air. Everything lay under a coat of gum.
>
> And then in the autumn the dry, palpitant air, harsh with static electricity, inflaming the body through its light clothing. The flesh coming alive, trying the bars of its prison. A drunken whore walks in a dark street at night, shedding snatches of song like petals. Was it in this that Anthony heard the heart-numbing strains of the great music which persuaded him to surrender for ever to the city he loved.[30]

What is so noticeable in this passage is its evocation of a condition in which the body is surrounded by an atmospheric intermingling of light, heat, and scent. The air, squeezed by a ceiling of clouds above, is suffused with the tiny yet visible particles of 'brick-dust' and, later, 'sea-damp.' The description plays upon the kind of synaesthesia referred to by Gumbrecht and Highmore also as the light is filtered through what would more usually be thought of as a straightforwardly olfactory experience: smelling the essence of lemons. Everything—with the body of the human subject being as much a thing as anything else in this landscape—lies under a 'coat of gum' and this merging of subject and object, body and landscape, reaches a peak with the ambiguity aroused by the 'light clothing' in the second paragraph: is this the clothing worn in the 'dry, palpitant air' or that very air itself, suffused with the light hum of an electrical charge? The flesh 'comes alive' in this passage, not only 'trying the bars of its prison' but also succumbing to the environment in which it has been thrown.

Passages like this saturate the quartet, with the text continually 'disclosing' Alexandria through the mood of the city. Concomitantly, there is a constant 'attunement' taking place in which, to use the phrasing of Guignon, Darley's capacity to be 'turned on' to events, people, and object around him is governed by the mood of Alexandria which has 'tuned him in.' In *Clea*, Darley returns to the city and claims to feel

> like the Adam of the medieval legends: the world-compounded body of a man whose flesh was soil, whose bones were stones, whose blood water, whose hair was grass, whose eyesight sunlight, whose breath was wind, and whose thoughts were clouds.[31]

This is an Alexandria not solely of outer dimensions but carrying an intensely inner register. To use Toni Morrison's phrase, as Gumbrecht does, to inhabit Alexandria is to be 'touched as if from the inside.'[32]

Such descriptive passages foreground an emphasis on *Stimmung*, but where else can the mood of the text be found? The majority of work that has been done on mood (and affect for that matter) has tended to focus on those aspects of text which seem least charged with the task of carrying meaning. Getting at what Hans-Georg Gadamer refers to as the 'volume' of the text has thus involved attending to its performative aspects: with performance in this sense carrying a range of meanings including the way in which a work might be physically spoken or sung, the use of visual images which may run counter to apparent meaning, the material forms in which a work of literature is housed and, most prominently, how the internal tones and rhythms of a text serve to 'perform' a singular presence.[33] In a recent special issue of *Textual Practice*, Alex Houen introduces a number of essays devoted to this latter approach, emphasising in his own introduction that language 'does not express feeling' so much as it 'does feeling' and that 'punctuation, vocabulary, and syntax each carry affect as part of their structure.'[34]

At the same time as this work, which is articulated in a context of continental philosophy and critical theory, has been taking place, an approach to 'literature and the emotions'—couched in the terms of analytical philosophy and contemporary psychology—has worked much more on the way in which emotional response interacts with the meaningful content of text. Taken in one sense, this is hardly a new claim.

Suzanne Keen thus introduces a recent special issue of *Poetics Today* on 'Narrative and the Emotions' by claiming that the literary scholar of 75 years ago would have little trouble in pairing these concepts.[35] In fact, she goes so far as to trace the lineage back to Aristotelian *catharsis*. At its best, this work is subtle and suggestive.[36] But what animates much of the work that Keen introduces is a concentration upon the closure (and closing emotion) that plot provides: *catharsis* occurs, after all, through the pity and fear that attends the conclusion of a tragedy in which the hero's reversal is fully recognised. Keen rightly makes a critique of Jenefer Robinson's book *Deeper than Reason* partially on these grounds, arguing that Robinson's exclusive attention to realist fiction produces a skewed account in which closure is assured. I would go further than this by challenging Robinson's reading of specific moments of high emotion within realist fiction as, ultimately, levers whose main function is to generate the desire to rationally understand through a process of 'cognitive monitoring' (Robinson's term).[37] Keen and the contributors to the special issue of *Poetics Today* are not quite so bound by this instrumental view of emotional response but the claims made do still often refer to a single emotion (sympathy, altruism) which generates an effect of pedagogical benefit: narratives make us feel the moral of a story rather than just rationally cognise it.[38]

In what remains of this chapter, I want to navigate something of a middle-ground between these approaches by picking up on a comment from Gumbrecht, who writes that aesthetic experience is formed from 'an oscillation (and sometimes an interference) between "presence effects" and "meaning effects."'[39] Taking this in the context of a discussion about mood, there is never a strict cut-off between the mood of the text and its meaningful content—so it is essentially limiting to look for mood only where meaning does not seem to adhere. At the other extreme, moods (and a more broadly conceived sense of the 'emotions') have too often been seen as conduits to aid in the construction of meaning. In order to bridge this gap it is useful to think about reversing the latter. In other words, rather than seeing mood as producing meaning we should attend to how meaning is embroiled in producing the mood of the text. And one of the ways this can be done is to think less about precisely *what* happens in the plot and more about *how* that plot happens.

The main driver of plot in *The Alexandria Quartet* is the city itself. On the opening page of *Justine*, Darley writes of 'the city which used us as its flora—precipitated in us conflicts which were hers and which we mistook for our own,' latterly reflecting that 'we are the children of our landscape; it dictates behaviour.'[40] Justine also talks of their affair as 'part of an experiment arranged by something else, the city perhaps' while Darley refers to the way in which the *cafard* (melancholia) of the city would, at times, seize Justine.[41] Tellingly, the city's agency is often described in a manner which plays upon the light but immersive touch of

Stimmung. Alexandria is thus described as 'breathing' on several occasions, while Justine comments that 'we are all in the grip of the emotional field which we thrown down about one another.'[42] At a contiguous point in the narrative 'the gravitational field of the city' is imagined as pulling people into it.[43] The behaviour which the city thus generates is primarily driven by a sensuality which characters seem powerless to control. So, Darley's affair with Justine is against his better judgement, his sense of morality, and his loyalty to Nessim. In *Mountolive*, the British diplomat, David Mountolive, is similarly unable to resist an impolitic attraction to Leila Hosnani. In fact, this particular volume is explicitly themed around Mountolive's desire, and failure, to 'act' autonomously in a political sense. Hamstrung by various political considerations and clearly affected by the onset of war, Mountolive also simply *feels* powerless in much the same way as Darley writes that 'at times she [Justine] spoke of going away: at times I did the same. But neither of us could move. We were forced to await the outcome with a fatality and exhaustion that was truly fearful to experience.'[44] A whole host of other characters, including Pursewarden, Mountolive, Scobie, Pombal, and Narouz, are similarly unable to resist what are ultimately self-destructive desires.

Reducing the mood of *The Alexandria Quartet* to a couple of basic descriptors is certainly not the intended outcome of this mood-reading. Having said that, what could be said with a fair degree of conviction is that there is a pervasive eroticism in the text which is connected both to the powerlessness referred to above and to the varieties of sensual experience which the city provides (the atmospheric 'coating' mentioned earlier). Lust, tension, and anxiety are 'in the air' just as heat and dust are subsumed within the body. But the entanglement goes further than this, as the 'highly determinate cultural world' of Alexandria—its ancient and modern history—is also imbricated in the text's mood: just as it acts as an agent in the plot, so too the city seems to have a memory in this sense. Darley writes explicitly with this in relation to Nessim:

> At this time he had already begun to experience that great cycle of historical dreams which now replaced the dreams of his childhood in his mind, and into which the City now threw itself—as if at last it had found a responsive subject through which to express the collective desires, the collective wishes, which informed its culture. He would wake to see the towers and minarets printed on the exhausted, dust-powdered sky, and see as if *en montage* on them the giant footprints of the historical memory which lies behind the recollections of individual personality, its mentor and guide: indeed its inventor, since man is only an extension of the spirit of place.[45]

Nessim is merely the 'responsive subject' of the city, created by memory and culture but also by 'towers,' 'minarets,' and 'dust-powdered sky.'

As the narrative develops, Darley, too, recognises and courts 'a desire to be claimed by the city, enrolled among its trivial or tragic memories.'[46] It is noticeable, then, that the first longer passage quoted in this essay ends with a reference to the city's most famous love affair, as Darley wonders: 'Was it in this that Anthony heard the heart-numbing strains of the great music which persuaded him to surrender for ever to the city he loved?'[47] What is combined here is a very specific referent of *Stimmung*—the haptic 'surrounding' of music which touches on the inside ('heart-numbing')—and a cultural precedent in the 'surrender' which Darley will make to Justine and Alexandria. The same entanglement can be seen when Justine is compared to that 'race of terrific queens which left behind them the ammoniac smell of their incestuous loves to hover like a cloud over the Alexandrian subconscious.'[48] In forming citizens as its 'flora' the city is aided by a history fertilised through a rich diversity of cultural influences. Darley thus writes of knowing Justine 'for a true child of Alexandria; which is neither Greek, Syrian nor Egyptian, but a hybrid: a joint.'[49] This melting pot of histories and cultures is intrinsically linked to the plot in that Nessim's justifies his actions on the basis that he is protecting the Egyptian Copts (of whom he is a member) from the rise of radical Islam by building an alliance with Palestinian Jews. But it is also connected to an anti-British thematic, most notably voiced by Pursewarden, which takes aim at the sterile homogeneity of colonialism and its attempt to flatten histories and beliefs. In some ways paradoxically, Durrell's text thus both attacks the evils of cultural and religious tension at the same time as it admonishes the failure to immerse oneself in such friction.[50]

There is one very important *caveat* to the preceding discussion, which is that it is questionable how accurate Durrell's rendering of Alexandria is. Ray Morrison has suggested that the quartet owes more to an immersion in Taoist philosophy than the particularities of Alexandrian life, while John Rodenbeck has been more condemnatory of Durrell, describing his writing as parading 'what appears to be a cynical indifference—perhaps even hostility—to the physical and historical underpinnings of what purports to be his subject.'[51] This remarkable statement is undermined by the fact that Rodenbeck sees the poetry of C.P. Cavafy as evoking a more authentic Alexandria at the same time as claiming that, without it, 'the Quartet would be in fact inconceivable.'[52] The internal contradiction of this stance aside, it does raise an interesting question about the authentic recapturing of mood. It is significant, for instance, that Darley finds the mood of Alexandria in a writing which is indebted to other writers, including Cavafy, and which takes place once he has left the city and is living on a Greek island. On the second page of *Justine*, Darley writes that 'I had to come here in order completely to rebuild this city in my brain—melancholy provinces which the old man saw as full of the "black ruins" of his life.'[53] From the beginning of the quartet, then, the possibility of a recollection which 'rebuilds' an authentic original is aided, but surely also undermined, by the recourse that must be made to the literary: the 'old man' referred to being Cavafy. References to the poet abound, often at extremely significant moments in the text. Thus, when Darley writes at length about Nessim and Justine's relationship, he imagines Nessim thinking with Cavafy:

> Was all the discordance of their lives a measure of the anxiety which they had inherited from the city or the age? 'Oh my God' he almost said. 'Why don't we leave this city, Justine, and seek an atmosphere less impregnated with the sense of deracination and failure?' The words of the old poet came into his mind, pressed down like the pedal of a piano, to boil and reverberate around the frail hope which the thought had raised from its dark sleep.[54]

This passage is connected to an endnote which directs the reader to Cavafy's poem, 'The City,' translated by Durrell and in which the 'black ruins' of the earlier reference appear. Cavafy's poem voices a desire to leave a city that imprisons the body and intrudes upon one's state of mind, its speaker referring to feeling 'confined among these dreary purlieus/Of the common mind' and of wandering the 'same mental suburbs.'[55] Similarly, Nessim's animus towards the city (which is aimed partly at its status as a colonial outpost which isolates it from the rest of Egypt) is vocalised through a sense of an atmosphere impregnated with emotion and which is a product of the city and the age. And the words of the poet reverberate like both a musical chord and the steam of boiling liquid—in other words, in the guise of the 'tone' and lightly atmospheric touch of *Stimmung*. Nessim recalls this poem as he himself thinks of leaving Alexandria—or is it that he thinks of leaving in the terms he does partly because Cavafy's poetry lives in the heat and dust of his city?

When it comes to mood, it is perhaps best to consider notions of original and representation as one further entanglement, the disentanglement of which should be resisted. As Darley comments, the city is 'half-imagined (yet wholly real).'[56] While this statement refers to the task of remembering an Alexandria that is now in his past, it also suggests that the experience of the city is partially an aesthetic encounter. Taken in this sense, mood and *Stimmung* can productively be connected to notions of aura. Indeed, this is precisely what Gernot Böhme has done in postulating a theory of aesthetics based on the idea of a 'production of atmospheres.' Böhme takes Walter Benjamin's aura as one of his starting points, noting that Benjamin refers to the aura as a

> strange tissue of space and time [...] which flows forth spatially, almost something like a breath or a haze—precisely an atmosphere.

Benjamin says that one "breathes" the aura. This breathing means that it is absorbed bodily, that it enters the bodily economy of tension and expansion, that one allows this atmosphere to permeate the self.[57]

In *Mountolive*, the writer Pursewarden makes a strikingly similar point, commenting that in the reception of art, 'artist and public simply register, like a seismograph, an electromagnetic charge.'[58] The aura of an artwork is autonomous—it does not produce its 'atmosphere' through the authentic reference to a prior reality but is marked only by, as Jean-Luc Nancy puts it, 'the coming into presence of some *presence*'—and it is encountered in a way that is strikingly similar to the attunement of *Stimmung* discussed in this essay.[59] It would therefore make sense to claim that it is precisely the internal mood of text which does most to produce its aura.

Conclusion

That the quartet's plot is constitutive of mood is, ultimately, a matter of its confluence with both the text's explicit evocation of *Stimmung* and its emplacement in a historically informed and 'highly determinate cultural world.' Of his own writing Darley comments that

> the solace of such work as I do with brain and heart lies in this—that only there, in the silences of the painter or the writer can reality be reordered, reworked and made to show its significant side. Our common actions in reality are simply the sackcloth covering which hides the cloth-of-gold—the meaning of the pattern.[60]

To return to the terms of affect theory and its critique, Darley thus sees his task as one of cognising meaning in retrospect and as an afterthought to instinctive immersion in the world. Yet, as the narrative progresses it is precisely this form of meaning which eludes his grasp. On the opening page of *Clea*, he thus writes:

> I had set out once to store, to codify, to annotate the past before it was utterly lost—that at least was a task I had set myself. I had failed in it (perhaps it was hopeless?) for no sooner had I embalmed one aspect of it in words than the intrusion of new knowledge disrupted the frame of reference, everything flew asunder, only to reassemble again in unforeseen, unpredictable patterns...[61]

As much as this passage articulates a failure to know, it is also one in which Alexandria's *Stimmung* can be felt. The patterns of meaning reassemble as the shifting sands of the desert sweep over the city, merging with the lapping waters of the shore and the Mareotis lake. And while these patterns never adhere enough to become an object of stable meaning, the interaction with each successive iteration *is* formed as an intentional relation to a cultural world characterised by a melting pot of histories and by friction and tension. In trying to remember discussions from his past, Darley not only comments that 'I can only remember the pattern and weight of these conversations, not their substance' but also notes that 'these are the moments which possess the writer [...] and which live on perpetually.'[62] Pattern, weight, mood, *Stimmung*, aura: Darley recalls what is also most memorable about Durrell's text—not the ultimate conclusions that might come out of its epistemological journey but the ontological being which that journey has in part produced. In other words, the confusing twists and turns of the plot are constitutive of an Alexandria which is a rich muddle of histories, cultures, and ethnicities and which is felt as a range of light touches which surround the body. Darley may be right to say that he has failed in something, or even in many things: but in registering the charge of Alexandria's *Stimmung*, the reader cannot feel that transmitting its mood has been one of them.

Notes

1 On the emotions, see Thomas Dixon, *From Passions to Emotions: The Creation of a Secular Psychological Category* (Cambridge: Cambridge University Press, 2003); Charles Altieri, *The Particulars of Rapture: An Aesthetics of the Affects* (Ithaca, NY and London: Cornell University Press, 2003); Jenefer Robinson, *Deeper Than Reason: Emotions and Its Role in Literature, Music, and Art* (Oxford: Clarendon, 2005); Berys Gaut, *Art, Emotion, and Ethics* (Oxford: Oxford University Press, 2007); Kirsty Martin, *Modernism and the Rhythms of Sympathy: Vernon Lee, Virginia Woolf, D. H. Lawrence* (Oxford: Oxford University Press, 2013). See also Suzanne Keen, 'Introduction: Special Issue on Narrative and Emotions,' *Poetics Today*, 32, 2011, pp. 1–53. On the body, see Elaine Scarry, *Literature and the Body: Essays on Populations and Persons* (Baltimore, MD and London: Johns Hopkins University Press, 1990); Steven Connor, *The Book of Skin* (London: Reaktion Books, 2004); Susan Stewart, *Poetry and the Fate of the Senses* (Chicago, IL: University of Chicago Press, 2002). Neither of these lists are exhaustive.
2 Rita Felski and Susan Fraiman, 'Introduction: Special Issue "In the Mood,"' *New Literary History*, 43, 2012, pp. v–xii; Ben Highmore and Jenny Bourne Taylor, 'Introduction: Special Issue "Introducing Mood Work,"' *New Formations*, 82, 2014, pp. 5–12.
3 Ben Highmore, 'Feeling Our Way: Mood and Cultural Studies,' *Communication and Critical/Cultural Studies*, 10, 2013, 427–38 (p. 427).
4 Melissa Gregg and Gregory Seigworth, 'An Inventory of Shimmers,' in *The Affect Theory Reader*, ed. by Melissa Gregg and Gregory Seigworth (London and Durham, NC: Duke University Press, 2010), pp. 1–25.
5 Eve Kosofsky Sedgwick, *Touching Feeling: Affect, Pedagogy, Performativity* (Durham, NC and London: Duke University Press, 2003); Brian Massumi, *Politics of Affect* (Cambridge: Polity, 2015).

6 Patricia Ticineto Clough and Jean Halley, *The Affective Turn: Theorizing the Social* (Durham, NC and London: Duke University Press, 2007); Marco Abel, *Violent Affect: Literature, Cinema, and Critique after Representation* (Lincoln and London: University of Nebraska Press, 2007); Lisa Blackman, *Immaterial Bodies: Affect, Embodiment, Mediation* (London: Sage, 2012); Adam Piette, 'Beckett, Affect, and the Face,' *Textual Practice*, 25, 2011, pp. 281–95; Ravit Reichman, *The Affective Life of Law: Legal Modernism and the Literary Imagination* (Stanford, CA: Stanford University Press, 2009).

7 Ruth Leys, 'The Turn to Affect: A Critique,' *Critical Inquiry*, 37, 2011, pp. 434–72 (p. 443).

8 Ibid., p. 450.

9 In the pages of *Critical Inquiry* alone, these include William E. Connolly, 'The Complexity of Intention,' *Critical Inquiry*, 37, 2011, pp. 791–98; Adam Frank and Elizabeth A. Wilson, 'Like-Minded,' *Critical Inquiry*, 38, 2012, pp. 870–7; Charles Altieri, 'Affect, Intentionality, and Cognition: A Response to Ruth Leys,' *Critical Inquiry*, 38, 2012, 878–81. See also Jonathan Flatley, 'How a Revolutionary Counter-Mood Is Made,' *In the Mood, Special Issue of New Literary History*, 43, 2012, pp. v–xii.

10 Ruth Leys, 'Affect and Intention: A Reply to William E. Connolly,' *Critical Inquiry*, 37, 2011, pp. 799–805. Ruth Leys, 'Facts and Moods: A Reply to My Critics,' *Critical Inquiry*, 38, 2012, pp. 882–91.

11 Altieri, 'Affect, Intentionality, and Cognition', pp. 879–80.

12 Gregg and Seigworth, 'An Inventory of Shimmers,' p. 1.

13 Martin Heidegger, *Being and Time*, trans. John Macquarrie and Edward Robinson (Oxford: Basil Blackwell, 1978), p. 174.

14 Ibid., p. 176.

15 Stephen Mulhall, *Heidegger and Being and Time* (London: Routledge, 1996), p. 76.

16 Hans Ulrich Gumbrecht, *Atmosphere, Mood, Stimmung: On a Hidden Potential of Literature*, trans. by Erik Butler (Stanford, CA: Stanford University Press, 2012), pp. 3–4.

17 Highmore's example of this is eating, where 'the cacophony of crunching might actually be part of the "flavor" of potato chips.' Ben Highmore, 'Bitter after Taste: Affect, Food and Social Aeshtetics,' in *The Affect Theory Reader*, ed. by Melissa Gregg and Gregory Seigworth (London and Durham, NC: Duke University Press, 2010), pp. 118–37 (p. 121).

18 Gumbrecht, *Atmosphere, Mood, Stimmung*, p. 4.

19 Gumbrecht's example of this is Thomas Mann's *Death in Venice* which is, of course, also deeply concerned with music. Ibid., p. 75.

20 Steven Connor, 'Cp: Or, a Few Don't by a Cultural Phenomenologist,' *Parallax*, 5, 1999, 17–31 (p. 18).

21 Jonathan Flatley, *Affective Mapping: Melancholia and the Politics of Modernism* (Cambridge, MA.: Harvard University Press, 2008), p. 16.

22 Charles Guignon, 'Moods in Heidegger's *Being and Time*,' in *What Is an Emotion?: Classic Readings in Philosophical Psychology*, ed. by Cheshire Calhoun and Robert C. Solomon (Oxford and New York: Oxford University Press, 1984), pp. 230–43 (p. 237).

23 Heidegger, *Being and Time*, p. 177.

24 Leys, 'Affect and Intentions', p. 802.

25 Keynote lecture at 'Mood—Aesthetic, Psychological and Philosophical Perspectives' conference, University of Warwick, 6–7 May 2016. Mood-reading thus has the potential to be a further mode of the 'surface reading' proposed by Stephen Best and Sharon Marcus. Stephen Best and Sharon Marcus, 'Surface Reading: An Introduction,' *Representations*, 108, 2009, pp. 1–21.

26 Highmore, 'Bitter after Taste', p. 119.
27 Lawrence Durrell, *The Alexandria Quartet* (London: Faber and Faber, 1968), p. 9.
28 Ibid.
29 Ibid., p. 338.
30 Ibid., p. 18.
31 Ibid., p. 700.
32 Gumbrecht, *Atmosphere, Mood, Stimmung*, p. 20.
33 On Gadamer, see Hans Ulrich Gumbrecht, *Production of Presence: What Meaning Cannot Convey* (Stanford, CA: Stanford University Press, 2004), p. 64. For various forms of performance, see William Eggington, 'Performance and Presence, Analysis of a Modern Aporia,' *Journal of Literary Theory*, 1, 2007, 3–18 (p. 6); Scott McCracken, 'The Mood of Defeat,' *New Formations*, 82, 2014, pp. 64–81; Patricia Waugh, 'Precarious Voices: Moderns, Moods, and Moving Epochs,' in *Moving Modernisms: Motion, Technology, and Modernity*, ed. by David Bradshaw, Laura Marcus, and Rebecca Roach (Oxford: Oxford University Press, 2016), pp. 191–213.
34 Alex Houen, 'Introduction: Affecting Words', *Special Issue of Textual Practice, Affects, Text, and Performativity*, 25, 2, 2011, pp. 215–32 (p. 217).
35 Keen, 'Introduction: Special Issue on Narrative and Emotions,' p. 4.
36 In the special issue of *Poetics Today*, see especially Miranda Burgess, 'On Being Moved: Sympathy, Mobility, and Narrative Form,' *Poetics Today*, 32, 2011, pp. 289–321.
37 Robinson, *Deeper Than Reason*.
38 For example, see Blakey Vermeule, 'A Comeuppance Theory of Narrative and Emotions,' *Poetics Today*, 32, 2011, pp. 235–53; Mary-Catherine Harrison, 'How Narrative Relationships Overcome Empathic Bias: Elizabeth Gaskell's Empathy across Social Difference,' *Poetics Today*, 32, 2011, pp. 255–88.
39 Gumbrecht, *Atmosphere, Mood, Stimmung*, p. 2.
40 Durrell, *The Alexandria Quartet*, pp. 17 and 39.
41 Ibid., pp. 28 and 49.
42 Ibid., p. 698.
43 Ibid., p. 729.
44 Ibid., p. 122.
45 Ibid., p. 143.
46 Ibid., p. 155.
47 Ibid., p. 18.
48 Ibid., p. 23.
49 Ibid., p. 698.
50 This reading of Durrell could be compared to Sianne Ngai's identification of feelings which are 'diagnostically concerned with states of *inaction*'—albeit Ngai uses a slightly different terminology and places genuine social experience at the core of her interpretations. Sianne Ngai, *Ugly Feelings* (Cambridge, MA: Harvard University Press, 2005), p. 22.
51 Ray Morrison, 'The City and Its Ontology in Lawrence Durrell's *Alexandria Quartet*,' *Mosaic: A Journal of the Interdisciplinary Study of Literature*, 46, 2013, pp. 55–70; John Rodenbeck, 'Alexandria in Cavafy, Durrell, and Tsirkas,' *Alif: Journal of Comparative Poetics*, 21, 2001, 141–60 (p. 156).
52 Rodenbeck, 'Alexandria in Cavafy, Durrell, and Tsirkas,' p. 149.
53 Durrell, *The Alexandria Quartet*, p. 18.
54 Ibid., p. 147.

55 Constantine P. Cavafy, 'The City,' in Lawrence Durrell, *The Alexandria Quartet*, (London: Faber and Faber, 1968), p. 201.
56 Durrell, *The Alexandria Quartet*, p. 209.
57 Gernot Böhme, 'Atmosphere as the Fundamental Concept of a New Aesthetics,' *Thesis Eleven*, 36, 1993, 113–26 (p. 117).
58 Durrell, *The Alexandria Quartet*, p. 482.
59 Jean-Luc Nancy, *The Birth to Presence*, trans. by Brian Holmes, (Stanford, CA: Stanford University Press, 1993), p. 389.
60 Durrell, *The Alexandria Quartet*, p. 20.
61 Ibid., p. 657.
62 Ibid., pp. 26 and 27.

References

Abel, Marco, *Violent Affect: Literature, Cinema, and Critique after Representation* (Lincoln and London: University of Nebraska Press, 2007).

Altieri, Charles, *The Particulars of Rapture: An Aesthetics of the Affects* (Ithaca and London: Cornell University Press, 2003).

———, 'Affect, Intentionality, and Cognition: A Response to Ruth Leys', *Critical Inquiry*, 38, (2012), 878–81.

Best, Stephen, and Sharon Marcus, 'Surface Reading: An Introduction', *Representations*, 108 (2009), 1–21.

Blackman, Lisa, *Immaterial Bodies: Affect, Embodiment, Mediation* (London: Sage, 2012).

Böhme, Gernot, 'Atmosphere as the Fundamental Concept of a New Aesthetics', *Thesis Eleven*, 36 (1993), 113–26.

Burgess, Miranda, 'On Being Moved: Sympathy, Mobility, and Narrative Form', *Poetics Today*, 32 (2011), 289–321.

Cavafy, Constantine P., 'The City', in *The Alexandria Quartet*, ed. by Lawrence Durrell (London: Faber and Faber, 1968), p. 201.

Clough, Patricia Ticineto, and Jean Halley, eds., *The Affective Turn: Theorizing the Social* (Durham, NC and London: Duke University Press, 2007).

Connolly, William E., 'The Complexity of Intention', *Critical Inquiry*, 37 (2011), 791–98.

Connor, Steven, 'Cp: Or, a Few Don't by a Cultural Phenomenologist', *Parallax*, 5 (1999), 17–31.

———, *The Book of Skin* (London: Reaktion Books, 2004).

Dixon, Thomas, *From Passions to Emotions: The Creation of a Secular Psychological Category* (Cambridge: Cambridge University Press, 2003).

Durrell, Lawrence, *The Alexandria Quartet* (London: Faber and Faber, 1968).

Eggington, William, 'Performance and Presence, Analysis of a Modern Aporia', *Journal of Literary Theory*, 1 (2007), 3–18.

Felski, Rita, and Susan Fraiman, 'Introduction: Special Issue "In the Mood"', *New Literary History*, 43 (2012), v–xii.

Flatley, Jonathan, *Affective Mapping: Melancholia and the Politics of Modernism* (Cambridge, MA: Harvard University Press, 2008).

———, 'How a Revolutionary Counter-Mood Is Made', *In the Mood, Special Issue of New Literary History*, 43 (2012), v–xii.

Frank, Adam, and Elizabeth A. Wilson, 'Like-Minded', *Critical Inquiry*, 38 (2012), 870–7.

Gaut, Berys, *Art, Emotion, and Ethics* (Oxford: Oxford University Press, 2007).

Gregg, Melissa, and Gregory Seigworth, 'An Inventory of Shimmers', in *The Affect Theory Reader*, ed. by Melissa Gregg and Gregory Seigworth (London and Durham, NC: Duke University Press, 2010), pp. 1–25.

Guignon, Charles, 'Moods in Heidegger's *Being and Time*', in *What Is an Emotion?: Classic Readings in Philosophical Psychology*, ed. by Cheshire Calhoun and Robert C. Solomon (Oxford and New York: Oxford University Press, 1984), pp. 230–43.

Gumbrecht, Hans Ulrich, *Production of Presence: What Meaning Cannot Convey* (Stanford, CA: Stanford University Press, 2004).

——, *Atmosphere, Mood, Stimmung: On a Hidden Potential of Literature*, trans. by Erik Butler (Stanford, CA: Stanford University Press, 2012).

Harrison, Mary-Catherine, 'How Narrative Relationshiips Overcome Empathic Bias: Elizabeth Gaskell's Empathy across Social Difference', *Poetics Today*, 32 (2011), 255–88.

Heidegger, Martin, *Being and Time*, trans. by John Macquarrie and Edward Robinson (Oxford: Basil Blackwell, 1978).

Highmore, Ben, 'Bitter after Taste: Affect, Food and Social Aesthetics', in *The Affect Theory Reader*, ed. by Melissa Gregg and Gregory Seigworth (London and Durham, NC: Duke University Press, 2010), pp. 118–37.

——, 'Feeling Our Way: Mood and Cultural Studies', *Communication and Critical/Cultural Studies*, 10 (2013), 427–38.

Highmore, Ben, and Jenny Bourne Taylor, 'Introduction: Special Issue "Introducing Mood Work"', *New Formations*, 82 (2014), 5–12.

Houen, Alex, 'Introduction: Affecting Words', Special Issue of *Textual Practice*: *Affects, Text, and Performativity*, 25, 2, (2011), pp. 215–32.

Keen, Suzanne, 'Introduction: Special Issue on Narrative and Emotions', *Poetics Today*, 32 (2011), 1–53.

Leys, Ruth, 'Affect and Intention: A Reply to William E. Connolly', *Critical Inquiry*, 37 (2011), 799–805.

——, 'The Turn to Affect: A Critique', *Critical Inquiry*, 37 (2011), 434–72.

——, 'Facts and Moods: A Reply to My Critics', *Critical Inquiry*, 38 (2012), 882–91.

Martin, Kirsty, *Modernism and the Rhythms of Sympathy: Vernon Lee, Virginia Woolf, D. H. Lawrence* (Oxford: Oxford University Press, 2013).

Massumi, Brian, *Politics of Affect* (Cambridge: Polity, 2015).

McCracken, Scott, 'The Mood of Defeat', *New Formations*, 82 (2014), 64–81.

Morrison, Ray, 'The City and Its Ontology in Lawrence Durrell's *Alexandria Quartet*', *Mosaic: A Journal of the Interdisciplinary Study of Literature*, 46 (2013), 55–70.

Mulhall, Stephen, *Heidegger and Being and Time* (London: Routledge, 1996).

Nancy, Jean-Luc, *The Birth to Presence*, trans. by Brian Holmes (Stanford, CA: Stanford University Press, 1993).

Ngai, Sianne, *Ugly Feelings* (Cambridge, MA: Harvard University Press, 2005).

Piette, Adam, 'Beckett, Affect, and the Face', *Textual Practice*, 25 (2011), 281–95.

Reichman, Ravit, *The Affective Life of Law: Legal Modernism and the Literary Imagination* (Stanford, CA: Stanford University Press, 2009).

Robinson, Jenefer, *Deeper Than Reason: Emotions and Its Role in Literature, Music, and Art* (Oxford: Clarendon, 2005).

Rodenbeck, John, 'Alexandria in Cavafy, Durrell, and Tsirkas', *Alif: Journal of Comparative Poetics*, 21 (2001), 141–60.

Scarry, Elaine, ed., *Literature and the Body: Essays on Populations and Persons* (Baltimore, MD and London: Johns Hopkins University Press, 1990).

Sedgwick, Eve Kosofsky, *Touching Feeling: Affect, Pedagogy, Performativity* (Durham, NC and London: Duke University Press, 2003).

Stewart, Susan, *Poetry and the Fate of the Senses* (Chicago, IL: University of Chicago Press, 2002).

Vermeule, Blakey, 'A Comeuppance Theory of Narrative and Emotions', *Poetics Today*, 32 (2011), 235–53.

Waugh, Patricia, 'Precarious Voices: Moderns, Moods, and Moving Epochs', in *Moving Modernisms: Motion, Technology, and Modernity*, ed. by David Bradshaw, Laura Marcus, and Rebecca Roach (Oxford: Oxford University Press, 2016), pp. 191–213.

11 Of Mood

A Sonic Repertoire

Mary Cappello

Preface

A non-genre that allows for untoward movement, apposition, and assemblage, that is one part conundrum, one part accident, and that fosters a taste for discontinuity: the essay might be mood's most companionate form.

Life Breaks In: A Mood Almanack, the book from which the following pieces are excerpted, is a collection of lyric essays and prose experiments that, in keeping with Hans Ulrich Gumbrecht's call to *essay* mood (in his *Atmosphere, Mood, Stimmung*), relies on what I call 'cloud-writing' to nudge mood into ever more intelligible forms.

Mood's aesthetic invitation to me as a writer was also its ineluctable challenge: not to chase mood, track it, or pin it down; neither to explain or define mood, but to notice it, often enough, to listen for it, and do something *like it* without killing it in the process.

Over the course of the ten years that I worked on this book, I came to consider that mood's relative abstractness or concreteness, its materialisation or its airy ethereality is never a preordained given. Rather, mood becomes apparent precisely according to the language we are willing to grant it, the extent to which we are willing to let it act upon our imaginations. Thus, I could not tell until I had finished composing my essays on mood that what I might have to offer was an alternative to the age old taxonomy of emotion that accompanies mood, considering it instead in terms of architecture and air, as envelope and sphere, as niche, sound, skin, and reverberation; as gravity, wave, voice, and hue; as temperature and tempo; as making and creating.

'Skeptical about the power of "theories" to explain atmospheres and moods' and doubtful around 'the viability of "methods" to identify them,' Hans Gumbrecht suggests that we rely more on

> the potential of counterintuitive thinking than on a pre-established 'path' or 'way' (the etymological meaning of *method*). Counterintuitive thinking is not afraid to deviate from the norms of rationality and logic that govern everyday life...Instead, it is set into motion by 'hunches'.
>
> (Gumbrecht, 17)

It is in that same experimental spirit that I composed *Life Breaks In*, following mood as a language rather than as a concept, and via a panoply of hints and cues. In these senses, my work moves in uncanny concert with Hans Gumbrecht's call to shift our modes of address and forms of inquiry in mood's name, never knowing in advance where we might arrive.

What new forms of writing does mood tempt us to create? How might mood exert an exciting pressure on our modes of public colloquy? Might the reading, the lecture, the panel discussion morph into 'mood rooms,' and what might characterise their collocations? These are the questions I am hopeful that we can, crossing disciplines and spaces, pursue.

'Of Mood: A Sonic Repertoire'

Excerpted and adapted from *Life Breaks In: A Mood Almanack©*, University of Chicago Press, 2016.

Mood Hint: *Life as a series of moods—like Picasso's Blue Period—tonal registers of being. Or a series of rabbit holes, or doors within doors, moods as rooms, rooms I have known in order to arrive at the place where I hear things.*

I. Oneiric

I'm sitting in an examining room while an otolaryngologist reads my chart. I've just turned fifty, but he remarks, 'You have the hearing of an eighty year old. There's no disease entity that has caused this,' he explains, and we've ruled out my having ever been a member of a heavy metal band. 'It's more like a natural deterioration that we see in people as they age, but in your case, it's happening much more rapidly.' And then he tries to exemplify my future with the mention of hearing aids—which seem acceptable to me—and lip-reading, which does not. There'd been an episode that precipitated my visit to the doctor, but I had waited at least a year or two to make the appointment. It was as simple a discovery as realising that Jean could hear the pitch of a digital thermometer that was hanging out of my mouth and I could not. I was in the middle of treatment for breast cancer at the time, and this discovery was rather low down on the list of things I was learning about myself. But then I started to notice that I was having trouble hearing my students—which got richer especially when I had to strain to hear them in classrooms where I was teaching courses on literature and sound—until it dawned on me: in the name of 'chemo brain,' doctors were beginning to admit that cancer and its treatments could affect a person's mood. But no one had mentioned that if chemotherapy had caused most of the hair on my body to fall off, mightn't it also have destroyed the hairs that governed hearing lodged in my inner ear? Clinicians are only just now beginning to acknowledge exactly that.

When a dime fell from a counter in a restaurant and I did not hear it hit the floor, Jean asked, with a touch of Isaac Newton meets Dr.

Caligari in her voice, 'You really didn't hear that? Let me do it again.' The diminution of a sense doesn't need to be experienced as a subtraction but as an opportunity for an entirely different relationship to the world. (Sure.) I may not have heard the dime hit the floor, but I was ultra-aware of the scent of clam chowder and the softness of Jean's overcoat to say nothing of the intimacy of an experimental mode that forever sparks the mood of our relationship. 'I'm not hearing anything,' I said as I watched the dime morph from metal washer to plastic bingo chip to cardboard disc, or so it seems retrospectively. When the bounce of its meeting linoleum or concrete—I can't remember which—produced no accompanying sound, I felt frightened but remained curious about the broken correspondences. Dropping the dime a third time and really concentrating, I thought I did hear an infinitesimally faint 'tic'—not quite the slap and ting I was expecting—it was more like the way a person with superhuman audition might claim to hear the tip of a pencil tapping through paper on the wooden surface of a desk from a very far distance in an amphitheater. I swear the movement of the object, shorn of sound, was both sped up and slowed down.

Do we ever perceive things as they are?

A dime hitting a floor sans sound, to a hearing person, is oneiric, a word I learned and never forgot from a professor of art history whose hair was as fine and voice as cavernously wispy as the meaning of the term: 'oneiric'—like a dream. Some paintings were part of an oneiric tradition, he explained. A painting could change your life, he said, describing one such metamorphic meeting in a museum, but, better, it could fill you with the Rilkean imperative in the poem that he read to us that *you* must change your life. I can hear still him across a gulf of thirty years making lessons in the form of lace at a Vermeer casement. There were bubbles in his voice like beads forever sunk inside a glass pane when he pronounced the words, 'the ba-roque,' prelude to our inauguration into a world of the overmuch. But when he asked us to turn our attention to the 'oneiric,' he cocked an ear and suggested we remain on the lookout for secular haloes that relied on something less immediate than sight. It was mood that he was asking us to attend to, and the only way to get there was by way of his hair and his voice, both of which were bathed in the mildest yellow.

*

Mood Hint: *Is to be awash in memory at bedtime to be summoned by or submerged by mood?*

II. Gong Bath

All I had said was 'mood' and 'sound,' and 'envelopes' in response to the question, 'What are you working on?,' when a friend of mine invited me to an event: it would require twenty dollars, she said, and would last for about an hour. She said she'd thought I'd really get a lot out of a 'gong bath.'

Immediately I pictured a take-me-to-the-river experience. I think I thought a midwife might be present. I needed to know if nakedness was a requirement, or if a bathing suit was optional. I imagined a toga, or endlessly unwinding winding sheet. The water would be turquoise-tinted and warm—bathtub warm but bubble-less. Everything would depend on my willingness to go under—to experience a form of suspended animation. No doubt sounds would be relayed to me—under-water healing sounds—to which I'd be asked to respond with my eyes closed all the while confident I would not drown.

Then I remembered how my mother was ever unable to float and how her fear of water fueled her determination that my brothers and I learn to swim early on. My mother can't swim, but throughout my childhood she writes poetry in response to the call of a nearby creek that she studies and meditates near. I maintain an aversion to putting my head under water even after I do learn how to swim. How can I ever push off or dive deep if my mother cannot float?

No memory will be as flush with pattering—*this is life!*—as the sensation that is the sound of the garden hose, first nozzle-tested as a fine spray into air, then plunged into one foot of water to refill a plastic backyard pool. The muffled gurgle sounds below, but I hear it from above. The nape of my neck is dry; my eyelids are dotted with droplets, and the basal sound of water moving inside of water draws me like the signal of a gong: 'get in, get out, get in.' The water is cool above and warm below, or warm above and cool below: if I bend to touch its stripes, one of my straps releases and goes lank. Voices are reflections that do not pierce me here; they mottle. I am a fish in the day's aquarium.

The gong bath turns out to be a middle-class group affair at a local yoga studio not a private baptism in a subterranean tub. The group of bourgeoisie of which I am a member pretends for a day to be hermits in a desert. It's summertime and we arrive with small parcels: loosely dressed, jewelry-free, to each person her mat and a pillow to prop our knees. We're to lie flat on our backs, we're told, and to try not to fidget. We're to shut our eyes and merely listen while two soft-spoken men create sounds from differently sized Tibetan gongs that hang from wooden poles positioned in a row in front of us. Some of the gongs appear to have copper-colored irises at their center. In their muted state, they hang like unprepossessing harbingers of calm.

At its furthest reaches, science's mood is poetry, at that point where it gives up on controlling the things it studies, agreeing instead to a more profound devotion to spare sounds whose tones the mysteries of existence brush up against asymptotically: the rustle of pages weighted with results, the fluttering of questions pondered in obscurity, the settling of a log on a forgotten fire, the hiss inside the grate. Even in its earliest incarnations, the science of acoustics turned to water as its scribe by dropping a pebble on a liquid surface—plunk—and watching the rings around it form. So, too, mood finds a home in circles and widening gyres: the geometry that accompanies mood—whether fore-, back-, sur-, or gr- is 'round.' And now these gongs waiting to be struck are also ringed, from the darkest centre to shimmering edge.

I know it will sound like I was tripping if I say I felt as though I was dropped down a watery chute inside a gong bath. The sounds slowed things down to the point of drugging of my inner voice: suddenly that voice was the cab of a hot air balloon that I would need to climb up into to enter should I ever feel the need to return to it. Is it possible for the mind to revert to pure sound? I began to have a feeling I'd never known before: my eyes weren't rolling backwards into my head—this wasn't exactly an ecstatic state; behind their closed lids, my eyes felt as though they were sliding to either side of my head. This must be what happens to us when we die, though I wasn't for that moment afraid of dying.

The lover's discourse—any word uttered by the beloved—takes up residence in the lover's body and rings there unstoppably. This pang that requires Roland Barthes to halt all occupation he calls 'reverberation.' Without the aid of microphones or speakers, the sound of gongs materialises and reverberates in the supine body—for my own part, I felt sound enter though the palms of my hands and the heels of my feet. In the concert hall, a cough or sneeze, whisper or crunch is a too ready reminder of the body of our fellows in the room. At a rock concert, we maybe sway or sweat together in a half-high haze but careful still to keep the edges of other bodies a-blur; we pitch our tent on the edges of group oblivion. In the gong bath, other bodies are nodal points that sound bounces off of. I felt sound bounce off the body of the person next to me, onto me, and on down the line; I felt it in my stomach like a pang.

Was I letting myself get all New Age kooky, producing a form of socially acceptable psychedelia that has no basis in fact? That sound can affect the central nervous system goes without saying. That sound can therefore be harnessed therapeutically to allay pain or alter the course of a disease has never been the drawing card of modern Western medicine. A little research can go a long way, and a student of mine once made me aware of prescribable sounds, or 'audioceuticals.' Vibroacoustic therapy is discounted as simply silly, along the order of overly priced vibrating easy chairs until someone gives a sound massage to a person with Parkinson's and finds that circulation is enhanced, and rigidity decreased. White noise as a treatment for ADHD, vibrating insoles to help the elderly maintain balance, or the space age sounding SonoPrep—a skin permeation device through which a blast of low-frequency ultrasonic waves opens a pore in the skin in lieu of a needle suggests territories we've barely begun to broach. Though neither I nor anyone I know has been offered a noninvasive therapy tool that can liquefy tumors of the prostate and the breast, or sonically bore a tiny hole into an infant's deformed heart valve, the sound technology and its practitioners apparently do exist.

What's this got to do with mood? Oceanographers tell us that sound moves faster in water than it does in air, but isn't air part liquid? They say they can measure qualities of sound that are impossible to hear. They observe that sound pushes particles together and pulls them apart, and that sound is the effect of a material's compression and expansion. When they add that the speed of sound in water is dependent on night or day, temperature, weather, and locale, I begin to feel I'm in the realm of sound with mood. So too when they describe a dolphin's 'kerplunk' as a slap of a tail on water to keep an aggressor at bay; when they note a whale's 'moans, groans, tones, and pulses,' and a seal's underwater 'clicks, trills, warbles, whistles and bells,' I begin to glimpse a mood part-sea.

A philosopher steps in and says the body itself is a skin stretched over resonant matter beneath. We are our own water-filled drums of emotionality and indigestion, of sounds and moods. A poet parts ways to say that water is sound; sound creates moods; all mood is aqueous sound.

It's the feeling a gong bath gives of encountering sound beneath a threshold, submerged, and then absorbed that makes me ally sound with mood as liquid. The gong bath doesn't affect my mood—it's the model for a mood; it is a mood, and it can't be reproduced. It says that mood and sound meet at the place of touching. Sounds touch me, and mood is the window of allowance, wide or narrow, to let sound in: my moods are equivalent to what I let myself touch, and be touched by in turn, but also what I have no choice in the matter of being encased in. A tongue stuck to a frozen pole; bare feet in mud. The bare of your back; the sting of my words. If I were a cat, touch would create a purring machine; if you over-touch me, I swat. Give us this day our daily sounds. How conscious are we of our ability to create our own soundscape exclusive of earbuds? How will you tune your day? What will you tune into with no instruments at your disposal but your whistle and gait?

Lest I seem to idealise my twenty-dollar experience, I should note that 50 minutes was way too long a time for listening to gongs. Five minutes would have had the same effect, but the gong players wanted to give us our money's worth.

Every gong bath since my first one has left me cold. They've really flopped.

In subsequent baths, I never got past the all-too-probable tendency to supply an image to every sound I heard, even entire narratives. Though the images were as unconsciously imbued, inexplicable, and private as those one experiences in dreams, I remained a foreigner stranded upon a shore and not a bather, immersing down and in. The images were dark: a boy shivering in his coat before drowning; my open mouth attempting but unable to pronounce Jean's name. There was a toucan and a typewriter, an avalanche of marbles, a body encased in wax. Having stirred up some unpleasantly tinged flotsam and jetsam, the Gong Bath left me feeling bereft, unlike great music 'that move[s] us…,' as Peter Kivy once wrote, 'because it is expressive of sadness,' not by 'making us sad.' Sad music puts us in an exalted mood, rendering us capable of experiencing the expression of sadness.

In order for a gong bath to work, sound has to obliterate language for a spell so we can touch mood's casement, its resonant shell. We have to be coaxed by sound to suspend our image-making tendencies even if pure mind like pure sound is impossible. But why should we try? After my first gong bath, I was convinced the phenomenon was going to become the audioceutical fad for twenty-first-century Americans. It could join the ranks of our half-understood borrowings from traditions not our own, providing an opiate to the all too comfortable classes, a soother to a whine. My prediction was a way of denying that I was in search of something, of an experience, deeply felt, and not just an observer doing fieldwork. I wanted to be invited to go under while you provide the sounds, to shed anticipation and bathe in curiosity, alive for a spell in the day's aquarium.

*

Mood Hint: *Some moods are the residue of a never completed cry—a wail?*

III. Sonophoto: Boy, Screaming

It must have been the absence of a flash at dusk combined with the relative shade of my backyard garden that yielded an entire roll of mostly blank birthday pictures that year. The conditions, combined with a cranky camera, weren't going to make it possible for any images to materialise, which must be why I received the one photo that partially did turn out— of four-year-old Kolya screaming—as a tonic. He's a trace in this soliloquising picture, and yet so vividly visible: there's a hue of a bare leg (it was summertime), and a broad white band of a striped shirt against the grey-green dark. Most especially, there's an audibly visible face, the angle of whose eyes shows the boy to be smiling—mischievously? triumphantly?—at the same time that he screams. His whole ghost-like figure tilts as if spinning inside the vertigo created by his cry, or maybe it just made the photographer woozy while the boy himself remained protected. This is my favorite detail: he's plugged his own ears with his fingers (Figure 11.1).

When Kolya was not that much younger, his father, my friend, Arthur, chalked up the extremity of Kolya's antics to the 'terrible twos,'

Figure 11.1 Sonophoto: Boy, Screaming.

but I never went in for that. The energy of Kolya's fervor was unique, or at least strictly his: he was his own heat-, light-, and energy-generating machine, which is how this photograph came to be. Against the absence of light and the possibility of a reproducible image, Kolya produces what physicists call *sonoluminescence*. Investigators still aren't entirely in agreement about how it happens, but they have observed emissions of regularly pulsing (in picoseconds) eerie blue light occasioned by high-frequency sound waves (just beyond the range of human hearing) as they bombard an air bubble suspended in water. Imagine finding ways to measure what goes on inside of tiny air bubbles as they react to sound, heat up, collapse, and emit a different form of energy: light. To say that Kolya's scream was sonoluminescent is far from scientifically accurate, but what he occasioned with his voice is more than metaphor, the literal projection of his being as an emanating source of temperature and tempo, of atmosphere and mood.

Now I wonder about the nature and quality of his photographed scream. How high was it pitched and to what extent did it muffle or mute the other ambient noises of that early evening background scene?

I once purposely left my camera home on a trip to an unfamiliar country, deciding to record nothing but a range of sounds as remembrance of the places we'd visited, from those that created an accidental ambiance—a voice suddenly singing in an alleyway—to those that alerted me to the distinctness of the place—the uncommon, to me, clapper that signaled an approaching train, cowbells on a hillside, voices in a restaurant, and especially the tune of clanking silverware floating through apartment windows at mid-day. I was convinced somehow that the sounds would offer a truer sense of the place than any two-dimensional picture plane could. If I reassembled the sounds when I got home, could I create something out-of-view about the place but immanent?

A video couldn't have accomplished the recreation of an atmosphere since sounds would be subordinated once again. Sounds by themselves, sounds and nothing but, have the effect of replacing us elsewhere. They bring us back, far, far back, and they bring us out and over to land in an extraneous zone, for sounds untethered are both reaching and vault-like, they emit a volume and an architecture, a substance and a shadow: but here I fall back on the language of images once again.

If we must have images—if we are never without images—and I do love my photograph of 'boy, screaming'—then how about a *sonophoto* or an *audiopic*? Neither a moving image, nor still images with wallpaper musical playlists made to match the images after the fact, a sonophoto asks to be a still image with, let's say, an accompanying audio chip as a record of the sounds that were synchronous with the subject caught that day at the very moment of its catching. For every predictable occasional shot, there'd have to be an unanticipated suite of sounds and voices, burps, and bumps to mark the pic as such and bubble up from it, and merge with it, to surround it like a sphere. Audiopics would register the tones that collectively jostle a moment's mood into being. Photographs might seem less bereft then. They'd not be lent a missing sound—don't get me wrong: the idea wouldn't be to animate the life we seek to reproduce, but to let it emerge and recede into its native sea of sound, albeit necessarily clipped and cut.

Here's where a challenge would have to be met because what would determine how long or short the photo's accompanying sound recording should be? A split second wouldn't do for a palpable mood song. You'd need at least several seconds for the sounds to be meaningful—or maybe not. Maybe the whole point of sonophotos would be to train our attention differently: to give us what we otherwise can't hear as distinguishing and vital and exceedingly short. It's the nature of sound to vanish, but memory seems to require the sense of a sustaining chain.

Would such sounds fizz around a photograph like tiny bubbles or create one large gelatinous frame?

'Froth,' according to an Aristotelian model of temperament and physique, 'is the euphoric counterpoint to black bile,' but the four humours only allow for choleric, phlegmatic, melancholic, and sanguine. This photograph of my boy screaming, though, could serve as a woodcut illustration to a type of 'mood euphoric' in which the figure has surrounded himself with a bubble of light. How long or short did he sustain it? That scream. Was it sharp and fleeting like a yelp or long and lasting far beyond the boundaries of a measured exhale? By the looks of Kolya's self-constructed earplugs, it was exceedingly loud and high-pitched. Was the whole point of the scream a test of how far he could throw his voice for how long?

Kolya used to like to run his fingers along the side of a balloon to make a squawking sound, then see how many squawks and pinches it would take until it popped. I used to like rubbing a balloon against the fuzzy surface of a rug, then take pleasure in the way it would stick with crackly static to different body parts. If I let Kolya's screaming photograph help me to remember one of my own mood cauls—a zone both sheltering and porous created by sound—I find myself returning to a very early scene from childhood set before the glow of a TV set, a glow that seemed an effect of its shutters-drawn evenly lambent droning. I almost wrote, 'in the dream,' but it wasn't a dream, it was an episode, and it wasn't an episode on TV but in my life. I was too young at the time to understand images or words, so it's not really possible that I was following whatever was on TV. I was held, however, inside the television's emanating light and the sounds that came through its coarse and fuzzy speaker. I was busy with the unselfconscious activity of cutting my own hair with a pair of blunt-edged, pink-handled, child-sized scissors. I wasn't trying to accomplish anything, but I was busy feeling something—something that sounded like what I sensed when I lost my feet inside of granules of sand on a beach. I was timelessly exploring, when a scream burst through that was at first my mother crying, 'Oh, no, Mary, what have you done!' followed by my own drop out of the zone and imitative screaming in turn.

The number of lessons I was to learn forced me to attention: (1) one is never to cut one's own hair—that's only something an insane person does; (2) scissors are not to be played with; (3) your own head is one thing and your doll's head is another, though you also shouldn't cut the hair off your doll; (4) bubbles are not safe zones; moods are easily broken by the cries of adults. Life breaks in to terminate the mood, leaving me to wonder whether moods have their own temporality, their own terminus based on their own end point. I mean, how long would my hair-cutting activity have gone on inside my bubble if I hadn't been stopped? When do you decide you are finished? When the body calls you back with hunger, a bowel movement, the need to sleep?

How long is the length of your scream? What form does your cry take? Which of your cries has gone unheard, unanswered? When is a mood the effect of a scream that doesn't require the presence of another?

We speak of people creating bubbles around themselves when we want to suggest a self-insulating shield of complacency, immunity, or ignorance. But insofar as we are all equipped with voices capable of generating heat and light, tone and atmosphere, we are all reliant on self-propelling mood spheres to carry us through our days. So much depends on the pliancy or porousness of our bubbles, their susceptibility to air currents or tendency to stick.

Within the first ten seconds of birth, each of us takes our first breath when our central nervous system responds to the sudden change in temperature. It sounds like a gasp. A developing baby produces two times more heat than an adult. A newborn might be covered in a thick waxy substance that helps a baby float in amniotic fluid. It will slough off in the baby's first bath.

When Kolya turned six, I gave him a story that I wrote for him about a cardinal. I can't remember the story's plot except that it was inspired by the suddenness of the bird's red presence in the garden one early April afternoon. I remember bestowing the bird with the power of anointing the boy who found him with just that: a mutually supervening presence of witnessing and being witnessed in turn. When Kolya turned eight, I gave him morning glory seeds since, never expecting to outpace his high-achieving sister, and, unbeknownst to him, greens flourished in the plot his parents had given over to his care. 'You have a green thumb,' I told him then. 'A green what?' he screwed up his face and scratched his head; inspecting his thumb through squinting eyes, he shrugged. 'Whatever,' he said, and, 'Hey! Will these morning glories climb the fence?'

I always gave Kolya books, but as he approached eleven and then twelve, finding the right gift became difficult. He'd moved through a *Minecraft* stage fervently and swiftly, and now his head lay buried in a game he played on his phone in which the physiognomies of actual soccer pros, tiny as cells under a microscope, scrabbled and pitched inside a field Kolya could hold in his hand.

'The best gift you can give a twelve-year-old boy,' a friend of mine explained, 'is a lava lamp.' She was right. He was thrilled. What's the deal with twenty-first-century boys and lava lamps? Their undulating bubbles in incandescent hues are mood simulators par excellence. They set a pace of even-keeled ejaculation for a boy on the brink of losing control. They're compressed screams, bottled, now gently gurgling.

Kolya rarely screams now. He's very dear, and very sweet. He's gentlemanly, and it almost breaks my heart the way he still hugs me unabashedly, still turning his ear to face my chest, the older we both get, hello and goodbye. The most recent footage I have of him once again places us in the garden. It involves water in slow motion, and the staged humiliation of being soaked by it. It's August, by the looks of it, when everything's at its blooming best and end. It's hot. Kolya is showing me and Jean and his father how to use an iPhone to make videos in slow motion. One video is elaborately staged but short and amusing: father and son face one another in their matching blue T-shirts. Kolya pushes his father whose rehearsed reflex—complete with over-blown exasperated facial expressions—is to toss the water from his wine glass onto Kolya as he bounces back. This is the point of the film: to capture water in slow motion as a beaded pelt and splat as it traverses a distance of two feet between two facing bodies. At the end of the water arc, droplets fall to make a necklace of dashes that punctuate Kolya's chest and chin. He's plastered, but beneath shut eyes, he beams a full-toothed grin.

Now the birds are aharmonic like those in an Amazonian rainforest while a slow ultradeep human voice can almost be heard to say, 'Don't ruin the i-phone.' This, no doubt, in reference to the liquid nature of the scene. The rose petals, singed at their edges, emit a pom-pom drumming, their scent made more sugary by the damp. Red geranium petals peal, and the dogwood releases its coppery downpour in the shade. The point of the game is to make something mind-bending, and in the process, to get drenched. Like his four-year-old scream, the gale is tuneless and unstoppable. It creates a mood of madcap inside an urban paradise. For five full seconds, we all laugh and laugh and laugh.

*

Mood Hint: *In English, we say "sunny mood" but never "moony mood."*

Mood Hint: *A friend of mine says people all his life described him as "moody," when he was really quite buoyant. "Moody" was a euphemism for what they didn't want to recognize as gay.*

IV. The Exciting or Opiatic Effect of Certain Words

The hypothalamic nuclei are connected to the cerebral cortex whose functioning underlies meaning—but how?—and also to the limbic lobe of the brain stem whose functioning underlies affects. At present we don't know how this transfer takes place, but clinical experience allows us to think that it does actually take place (for instance, one will recall the exciting or sedative, 'opiatic,' effect of certain words).
From Julia Kristeva, *Black Sun: Depression and Melancholia*

When Julia Kristeva talks about the sedative or opiatic effect of certain words, I don't think she has in mind the mood-altering capacity of the meanings that accompany words—those bulky overcoats—even though that word ('meaning') appears in her gloss. I suspect she's talking about words as sound forms whose texture and timbre have the power to, as the saying goes, touch something in us, and in the touching, to either create a new mood, if such a thing is possible, or to conjure the residue of a mood that's gone missing. Psycho-phonologists read high-frequency sounds as capable of producing states of heightened awareness in us humans, acting as they do on the cochlea, whereas low-frequency sounds can calm us to the point of stasis and torpor: if the liquid inside the semicircular canals of the ear's vestibule is made to rotate enough, by repeated low-frequency drumming, say, a state of trance is the result. Then we are said to be 'captives of our vestibules.'

But what about the effect of language on our 'neurobiological networks?' Is it possible to identify words that at one time made us happy exclusive of 'candy?' And how about words that exert a drone or din? Just as worry is easier to bear in a particular place, so worry is easier to bear surrounded by particular words. Can words in themselves have this power or does it depend on the quality of the air through which words move? There's the rub: doesn't it all come down to voice, the ineluctable wooing of one by the other—word and voice, ear and tongue and throat, lips and lungs? If pronounced in *her* voice, all words create the best mood in me. That's the ticket. All distinctions fall away.

Use the next full minute to list words that come to mind as likely to produce a soothing or pleasant mood in you. Go!

> denizen versus citizen
> hula hoop versus tire iron
> glockenspiel versus man-o'-war
> harmonica versus accordion
> charlotte, but now we're back to ice cream, or dessert.

Swarthy, swatch, and glade; recluse and surcease; recant and disuse; delve, shelve, elve; elevate and conjugate. Jugular and jaguar. Constantinople. Fructify. Gina Lollobrigida. Riffraff. Rinky-dink. Edgeless. Leavening. Sausalito. Somersault.

The mood-producing effects of such words must have to do with the nap of each person's individual fur, each person's causeway-like zags, marbleised or plush, the orientation and density of our inner and outer linings. And maybe, too, with the mechanics of an accented rise and fall of the voices that originally coaxed us into being, 'Come out, come out,' they said, 'for now it's time to come out.' Or, 'sleep, now—there, there—it's time to sleep.'

We leave it to poets to return language to its roots in the body, to restore language's place amid the elements, earth, air, fire, and water. A sentence can move as mesmerically as a reversing falls like the small and quiet ones hidden inside trees more majestic than those that pound for pound and measure for measure weight of their force drawn down or up the sentence sentenced to reverse itself to meet but not to find itself again drawn back upon itself not by itself alone upon a pad this pen and that heart draws it forth and back until a feeling is produced by it and then it stops.

We turn to poets or to the poets we, ourselves, become when called to attention by distillates even in the most analytic prose. Then I gather such phrases for their capacity to say everything that needs to be said, that are in themselves all the mood-thought we need to understand depression, (for example), as from, Kristeva the word-pools,

> "institutionalized stupor"
> "prisoners of affect"
> "the delights of suffering"
> "nychthemeral rhythms"
> "our most persistent despondencies"
> "to tame and cherish sadness as an object for lack of another"
> "a lucid counterdepressant"
> "to unfold language's resources"
> "our basic homeostatic recourses"
> "faced with the impossibility of concatenating"
> "learned helplessness"
> "playing dead"
> "psychic crypts" or "psychic voids."

In order to effect a mood out of language, need a writer put words through the same process that herbs are subjected to in the creation of mood-enhancing cordials? Steeping, distilling, infusing, and macerating, all of which share the requirement of soaking and softening, condensing and extracting, supply the idea of a liquid aesthetic, and who wouldn't wish to produce in a fellow being the combination hum and high of cranberries soaked in bourbon?

Maybe a poet's charge is to unsteep words and in doing so to perform an only seemingly simple operation of extraction, to allow us to hear what we never hear inside the words we always hear, for I know I am put in a mood part joyful and part curious—not an opiatic mood but a wakeful one—when met with the word 'seemly' over and against the more commonplace unseemly; when prompted to imagine a 'shevled' rather than dishevelled appearance; to be made to consider what 'whelms' me as distinct from what overwhelms me; to comprehend the way in which each repetition is a renewed 'petition'; to find loose leaf pages—a 'quire'—at the centre of all requirements and inquiries; to posit positively against the force of certain words' tendency to exist only in negation—to eke out the 'choate' in the inchoate, the 'ane' in the inane—to 'bibe,' and 'bue' without a consuming '-im': to saturate.

Occasionally you'll hear it on the radio, how the confident mood of capitalism turns hysterical. Then mad throngs storm the vestibules of Walmart intent on a widescreen TV, trampling to death a guard in the process. What words create the frequencies to inspire mass motility numb to the sound of voice and tongue and throat, lips and lungs, heart and mind and memory pulsing underfoot? I think of Thoreau's different drummer, of Dickinson's poetry of tilt and whirl. I wonder if poetry undelivered, distant but there, poetry requiring that we crane just long enough to pause indeterminately can avert the disaster of stampede.

Works Consulted

Oneiric

Prevenas, Nick, 'UA Cancer Center Surgeon Assists Patients Suffering from Chemotherapy-Related Hearing Loss', University of Arizona Cancer Center, Updated 26 February 2013. http:// surgery.arizona.edu/in-the-news/ua-cancer-center-surgeon-assists-patients-suffering-chemotherapy-related-hearing-loss.

Gong Bath

Barthes, Roland, *A Lover's Discourse: Fragments*, trans. by Richard Howard (New York: Hill and Wang, 1978).

Field, Eleanor Selfridge, 'Experiments with Melody and Meter, or the Effects of Music: The Edison-Bingham Music Research', *Musical Quarterly*, 81 (Summer 1997), 291–310.

Graduate School of Oceanography and Marine Acoustics, University of Rhode Island, 'Discovery of Sound in the Sea'. www.dosits.org.

Histotripsy Group, 'Non-invasive Ultrasonic Tissue Fractionation for Treatment of Benign Disease and Cancer–"Histotripsy"', Biomedical Engineering Department, University of Michigan. www.histotripsy.umich.edu.

Kahn, Douglas, *Noise, Water, Meat: A History of Sound in the Arts* (Cambridge, MA: MIT Press, 2001).

Kercher, Sophia, 'Sound Baths Move from Metaphysical to Mainstream', *New York Times*, 15 August 2015. www.nytimes.com/2015/08/16/fashion/sound-baths-move-from-metaphysical-to-mainstream.html?r=0 [accessed 15 August 2015].

King, Lauren, Quincy Almeida, and Heidi Ahonen, 'Short-Term Effects of Vibration Therapy on Motor Impairments in Parkinson's Disease', *NeuroRehabilitation*, 25 (2009), 297–306.

Lanza, Joseph, *Elevator Music: A Surreal History of Muzak®, Easy-Listening, And Other Moodsong®* (Ann Arbor: University of Michigan Press, 2004).

Sonophoto: Boy, Screaming

Anderson, Ben, 'Affective Atmospheres', *Emotion, Space and Society*, 2, 2 (December 2009), 77–81.

Böhme, Gernot, 'Atmosphere as the Fundamental Concept of a New Aesthetics', *Thesis Eleven*, 36 (1993), 113–26.

Carson, Anne, 'The Gender of Sound', in *Glass, Irony and God* (New York: New Directions, 1995), pp. 119–39.

Chion, Michel, *The Voice in Cinema*, trans. by Claudia Gorbman (New York: Columbia University Press, 1999).

Diaconu, Mădălina, 'Patina—Atmosphere—Aroma: Toward an Aesthetics of Fine Differences', *Analecta Husserliana*, 92 (2006), 131–48.

Heschong, Lisa, *Thermal Delight in Architecture* (Cambridge, MA: MIT Press, 1999).

MedLine, "Changes in the Newborn at Birth", Updated 12 April 2013. www. nlm.nih.gov/medlineplus/ency/article/002395.htm.

Putterman, Seth J., 'Sonoluminescence: Sound into Light', *Scientific American*, 272, 2 (February 1995), 32–7.

Sloterdijk, Peter, 'The Siren Stage: On the First Sonospheric Alliance', in *Bubbles*, *vol. 1 of Spheres: Microspherology*, trans. by Wieland Hoban (LosAngeles, CA: Semiotext(e), 2011), pp. 477–521.

The Exciting or Opiatic Effect of Certain Words

Kristeva, Julia, 'Life and Death in Speech', in *Black Sun: Depression and Melancholia*, trans. by Leon S. Roudiez (New York: Columbia University Press, 1989), pp. 31–68.

Name Index

Note: Page numbers followed by "n" denote endnotes.

Subject Index

Note: Page numbers followed by "n" denote endnotes.

Printed in Great Britain
by Amazon

33896201R00132